THE REIGN OF ANTICHRIST

By
R. GERALD CULLETON

*"Lord wilt Thou at this time restore the Kingdom of Israel? . . . It is
not for you to know the times or dates which the Father has fixed . . ."*
Acts 1:6-7

*"Let no one deceive you . . . The day of the Lord will not come
unless the apostasy comes first and the man of sin is revealed . . . who
. . . gives himself out as if he were God."*
2 Thes. 3-4

TAN Books
Charlotte, North Carolina

ISBN: 978-0-89555-047-7

Cover image and design by Mike Dellinger.

Printed and bound in India

TAN Books
Charlotte, North Carolina
www.TANBooks.com
2012

PUBLISHER'S PREFACE

Originally issued in 1951, the *The Reign of Antichrist* forms a companion volume to *The Prophets and Our Times* (1941) and is very much like the latter in scope and content. Two important differences in the books, however, should be noted: *The Reign of Antichrist* comprises Biblical prophecies as well as saintly prophecies; whereas, *The Prophets and Our Times* covers saintly prophecies almost entirely. Secondly, *The Reign of Antichrist* deals with a slightly different period of time, that, obviously of *the individual* Antichrist; *The Prophets and Our Times* deals with the period just before the reign of Antichrist, a period dominated by the Great Monarch. A careful reading of these two books will indicate that the time of the Great Monarch more or less prefigures that of Antichrist, although the two personages have generally reversed roles; that is, the times of both men are calamitous for the Catholic Church and for society. The Great Monarch's ascension to power ends the turmoil and initiates an unprecedented peace; on the other hand, Antichrist's coming to power ends the great peace and prosperity of the Great Monarch and heralds the most dreadful situation for both Church and society, which situation ends in the second coming of Our Lord.

The present work is by no means perfect, and all readers should recognize this before they start. Our purpose in reprinting it is twofold: It *is* a wonderful source book, one from which students of the subject can make an excellent beginning and from which, perhaps some really good student of eschatology, using other existing sources also, can give us a truly authoritative work on the subject. Secondly, there is practically nothing in print in this area that is even remotely reliable. *History of Antichrist*, by Rev. P. Huchede (1884) is a notable exception, being not only authoritative, but brief and highly readable. Our suggestion is that this book be read before *The Reign of Antichrist*, if possible, or at least shortly thereafter; it is an excellent outline of Catholic teaching relative to Antichrist. A first reading of Father Huchede's book should be followed by one where the reader looks up all the Biblical passages cited there. In this manner, the subject becomes extremely clear. Father Huchede bases his thesis upon Scripture, Tradition, and the Fathers and Doctors of the Church. Father Culleton, however, actually *quotes* the passages from scripture and the Fathers and Doctors of the Church, plus gives numerous sources of written tradition; added to these, moreover, he quotes many saints and holy people who possessed the gift of prophecy themselves. Having all these prophetic passages under one cover singularizes *The Reign of Antichrist* as a unique and valuable book in its field.

A word of warning needs to be interjected here. Saintly prophecies are not "of faith" (*de fide* pronouncements) and most of the Biblical prophecies regarding Antichrist have not been given official interpretation; consequently, we must observe precaution in interpreting them and in basing our actions upon them, especially until the Church has made judgment in their regard. Nonetheless, these prophecies, both Biblical and saintly, were given and intended for our enlightenment and should not be casually put aside. "Despise not prophecies," says St. Paul, "but prove all things." (1 *Thes.* 5:20-21). Also he tells us, "Follow after charity, be zealous for spiritual gifts; but rather that you may prophesy . . . He that prophesieth, speaketh to men unto edification, and exhortation, and comfort . . . He that prophesieth, edifieth the church . . . For greater is he that prophesieth, than he that speaketh with tongues." (1 *Cor.* 14:1,3,4,5). We would indeed be most foolish if we debunked the prophecies Father Culleton has gathered together here, for they form an impressive collection, probably the most thorough treatment on the subject in print. Perhaps it is even providential that the book is being reissued at this time, along with *The Prophets and Our Times* as well. Together, these two books tell quite a story about the future. And the great divergence of the sources of the prophecies cited is itself the most compelling argument for their validity.

Needless to say, the doctrine on Antichrist is very much a part of our Catholic theology and Tradition, and as such, must be considered carefully by all men, the learned and the unlearned alike, for the Antichrist, when he comes, will affect the lives of all men. Based upon the firmness of their faith and the correctness of their knowledge, men will either apostatize or remain faithful to Christ and His Church. Thus, it will be seen that a knowledge of the prophecies regarding Antichrist is of an immensely practical nature.

We have omitted from the book the secret messages of the La Salette apparition (1846—approved by the Church in 1851), and the reader will find under Number 337 on page 163 a note to this effect. Pages 164 through 170 are missing entirely and only part of pages 163 and 171 appear. In the proper place we have explained why this was done. Other than that, a correction has been made concerning the "Secret of Fatima" on page 186. The wording of the original edition was not precisely what it should have been, and the author issued with each book a preface sheet containing also some corrections; this particular correction we have thought to include new in the body of the book, as well as two others of merely typographical nature. The balance of the author's loose-leaf enclosure has been added as the "Author's Preface."

Some readers no doubt will question Father Culleton's including Number 315, the prophecy of Michael Nostradamus (page 144) because Nostradamus was an astrologer, or at least a student of that subject. Presumably, this was due to Nostradamus' great overall accuracy as a prophet. Although Jewish by birth, he was a Catholic and apparently a very devout one. Moreover, he believed his prophetic foresight was so accurate that he scrambled his quatrains (the enigmatic, four-line verses in which he cast most of his prophecies), in order that people would not be too frightened of the future. Cultivation of the occult sciences is of course forbidden, but to what extent he relied upon astrology to make his predictions, if at all, I do not know. Nonetheless, his reputation for accuracy is great; however, in the particular predictions Father Culleton quotes here, he seems to have made several errors. But the same is true for the predictions of Father Theophilus Reisinger, O.F.M., Cap. (No. 369; page 222), the renowned exorcist of Earling, Iowa fame, popularized by the booklet *Begone Satan*.

This leads immediately into the question of errors in saintly prophecies. Does this obvious element of error vitiate the entire book. I do not believe it does, and for the following reasons: First, prophecies are about the future, and events, spiritually speaking, are greatly dependent upon the moral quality of human lives; when mankind improves his behavior, he can forestall or remove immenent catastrophe from happening. The prophet might be predicting in the sense of "if conditions do not change, then. . ." Second, a prophet may simply be misquoted. Third, he may be misinterpreted. And finally, the person in question may not in fact have the prophetic gift, as I believe is the case with Father Reisinger, whose forte or charisma was exorcism; the prediction given by him was through a second party, a mystic who received a locution.

Over all, however, the reader will see that most of Father Culleton's book contains passages that tend to support one another and which in general elucidate what Sacred Scripture has to say on Antichrist, and it is for this reason that we have reissued his book. May it bring enlightenment to its readers on this sorely abused subject, and may it inspire people today to turn to a serious spirituality in their lives, as the only valid bulwark to the onslaught of "the man of sin," a spirituality including prayer, penance, good works, spiritual reading, and frequenting the Sacraments, the formula laid down by the saints for spiritual perfection. This, after all, should be the end result of all our reading—growth in holiness so that we may earn salvation through the merits of Our Lord Jesus Christ, no matter what it may be our fate to live through.

Thomas A. Nelson
July 1, 1974
Feast of the Precious Blood

ADDENDUM

In the first TAN edition of *The Reign of Antichrist* (1974), we omitted the secret messages of the La Salette apparition (1846—approved by the Church in 1851). This included pages 164 through 170 and parts of pages 163 and 171. We had read in various publications that the Holy Office in Rome had issued a decree on December 21, 1915, against publication of various versions of these two secret messages. However, in a very illuminating article on the subject of La Salette, entitled *The Secret of La Salette—Little Apocalypse of Our Lady* (Big Rock Press. Leesburg, Virginia. 1974. p. 3) Solange Hertz clarifies the nature of this decree, showing that the proscription is against publishing *interpretations* of the secret messages, and *not* against publishing the messages themselves. That decree states: "It has come to the knowledge of this Supreme Congregation that there are still persons, even ecclesiastics, who, in spite of the answers and decisions of the Sacred Congregation itself, continue by books, pamphlets and articles published in periodicals, whether signed or anonymous, to discuss the question of the Secrets of La Salette, its various texts, its adaptations to our present times or to the future, and these, not only without the approbation of their Bishops, but even in spite of their express prohibition. In order that these abuses, which are harmful to true piety, and seriously attack ecclesiastical authority, may be repressed, the same Sacred Congregation orders the faithful of all countries to abstain from treating and discussing this said question, under whatsoever pretext or form, either in books, pamphlets or articles signed or anonymous, or in any other way . . . This Decree is not, however, contrary to the devotion of the Blessed Virgin invoked and known under the title of Reconciler of La Salette." (*Prophecy for Today*. Edward Connor. Apostolate of Christian Action. Fresno California. 1963. p. 19.) The gist of the decree, obviously, is to silence *discussions* of the secret messages, many of which bordered on anti-clerical. Consequently, we have added Father Culleton's original material on the subject in this edition of the book (1978).

TABLE OF CONTENTS

EDITOR'S PREFACE

Father Gerald Culleton lost his life in an automobile accident, February 19, 1950. He was on his way to say Sunday Mass in his mission church when his car struck a truck in the thick fog. This was at the place called Traver on U. S. Highway 99. He is buried in Holy Cross Cemetery, Fresno, California.

The manuscript for this book was pretty well completed when he died. The index and bibliography only were missing. These and two quotations have been added by the editor; also a couple of prophecies since repudiated by Church authority have been omitted, as has a large section from the introduction. This was necessary to keep the size and price down.

It is most important that readers understand that inclusion of any private prophecy in this book does not in any way indicate that it is approved by the Church or even by the author of this work. This is merely an historical presentation of oracles that at the moment are read by good Christians.

The author, as a rule, avoids expressing his own views. Now that he has gone to his reward we may well ask just what were those views. Did he expect Antichrist in the 1950's? So far as we can learn he held no definite personal views as to the time of Antichrist's appearance. He did believe, however, that private prophets expected a very great anti-Christian movement (or an antichrist more fierce than any yet encountered) in this present decade. This person or movement would set out to conquer the world and would be at first very successful. The attempt would be defeated just when it would seem about to overcome the last remnant of opposition. As is natural he felt that if these prophets are true, Communism is this anti-Christian force.

As to the object which would defeat this force he was not at all sure. Would it be a person and thing still more evil, namely the Antichrist par excellence, or a Christian organization under a personage often called in prophecy the Great Monarch, or a more apparent miracle (such as three days darkness), or something that would typify the Second

Coming of Christ? He found the prophets too diversified to find an answer to this question. The diversity need not mean contradiction, for each prophet may speak of different times or different phases of the same time.

Some private prophets give very precise dates. This is one of the simplest ways of eliminating a prophecy from the realm of truth. If the date arrives and the words are not fulfilled then evidently God has not spoken, or if he has, he meant one of many antichrists and the prophet thought he meant the Antichrist.

The author did not hope to be able to make a collection of prophecies all of which would be true. All he could do was bring together all which at the moment seemed likely to be trustworthy. Just as Satan has a hand in false religions, chiefly because they tend to make religion itself ridiculous, so also does he take a hand in false prophecy, again in an effort to make all prophecy ridiculous. Nevertheless, just as the true religion shall survive and prove itself, so also shall those prophecies that are true survive and prove themselves. If one or other prophecy recorded in this book be repudiated, let it be understood that others still stand.

Father Culleton wrote his first book **THE PROPHETS AND OUR TIMES** at the suggestion of Monsignor (later Bishop) Philip G. Scher, who was the pastor when he was an assistant at Monterey. The book itself was written somewhat later when father was pastor at Taft, California (1934-1944). It was widely read having gone through three editions totaling 12,500 copies. Most purchasers who wrote the author complained that so many had borrowed their copies that the book was literally read to pieces.

Father was born at Fresno, California, September 10, 1902 of Irish immigrant parentage: Patrick J. Culleton, of Coolgraney, Co. Kilkenny and Mary J. McCrory of Aghagallon, Co. Antrim. He was one of four children. After the grammar and high grades at the local parish school, he went to Santa Clara College. Having decided to be a diocesan priest, he transferred to St. Patrick's Seminary, Menlo Park, California and three years later went to the American College in Rome, where he was ordained March 24, 1928. He has a brother a priest and a sister and aunt in the convent.

After assistancies at Hanford, Monterey, Salinas, and

San Luis Obispo, he became pastor of Taft and then of Wasco. He contracted undulant fever in the latter place and was sent to the cooler climate cf Soledad, where he was Chaplain at the Medium Security Prison. It was while he was in Wasco and Soledad that he collected and arranged the material for this book. The typing was done by one of the Soledad prisoners.

His health was restored somewhat at Soledad. He was then given a district in the San Joaquin Valley to develop into a parish. This was July 29, 1949. By February 20, 1950, he had built a rectory and otherwise developed the place to the point where on that day Bishop Aloysius J. Willinger established the parish of the Sacred Heart, Exeter, with Father Culleton as its first pastor.

Father had not been well for some weeks before his death, which he expected without knowing why, and which he asked cthers to help him prepare for. He had special devotion to the Holy Ghost, Saints Michael, Gabriel of our Sorrowful Mother, Gemma Galgani, and Maria Gecretti, and great faith in relics and sacramentals. He always gave ready submission to the desires of his superiors.

The manuscript for this book passed by will to Father's bishop, who gave it to us with permission to print and distribute it.

PREFACE

It has not been my intention to inject myself or my personal opinions into this book. On the whole it is not to be considered so much a theological as an historical presentation. The purpose has been to put into the hands of as many readers as possible the thoughts of many different persons, all of them pious and some of them learned. In all cases where I could detect any intention to deceive, the material has been excluded. In other cases, and this is really my only intrusion, when a statement seemed to me in need of clarification or of modification from a doctrinal point of view, I have added a footnote or remarks in parenthesis.

Were it not for a book such as this, it would be humanly impossible for the ordinary person, lay or clerical, to get an over-all picture, in original sources, of the thought of true believers on the Antichrist through the long centuries that the Antichrist idea has formed an indispensible segment of divine teaching. This because Antichrist literature is widely scattered and for the most part in books long out of print and besides closed to the ordinary person in that they are not in the English language.

I do not pretend to have satisfied the requirements of scholars in the presentation of these texts; but I do not write the book for scholars. They can look up the material for themselves. Were the texts to be issued in the critical manner of the scholar, the lifetime of one man and the wealth of many could not have produced this book and when it was produced, no one but a scholar could or would have read it.

I am not satisfied myself with some of the sources; but I doubt that any serious errors, that have not been pointed out, have crept into the books that I have used Some of the translations, too, are imperfect; but not so imperfect that they distort the original.

A really good book on Antichrist by several scholars working together and in libraries, which my busy life in a parish made impossible, is surely in order. I will be the first to hail the man or men who will issue a better book on this fascinating subject.

The Author

November 16, 1949

Author's Preface

This first edition of THE REIGN OF ANTICHRIST has been printed at the request of and exclusively for several persons who own and appreciate a copy of THE PROPHETS AND OUR TIMES. It is a second volume along the same idea.

Apart from being the first attempt in any language to give a complete picture of the Antichrist of prophecy, this work also lays claim to being the first genuine book printed with paper plates instead of with type, or the zinc plates heretofore in use.

We have issued the book as a printed manuscript but as noted at the end of the Editor's Preface, it is issued with the bishop's permission. To assure our readers, however, we submitted the book in its present form to the book censor for the Diocese of Monterey-Fresno, Reverend Amancio Rodriguez, S. T. D. His reply is as follows:

"I have examined the book, THE REIGN OF ANTI-CHRIST, and found nothing in it against Faith or Morals. However, it should be noted at the beginning that the scriptural texts never have received an authentic interpretation by the church and that in the case of private revelations they are only matter of private opinion."

If this edition meets with favor we shall issue another for the general public. Meanwhile, we will appreciate your criticism and any information you may have on additional prophecies, old and new.

INTRODUCTORY CHAPTER

Since the author or rather the compiler of this book has no merit as a theologian, he has felt that he will perform a better service if he lets others do most of the talking. For this reason, even this introduction will come almost entirely from the mouths of men whose knowledge and ability are beyond doubt.

The fundamentals of the Christian idea of Antichrist are in the **Second Epistle to the Thessalonians** and in the **Apocalypse,** so we will hear what Father Prat has to say about the former and Father LeFrois about the latter. Most theologians devote very little space to Antichrist so we have chosen to translate from the work of Father Hervé whose comments are typical. I have interjected a few remarks in parenthesis. Neglect them if you wish.

The only point I am forced to make deals with an opinion now quite widespread, that the times of Antichrist are upon us. The only reason I speak is because I have found no one without preconceived ideas whom I can quote.

First: Several have told me that Antichrist is already born. One puts him in Pennsylvania, another in Illinois, a third in Iraq; a fourth has informed me that he already has temples in the four corners of the earth, one corner being Chicago and another Los Angeles. Christ has said, "If they say, lo, here is Christ or there, go ye not out to look." If I err not, this means we should not bother with these rumors. When Antichrist comes, the whole world will know him, the elect for what he is, the rest for what he is not.

Second: It is said that the times in which we live fit very well into those which will immediately precede the coming of Antichrist. This is not for me to judge. They are indeed evil times. They are more intensely and widespreadly evil than any that have existed since Constantine. They will, no doubt, get worse. The Church will suffer much more than She now suffers. But whether what we now see or may live to see is any more than one of the numerous eras which are to precede Antichrist, I do not know. There are those quoted in this book who say we are near the times of Antichrist. Who am I to say they are wrong? But on the other hand, who are they, that we are to believe them. We do not doubt their good faith. The value of their word we know not.

Antichrist According to Saint Paul's Epistles

In 2 **Thess.** 2:3-12 Saint "Paul merely recalls here, with a few allusions, some features of his oral preaching. He takes it for granted that the Thessalonians are familiar with these ideas, for the instructions given to the neophytes always included a chapter on the last things associated with the parousia. (1) The Apostle contents himself with refreshing their memory of them. He formerly taught orally, and now he repeats in writing — but in terms the conciseness of which makes them enigmatical for us — that the last day is to be preceded by two great crises — the apostasy and the appearance of Antichrist. He speaks of both as of things well known which do not need explanation.

"The apostasy indicates certainly a religious defection, a revolt against God or his representatives. It appears to be closely connected with the acts and wonders wrought by the great adversary. The latter, formally distinguished from Satan, who lends him his aid and uses him as an agent, is described with the traits and characteristics of the persons of whom he is the antitype. He will lift himself up above all that is God or is called God, like Antiochus Epiphanes; he will give himself out for God and will wish to be treated as God, like the Prince of Tyre in Ezechiel and the King of Babylon in Isaias; he will sit in the very Temple of God, like the abomination of desolation predicted by Daniel.

"These reminders are not so much new prophecies as allusions to old texts; it is not necessary to expect the literal verification of them, they are symbols realizable according to a law of proportion unknown to us. When we read that the Lord Jesus 'will destroy the wicked one with the spirit (breath) of his mouth,' these words recall to us the way in which the Son of David, according to Isaias, is to destroy impiety; but what can we conclude from them as to the real way in which those things will take place? What is said, aside from figures of speech, is that Antichrist will work

---

(1) Second coming of Christ.

2

false miracles, signs and wonders, will seduce a great many souls, and also cause a schism in the Church, but that he will finally be conquered, and that his fall will be the signal for the parousia.

"In one point only does Paul go beyond his predecessors. He speaks of an obstacle which hinders the immediate coming of Antichrist, and gives us the following description of it: It is a person or something personified (masculine), and at the same time a physical or moral force (neuter). The obstacle is already active and it checks the mystery of iniquity; it prevents the advance of the wicked one. As soon as this obstacle disappears the field will be open to Antichrist whose appearance seems likely to precede but shortly the appearance of the Son of God. What is this obstacle? The Thessalonians had learned what it is from the mouth of the Apostle, but we are ignorant of it now, and everything leads us to suppose that we shall always be ignorant of it. The proverbial obscurity of this passage has given rise to innumerable solutions.

"With brotherly unanimity, Albigenses, Waldenses, Hussites, the disciples of Wyclif, of Luther and Calvin, and ancient and modern Anglicans, down to the nineteenth century, have seen in Antichrist the Pope and in the obstacle which opposes the triumph of the former, first the Roman Emperor and later the German Emperor. In 1518, when the first ideas of revolt were fermenting in him, Luther had a slight suspicion that the Pope might indeed be Antichrist; in 1519, he was almost sure of it, and at the end of that year, when the rupture with Rome was complete, he had become entirely certain of it. Ten years later, he was indignant that the Augsburg confession had made no mention of such a fundamental article of faith. The mistake was remedied at Smalkalde, where it was declared that 'the Pope is the true Antichrist who has elevated himself against Christ and above him.'

"The only divergence among the Protestants is that some have admitted two Antichrists — one for the East, namely Mohammed and Islam; the other for the West, the Pope and the Papacy. One bolder commentator has even discovered that if the Pope is always Antichrist, of course the mystery of iniquity is Jesuitism, while the temple of God is the pure Lutheran doctrine, and the obstacle which resists the advent, not of Antichrist, as the text of St. Paul requires, but of Jesus, is still the Pope. It is not long since the Lutherans, Calvanists and Anglicans gave up this exegesis, which was for them more sacred than the most solemn definition of faith is for us. So difficult to uproot are the prejudices of sect and caste, strengthened by habit and education!

"As for the rationalists, they all declare that the prophecy of St. Paul has not been fulfilled and never will be. It is only a dream of the Apostle. But when they try to say precisely what the object of this dream is, they are so divided that it is impossible to find two of them with the same opinion.

"Nor can we say that Catholic commentators are any more agreed. However, in spite of infinite divergences of detail, they almost all regard the parousia as the personal return of Jesus Christ coming to judge the living and the dead; they see in Antichrist an individual, although St. Augustine thinks rather of a tendency; in the apostasy they see a defection and a revolt, either religious or political, or both at the same time; in the mystery of iniquity, either Nero and the persecutors, or heretics and schismatics; in the temple of God, either the Temple of Jerusalem rebuilt or the Christian Church; finally, in the obstacle, they see either the Roman Empire or its heir, the Christian State. But what State today constructs a dyke against the invasion of evil? In despair of finding any other solution, some are forced to hold that it is the faith still living in many hearts or the command to preach the Gospel throughout the world.

"Not only is the 'obstacle' not yet found, but we doubt whether it has ever been looked for in the right direction. Paul keeps to the ideas of Jewish and Christian eschatology. Like Daniel and St. John, he describes a conflict between good and evil, which has its echo on the earth, but the scene and principal seat of which are elsewhere. It is, in fact, Satan who begins it and maintains it, helping his tool with all his might. The antagonist must be a power of the same

4

order. In the prophecy of Daniel it is the commander of the heavenly hosts, the chief of the people of God, Michael, who takes up the cause of the holy nation, especially at the time of the great tribulation and on the eve of the resurrection of the dead. In St. John it is still Michael at the head of his angels who fights against the Dragon, the old Serpent, Lucifer, the Devil, Satan, and who finally wins the victory for Christ.

"The struggle between Michael and Satan goes on through the centuries. There is no need of interrogating the Apocrypha — the Book of Enoch, the Testament of the Twelve Patriarchs, or the Apocalypse of Moses — to know what a leading role the Archangel Michael is to play at the last day. It is he, according to St. Paul — the thing is scarcely doubtful — who will give the signal for the resurrection and the judgment. Will it not be also he — the protector first of the Synagogue and then of the Church — who with his legions will bar the passage of the powers of hell until the fulness of time? All the features of Paul's description are applicable to him; a personal being, he commands an army and represents a force; he is immortal, and his fight against Satan, begun in the apostolic epoch, runs on through history to its final climax. If his momentary disappearance signified a defeat or a destruction this character would not be applicable to him, but the Apostle's words do not mean this, and need not be thus understood. Until the baffled exegetes have found a better solution it is here that we shall seek for the mysterious 'obstacle' that retards the appearance of Antichrist." (Fernand Prat, S.J., **The Theology of St. Paul**, 1927. Vol. I, pp. 79-83).

Antichrist According to the Apocalypse

"Despite the fact that the spiritual or ideal interpretation of the Apocalypse, elaborated chiefly by Father Allo, O.P., has gained many adherents in the past forty years, there is an ever increasing number of authors who, along the lines of the earliest Church Fathers, prefer to give an eschatological interpretation to the greater part of that prophetical book of the New Testament. It would be interest-

5

ing to see what such an interpretation would offer in detail. A summary picture would probably result as follows.

"The Apocalypse is chiefly the grand finale of the Kingdom of God on earth, the completion of all prophecies in a final synthesis.

"Part I (1:9-3:22) depicts the First Age of the Church with its needs and impending trials. Part II (4:1-20:15) sets forth the Final Age of the Church. Such a combination of events widely separated in time is common to the prophetic vision. However, a connecting bridge between the two eras is probably given in a second fulfillment of Part I, namely, the typical sense of the Seven Letters.

"Part II opens with the Almighty Judge seated in judgment together with His heavenly court (Apoc. 4:1-5:14). His final decrees for mankind are in the sealed scroll. But He has given all judgment to the Son (John 5:22), so it is the Lamb, once slain by man, who executes these decrees on man, through the mediation of the angelic world. Part II has two sections.

"Section One (6:1-11:19) portrays the great distress among the nations on account of the calamities which the Lamb allows to overtake the world in punishment for unbelief. These calamities are in origin terrestrial (ch. 6), celestial (ch. 8), and infernal (ch. 9). Even a foretaste of hell is given to mankind before the great day of reckoning. Also in St. Luke's eschatological chapter, there is a clear distinction made between ordinary wars and insurrections on the one hand, and **universal** war, calamity, famine and death on the other. The latter is the sign of the coming judgment (Luke 21:9 and 10-11).

"The period of great distress coincides with the 'Major Apostasy' of 2 Thess. 2:3 and with the end of the 'Time of the Gentiles.' After describing the destruction of Jerusallem, Jesus said: 'And Jerusalem will be trodden down by the Gentiles until the times of the nations to be fulfilled' (Luke 21:24). The great distress brought physical death to many on earth, but like in the days of the flood (see 1 Peter 3:20), many found repentance before death and washed their robes in the blood of the Lamb, and an innumerable crowd remained faithful to Him unto death (Apoc. 7:9-14).

"At this juncture there is place for the conversion of the Jews (as a whole) (see Rom. 11:13-25). 'A partial blindness only has befallen Israel until the full number of the Gentiles should enter, and thus all Israel should be saved' (Rom. 11: 25). So the Church of the Last Age (represented by the 144,000 of chapter 7, sealed from both spiritual and physical harm) shall come through unscathed, and shall once more be (predominantly) Israelitic. It shall continue so to the end, marked (sealed) by God, like Israel of old in Egypt, as His own people. But the nations fall back into unbelief (Luke 18:8).

"Israel's conversion is brought about by the preaching and miracles of Elias during the great distress. 'Behold I will send you Elias the prophet before the coming of the great and dreadful day of the Lord. And he shall turn the heart of the children to the fathers; lest I come and strike the earth with anathema' (Mal. 4:5-6). 'Elias is indeed to come and will restore all things' (Mt. 17:11). True Israel is now spiritual; the material-minded and worldly Jews are rejected, as symbolized in the measuring cf the Temple (Apoc. 11:1-2).

"Henoch is the second witness sent back to preach penance in preparation for the coming of the reign of Antichrist. It seems that his mission is to the nations, so that they have an opportunity of salvation to the end (see Sir. 44:16). Jude 14-15 also hints at Henoch's mission in the latter days. The ministry of the two witnesses lasts 'three and a half years' (Apoc. 11:3), which coincides with the first half of Daniel's last 'year-week' (Dan. 9:26-27), whereas the second half of that 'year-week' coincides with the reign of Antichrist (who also reigns for three and a half years or 42 months in Apoc. 13:5) and makes desolate all religion, only to sit in the temple of God and give himself out to be God (2 Thess. 2:4). This is either a typical fulfillment of Daniel's last year-week, or there was a suspension in Daniel's vision after the seven plus sixty-two weeks until the time of the nations be fulfilled, and then the vision is resumed with the last year-week concerning Daniel's own people: Israel.

"Section Two of Part II (12:1-20:15) portrays the godless reign of a personal Antichrist, and the subsequent utter destruction of his kingdom, metropolis, and devotees. The stage is prepared by showing the Church of the Consummation fitted out with the characteristics of the Virgin-Mother, invulnerable in this attire against the attacks of the fierce dragon. Yet the dragon prepares to engulf her in a last supreme onslaught (ch.12).

"Beast number one is collective Antichrist persecuting the People of God from its very beginnings on earth down through the centuries (ch. 13). This it does through its seven heads but chiefly through him who caps all seven, namely, personal Antichrist, who sums up in himself all the perversity of the seven. Thus he is the eighth (Apoc. 17: 11). Seven heads which endeavored to engulf God's people on earth from the beginning of its existence are: Egypt (Pharao), Assyria, Babylonia, Medo-Persia (under Artaxerxes Ochos), Greco-Macedonia (in the Seleucides), Totalitarian pagan Rome (the sixth head) and a world empire of latter times. Symbolism (like in Daniel) fluctuates between a collective and a personal being, namely, an empire and a chief representative of that empire, e.g., the sixth head is represented as both empire and chief head of that empire (see 17:9). Daniel's fourth beast with the ten horns (Dan. 7:17-25) coincides with this beast of the Apocalypse in its sixth head (Apoc. 17:10). Ten horns are those state-kingdoms which follow upon the break-up of the Roman Empire and (eventually) persecute the Church.

"Beast number two is a false Elias heralding the advent of the false Christ (Antichrist in person). By diabolical signs he succeeds in bringing over the infidel world to Antichrist. St. Paul states that this deception is also a punishment for unbelief in Christ's Gospel of truth and love (2 Thess. 2: 9-12). Antichrist's name is given a numerical value: 666. Fulfillment alone can give certitude to this riddle. The Hebrew letters of Nero (n) Kaisar amount to 666. If this is the meaning of St. John, then Antichrist will come in the spirit of Nero (the sixth head), so that the horrible beast lives again (Apoc. 13:3).

8

The Marian Church of the Consummation has nothing to fear from the Antichrist, for he cannot extinguish her. God gives her supernatural aid (Apoc. 12:6). She is now virginal in the purity of her conduct and her devotedness to the Lamb. Her imitation of the Lamb is unexcelled (14:4). Mindful of the advice of St. Paul (1 Cor. 7:26-31), all live the virginal ideal. The time is at hand.

"Destruction of Antichrist's metropolis and works is accomplished by angelic powers in the pouring out of the bowls of God's wrath (ch. 16). Personal Antichrist and False Elias are overcome and cast into hell by the personal coming of Christ in glory (19:11-21).

"Millenium: Since the Holy Office decreed (July 21, 1944) that it cannot be safely taught that Christ at His Second Coming will reign visibly with only some of His saints (risen from the dead) for a period of time before the final and universal judgment, a spiritual millenium is to be seen in Apoc. 20:4-6. St. John gives a recapitulation of the activity of Satan, and the spiritual reign of the saints with Christ in heaven and in His Church on earth. When Christianity triumphed over the Beast (in its sixth head, the pagan Roman empire) Satan was chained. With the re-appearance of the Beast in the anti-Christian world empire (the seventh head), he will be unchained, and muster all his forces against the Church until the peak of the persecution under Antichrist (the eighth). Meanwhile, the church enjoyed the millenium with Christ enthroned among the nations.

"Part III (Apoc. 21-22) deals exclusively with the new heaven and the transformed earth, the new Jerusalem, Paradise, and eternal happiness. It harkens back to the first three chapters of Genesis. Mankind is restored forever to God's love and friendship, but through the Lamb and the Virgin (22:1-3). And the river of God's Love shall quench the thirst of the sons of God forever. And they shall be like unto God (22:4-5)."

(Bernard J. LeFrois: "Eschatological Interpretation of the Apocalypse" in The Catholic Biblical Quarterly, Vol. XIII, pp. 17-20. This text has been added by the editor).

"Christ Himself has given the signs which precede the end of the world, adding, 'When you see all these, know that it is **near,** (yes) at the door'. (Matt. 24:14)

"The chief signs follow:

I. **The preaching of the Gospel in the entire world**—'This Gospel will be preached in testimony to all nations, and then will come the end' (Matt. 24:33). From this it is certain that the end of the world will not occur before the Gospel has been preached in all nations; but it does not follow the end will be immediately after that. (Neither do we know what preaching of the Gospel implies; but it likely means that every community in the world must be given sufficient information on the true and only Church of Christ that the people will be guilty of grave sin if they do not accept the truth).

II. **The great defection from the Faith and the appearance of Antichrist**—'Unless the defection comes first and the man of sin be revealed . . . the day of the Lord is not imminent'. (II Thess. 2:1-4).

This defection or apostasy is one from God and his Christ, one of nations which will combat and try to abolish the Church. The Church, of course, will be preserved to the very end; although those who are not among the 'elect' and 'whose names are not written in the book of life' will follow Antichrist (Matt. 24:12; Luke 18:8; Tim. 4:1; Apoc. 13:8).

It is when this apostasy is at its highest that 'there will appear the evil one, whom (however) the Lord Jesus will (a) slay with the breath of His mouth and (b) destroy by the light of His coming' (II Thess. 2:8). (Whether these two judgments of Christ are one and the same or two different punishments is not clear nor if two is there anything here to indicate that they are contemporary. If one refers to death of the body and the other to a formal condemnation to Hell on the last day, there is nothing indicating the time that is to elapse between the two).

Antichrist has precursors for already from the beginning the fight against Christ was begun; but it will be **greatest at the end of the times** when the **man of sin** appears (This phrase **end of time** or **latter times** could mean the whole Christian era or any part of it at least so it was used by St. John who told his followers: Because Christ is now opposed, we know we are in the latter times. I John 2:18).

This adversary of God will pass himself off as God and, 'according to the operation of Satan', he will be strong 'in every power and signs and lying wonders and in every seduction of evil' (II Thess. 2:9-11). Antichrist is not a perscnification of persecution against the Church; but a special definite person. He is so referred to by St. John and segregated from indefinite antichrists. The Apostle always refers to him in the singular, for example, man of sin, son of perdition, the adversary, the evil one, etc. On the other hand a group could not propose itself for worship in a temple. Moreover, the Fathers and theologians traditionally have referred to him as a single definite person.

III. **The return of Elias and Enoch**—Two witnesses precede the coming of Christ as Judge and fight against Antichrist (Apoc. 11:3ss). One of them is Elias as is clear from Malachias (4:5-6), St. Matthew (17:10ss), and St. Luke (1:17). The other will be Enoch according to many Fathers, based on **Ecclesiasticus** (44:16) 'Henoch was transferred into Paradise that he may give repentance to the nations.' Others, however, think the second witness will be Moses or Jeremias.

IV. **The conversion of the Jews**—This conversion will be made chiefly by the preaching of Elias. St. Paul says, 'Blindness in part has happened in Israel until the fulness of the Gentiles should come in. And so all Israel should be saved as it is written, He shall come out of Sion and deliver and shall turn away ungodliness from Jacob'. This is the origin of the Christian persuasicn of the conversion of Israel at the end of the world.

V. **Many prodigies in the heavens and on earth** (Luke 21:25-26)." Father Hervé adds, "These signs are, of course, **rather indefinite** and the time of Christ's Second Coming cannot be known for certain from them."

(J. M. Hervé: **Manuale Theologiae Dogmaticae**, Vol. IV, Sec. 623.)

11

CHAPTER I

PROPHETIC TEXTS FROM THE BIBLE

We have used the Old Testament Scriptures as they exist in English in the Douay Version. This is the translation in common use among Catholics and the only complete Bible in the English language. It is translated from the Latin Vulgate in comparison with the Hebrew and Greek texts as they were recognized in A.D. 1582.

This version has several advantages. First, it is a translation of the whole canonical Old Testament. The non-Catholic versions leave out several books and parts of books. The Protestant divines chose to admit as sacred only those books which the Jewish rabbis, who refused to accept Christ, decided to retain in the Jewish Bible. This selection was made by the rabbis not earlier than two hundred years after the birth of Christ therefore long after Judaism had ceased to be guided by the Holy Ghost, as the true religion must be guided, and by a group of men without authority even under the Mosaic Law. Priests, Prophets, and Kings and not teachers (rabbis) represented Jehovah (Yahwey in Hebrew) in the Old Dispensation.

Modern Jewish authors (1) readily admit that the rabbis of the early Christian times repudiated or reinterpreted all Jewish literature which could be produced in support of the claims of Jesus Christ, himself a Jew, the last of the true Jews, and the one who from the beginning of time was destined to turn Judaism into a religion for all men of good will and not for just one particular race irrespective of the will, good or otherwise, of the members of that race.

Second, the Douay version has the approval of the successor of St. Peter and all the bishops of the Church Universal, whereas the chief and basic Protestant Bible contents itself with the approval of King James of England and the parliament of that nation. As is evident even to the most superficial students of Sacred Scripture there is nothing in the Bible, or elsewhere, except the laws made by Englishmen, that gives an English or any other King or any civil government any

(1) E.g. Waxman: **A History of Jewish Literature, Vol. I.**

12

right whatever over the Word of God. "Thou art Peter and upon this rock I will build my church." "Whatsoever thou shalt bind shall be bound." These words refer to Apostles and their successors exactly as they were spoken to Peter alone or Peter with all. Kings, princes and dead limbs cut off into national or autonomous churches have no authority over God's word and much less so has each man just because he happens to be born.

Third, the Vulgate, from which the Douay derives, not only resulted from manuscripts hundreds of years older than those used by King James' men but derived from a canon (i.e. list of Sacred Books), which the whole Church for 1600 years before Luther held to be Sacred. In fact the Septuagint Greek Bible, the Bible used by Greek speaking Jews and gotten together long before Christ and when no one "had an ax to grind," is the true index to the books which the pre-Christian Jews and all the first Christians held sacred. The Septuagint has the same books as the Vulgate and in fact it was used as a guide by the translators of the Vulgate 1200 years before the first Protestant was born and just about the time that the Jewish rabbis were deciding that they wanted no part of some of the texts their ancestors had venerated.

For these then and many other reasons we use the Douay version considering the King James and its filial versions fit reading for a study of the English language but not for an impartial survey of the Word of God.

While it would have made this book much shorter to have given only the Scriptural references letting each one go to his own Bible, we reproduce the texts here to save time for our readers, and so that standing alone and in the usual paragraph form they may be more easily integrated with each other and with private prophesies.

201a. *Genesis* On Henoch

"And Jared lived a hundred and sixty-two years, and begot Henoch . . . And Henoch lived sixty-five years, and begot Mathusala. And Henoch walked with God: and lived after he begot Mathusala, three hundred years, and begot sons and daughters. And all the days of Henoch were three hundred and sixty-five years. And he walked with God, and was seen no more: because God took him." (5: 18-24).

b. **This text is used by those who say Antichrist will be from the Tribe of Dan.**

"Dan shall judge his people like another tribe in Israel. Let Dan be a snake in the way, a serpent in the path, that biteth the horse's heels that his rider may fall backward" (49: 16-17). Cf. also Gen. 3:1 ff; Deut. 13:1 ff; Job 4:8 ff. All of Genenis 49 is on the last days but not all on Anti-Christ.

202. *Deuteronomy* On False Prophets

"If there rise in the midst of thee a prophet or one that saith he hath dreamed a dream, and he foretell a sign and a wonder, and that come to pass which he spoke, and he say to thee: Let us go and follow strange gods, which thou knowest not, and let us serve them: Thou shalt not hear the words of that prophet or dreamer: for the Lord your God trieth you, that it may appear whether you love him with all your heart, and with all your soul, or not" (13:1-3).

203. *III Kings*

Chapters 17 to 19 and Chapter 21: 17-29 recount at length the story of Elias the Prophet and his dealings with Achab King of Israel. While a reading of this part of the Bible is essential for a life of the prophet there is little or nothing to be found there concerning the role he is to play in the last days. Subsequent students, however, may have remembered the following words when they dealt with the end of time.

a. And the word of the Lord said to Elias, "go forth, and stand upon the mount before the Lord overthrowing the mountains, and breaking the rocks in pieces: the Lord is not in the wind, and after the wind an earthquake: the Lord is not in the earthquake. And after the earthquake a fire: the Lord is not in the fire, and after the fire a whistling of a gentle air. And when Elias heard it, he covered his face with his mantle, and coming forth stood in the entering in of the cave, and behold a voice unto him, saying: What dost thou here, Elias? And he answered: With zeal have I been zealous for the Lord God of hosts: because the children of Israel have forsaken thy covenant: they have destroyed thy altars, they have slain thy prophets with the sword, and I alone am left, and they seek my life to take it away. And the Lord said to him: Go, and return on thy way through the desert to Damascus: and when thou art come thither, thou shalt anoint Hazael to be king over Syria. And thou shalt anoint Jehu the son of Namsi to be king over Israel: and Eliseus the son of Saphat, of Abelmuela, thou shalt anoint to be prophet in thy room. And it shall come to pass, that whosoever shall escape the sword of Hazael, shall be slain by Jehu: and whosoever shall escape the sword of Jehu shall be slain by Eliseus. And I will leave me seven thousand men in Israel, whose knees have not been bowed before Baal, and every mouth that hath not worshipped him . . ." (19: 9-18).

b. "Because he hath humbled himself for my sake I will not bring evil in his days, but in his son's days will I bring the evil upon his house" (21: 29).

204. *IV Kings*

Chapter 1 continues the life of Elias under the son and successor of Achab and does not enlighten us on the prophet's eschatological role, but the following is, of course, important.

"And it came to pass, when the Lord would take up Elias into heaven by a whirlwind, that Elias and Eliseus were going from Galgal. And Elias said to Eliseus: Stay thou here, because the Lord hath sent me as far as Bethel. And Eliseus said to him: As the Lord liveth, and as thy soul liveth, I will not leave thee.

"And when they were come down to Bethel, the sons of the prophets, that were at Bethel, came forth to Eliseus, and said to him: Dost thou know that this day the Lord will take away thy master from thee? And he answered: I also know it: hold your peace. And Elias said to Eliseus: Stay here because the Lord hath sent me to Jericho. And he said: As the Lord liveth, and as thy soul liveth, I will not leave thee.

"And when they were come to Jericho, The sons of the

prophets that were at Jericho, came to Eliseus, and said to him: Dost thou know that this day the Lord will take away thy master from thee? And he said: I also know it: hold your peace. And Elias said to him: Stay here, because the Lord hath sent me as far as the Jordan. And he said: As the Lord liveth, and as thy soul liveth, I will not leave thee; and they two went on together. And fifty men of the sons of the prophets followed them, and stood in sight at a distance: but they two stood by the Jordan.

"And Elias took his mantle and folded it together, and struck the waters, and they were divided hither and thither, and they both passed over on dry ground. And when they were gone over, Elias said to Eliseus: Ask what thou wilt have me to do for thee, before I be taken away from thee. And Eliseus said: I beseech thee that in me may be thy double spirit. And he answered: Thou hast asked a hard thing: nevertheless if thou see me when I am taken from thee, thou shalt have what thou hast asked: but if thou see me not, thou shalt not have it.

"And as they went on, walking and talking together behold a fiery chariot, and fiery horses part them both asunder: and Elias went up by a whirlwind into heaven. And Eliseus saw him, and cried: My father, my father, the chariot of Israel, and the driver thereof. And he saw him no more: and he took hold of his own garments, and rent them in two pieces.

"And he took up the mantle of Elias, that fell from him: and going back, he stood upon the bank of the Jordan, And he struck the waters with the mantle of Elias, that had fallen from him, and they were not divided. And he said: Where is now the God of Elias? And he struck the waters and they were divided, hither and thither, and Eliseus passed over. And the sons of the prophets at Jericho, who were over against him, seeing it said: The spirit of Elias hath rested upon Eliseus. And coming to meet him, they worshipped him, falling to the ground" (2: 1-15).

205. II Paralipomenon
In this book is recorded the story of Elias and Joram King of Juda (21: 12-19). It is not to our purpose. Prophesy 3 in

our first book describes the unsettled conditions that will prevail when Israel is refounded. It too is from this Sacred Book.

206. *Psalms*

In our former work prophesies 4a to c either refer to the latter times or inspired Christian prophets.

207. *Wisdom*

Prophesy 5 in the former book describes our modern world quite well and was meant for any age which turns it back on the Creator.

208. *Ecclesiasticus* or **Ben Sirach**

This book written about 275 years before Christ is the first known to us which speaks of future roles assigned to the prophets Henoch and Elias. The author, however, is not and does not claim to be, a prophet. He merely sets down the commonly held Jewish teaching of his time.

a. "Henoch pleased God, and was translated into paradise, that he may give repentance to the nations" (44: 16).

b. "No man was born upon earth like Henoch: for he also was taken up from the earth" (49 :16).

c. "And Elias the prophet stood up, as a fire, and his sword burnt like a torch. He brought a famine upon them, and they that provoked him in their envy, were reduced to a small number, for they could not endure the commandments of the Lord. By the word of the Lord he shut up the heaven, and brought down fire from heaven thrice. Thus was Elias magnified in his wondrous works. And who can glory like to thee? Who raisest up a dead man from below, from the lot of death, by the word of the Lord God. Who broughtest down kings to destruction, and brokest easily their power in pieces, and the glorious from their bed. Who heardest judgment in Sina, and in Horeb the judgments of vengeance. Who anointedst kings to penance, and madest prophets successors after thee. Who wast taken up in a whirlwind of fire, in a chariot of fiery horses. Who art registered in the judgments of times to appease the wrath of the Lord, to reconcile the heart of the father to the son, and to restore the tribes of Jacob. Blessed are they that saw thee, and were honoured with thy friendship. For we live only in our life, but after death our name shall not be such. Elias was indeed covered with the whirlwind, and his spirit was filled in Eliseus." (48: 1-13a).

209. Isaias

In our former book prophesy 8 contains extracts descriptive of the confusion of the latter days and also a section on the eventual universal peace and unity of faith. There follows here words that have yet to be completely fulfilled. In fact Ecclesiasticus (48: 26, 27) says that Isaias foresaw the things that would come to pass at last.

a. "The noise of a multitude in the mountains, as it were of many people, the noise of the sound of kings, of nations gathered together: The Lord of hosts hath given charge to the troops of war. To them that come from a country afar off, from the end of heaven: the Lord and the instruments of his wrath, to destroy the whole land. Howl ye, for the day of the Lord is near: it shall come as a destruction from the Lord. Therefore shall all hands be faint, and every heart of man shall melt, And shall be broken. Gripings and pains shall take hold of them, they shall be in pain as a woman in labour. Every one shall be amazed at his neighbour, their countenances shall be as faces burnt. Behold, the day of the Lord shall come, a cruel day, and full of indignation, and of wrath, and fury, to lay the land desolate, and to destroy the sinners thereof out of it. For the stars of heaven, and their brightness shall not display their light: the sun shall be darkened in his rising, and the moon not shine with her light. And I will visit the evils of the world, and against the wicked for their iniquity: and I will make the pride of infidels to cease, and will bring down the arrogancy of the mighty" (13:4-11).

b. "Hell below man in an uproar to meet thee at thy coming, it stirred up the giants for thee. All the princes of the earth are risen up from their thrones, all the princes of nations. All shall answer, and say to thee: Thou also art wounded as well as we, thou are become like unto us.

"Thy pride is brought down to hell, thy carcass is fallen

down: under thee shall the moth be strewed, and worms shall be thy covering. How art thou fallen from heaven, O Lucifer,who didst rise in the morning? how art thou fallen to the earth, that didst wound the nations? And thou saidst in thy heart: I will ascend into heaven, I will exalt my throne above the stars of God, I will sit in the mountain of the covenant, in the sides of the north. I will ascend above the height of the clouds, I will be like the most High. But yet thou shalt be brought down to hell, into the depth of the pit.

"They that shall see thee, shall turn toward thee, and behold thee. Is this the man that troubled the earth, that shook kingdoms, that made the world a wilderness, and destroyed the cities thereof, that opened not the prison to his prisoners? All the kinds of the nations have all of them slept in glory, every one in his own house. But thou art cast out of thy grave, as an unprofitable branch defiled, and wrapped up among them that were slain by the sword, and art gone down to the bottom of the pit, as a rotten carcass" (14: 9-19). cf. 11:4; 66:15 ff.

210. Jeremias
Prophesy 9 in our earlier work deals at length with false prophets and speaks of terrible chastisements that will follow widespread evils. All the things foretold have not yet been accomplished.

211. Ezechiel
Prophesy 11 like 9 mentioned above deals with false prophets and chastisements. There follows the extensive extracts whence has flowed subsequent literature on Gog and Magog.

"Son of man, set thy face against God, the land of Magog, the chief prince of Mosoch and Thubal: and prophesy of him, and say to him: Thus saith the Lord God: Behold, I come against thee, O Gog, the chief prince of Mosoch and Thubal...

"After many days thou shalt be visited: at the end of years thou shalt come to the land that is returned from the sword, and is gathered out of many nations, to the mountains of Israel which have been continually waste: but it hath been brought forth out of the nations, and they shall all of them dwell securely in it. And thou shalt go up and come like a storm, and like a cloud to cover the land, thou and all thy bands and many people with thee.

"Thus saith the Lord God: In that day projects shall enter into thy heart, and thou shalt conceive a mishievous design. And thou shalt say: I will go up to the land which is without a wall, I will come to them that are at rest, and dwell securely: all these dwell without a wall, they have no bars nor gates: To take spoils and lay hold on the prey, to lay thy hand upon them that had been wasted, and afterwards restored, and upon the people that is gathered out of the nations, which hath begun to possess and to dwell in the midst of the earth.

"Saba, and Dedan, and the merchants of Tharsis, and all the lions thereof shall say to thee: Art thou to take spoils? behold, thou hast gathered thy multitude to take a prey, to take silver, and gold, and to carry away goods and substance, and to take rich spoils.

"Therefore, thou son of man, prophesy and say to Gog: Thus saith the Lord God: Thou shalt not know, in that day, when my people of Israel shall dwell securely? And thou shalt come out of thy place from the northern parts, thou, and many people with thee, all of them riding upon horses, a great company and a mighty army. And thou shalt come upon my people of Israel like a cloud, to cover the earth. Thou shalt be in the latter days, and I will bring thee upon my land: that the nations may know me, when I shall be sanctified in thee, O Gog, before their eyes.

"Thus saith the Lord God: Thou then art he, of whom I have spoken in the days of old, by my servants the prophets of Israel, who prophesied in the days of those times that I would bring thee upon them. And it shall come to pass in that day, in the day of the coming of Gog upon the land of Israel, saith the Lord God, that my indignation shall come up in my wrath. And I have spoken in my zeal, and in the fire of my anger, that in that day there shall be a great commotion upon the land of Israel: So that the fishes of the sea, and the birds of the air, and the beasts of the field, and every creeping thing that creepeth upon the ground, and all men that are upon the face of the earth, shall be moved by my presence: and the mountains shall be thrown down, and the hedges shall fall, and every wall shall fall to the ground. And I will call in the sword against him in all my mountains, saith the Lord God; every man's sword shall be pointed against his brother. And I will judge him with pestilence, and with blood, and with violent rain, and vast hailstones: I will rain fire and brimstone upon him, and upon his army, and upon the many nations that are with him. And I will be magnified, and I will be sanctified: and I will be known in the eyes of many nations: and they shall know that I am the Lord.

"And thou, son of man, prophesy against Gog, and say: Thus saith the Lord God: Behold, I come against thee, O Gog, the chief prince of Mosch and Thubal. And I will turn thee round, and I will lead thee out, and will make thee go up from the northern parts: and will bring thee upon the mountains of Israel. And I will break thy bow in thy left hand, and I will cause thy arrows to fall out of thy right hand. Thou shalt fall upon the mountains of Israel, thou and all thy bands, and thy nations that are with thee: I have given thee to the wild beasts, to the birds, and to every fowl, and to the beasts of the earth to be devoured. Thou shalt fall upon the face of the field: for I have spoken it, saith the Lord God.

"And I will send a fire on Magog, and on them that dwell confidently in the islands: and they shall know that I am the Lord. And I will make my holy name known in the midst of my people of Israel, and my holy name shall be profaned no more: and the Gentiles shall know that I am the Lord, the Holy One of Israel ...

"And it shall come to pass in that day, that I will give Gog a noted place for a sepulchre in Israel: the valley of the passengers on the east of the sea, which shall cause astonishment in them that pass by: and there shall they bury Gog, and all his multitude, and it shall be called the valley of the multitude of Gog ...

"And all the people of the land shall bury him, and

21

it shall be unto them a noted day, wherein I was glorified, saith the Lord God . . .

"And I will set my glory among the nations: and all nations shall see my judgment that I have executed, and my hand that I have laid upon them. And the house of Israel shall know that I am the Lord their God from that day forward" (38: 1 to 39: 22). cf. 7: 11 and 28.

212. Daniel

Neither the Prophet Daniel nor any other pre-Christian author has used the word Antichrist. In fact that word is used in but one context of the **New Testament.** It does not appear at all in the **Apoclypse.** Despite this it is universally agreed that in the **Book of Daniel** we find the earliest uncontested reference to the personage now known as Antichrist. It is further agreed that the **Apoclypse** develops ideas that were first given to the world by the Prophet Daniel.

a. "Behold . . . a great statue . . . and the look thereof was terrible. The head . . . was . . . gold . . . the breast . . . silver . . . the belly and thighs . . . brass the legs iron and the feet part iron and part clay. A stone cut out of a mountain without hands struck the statue and the feet and broke them. Then the iron, clay, brass, silver and gold was broken and became like chaff and were carried away by the wind but the stone became a mountain which filled the whole earth.

"This is . . . the interpretation . . . Thou (Nabuchodonosor King of Babylon) art the head . . . after thee shall rise up another kingdom (Medes and Persians), and a third kingdom shall rule all the world (Alexander the Great), and the fourth kingdom shall be as iron . . . (and) shall break and destroy all these (Roman Empire).

"And whereas thou sawest the feet and the toes, part of potter's clay and part of iron, the kingdom shall be divided, but yet it shall take its origin from the iron, according as thou sawest the iron mixed with the miry clay. And as the toes of the feet were part of iron, and part of clay, the kingdom shall be partly strong, and partly broken. And whereas thou sawest the iron mixed with miry clay, they shall be mingled indeed together with the seed of man, but they shall not stick fast one to another, as iron cannot be mixed with clay.

"But in the days of those kingdoms the God of heaven will set up a kingdom (the Church of Christ) that shall never be destroyed, and his kingdom shall not be delivered up to another people; and it shall break in pieces, and shall consume all these kingdoms, and itself shall stand forever. According as thou sawest that the stone was cut out of the mountain without hands, and broke in pieces the clay, and the iron, and the brass, and the silver, and the gold, the great God hath shown the king what shall come to pass hereafter, and the dream is true, and the interpretation thereof is faithful." (2:31-45).

b. "Four great beasts . . . came up out of the sea. The first was like a lioness and had wings (Chaldean Empire) . . . another beast like a bear (Persian Empire) . . . another like a Leopard (Grecian Empire) . . . a fourth beast terrible and wonderful . . . It had great iron teeth (Roman Empire) . . . It had ten (1) horns. I considered the horns, and behold another little horn (2) sprung out of the midst of them: and three of the first horns were plucked up at the presence thereof . . . and behold eyes like the eyes of a man were in this horn, and a mouth speaking great things . . .

"I beheld because of the voice of the great words which that horn spoke, and I saw that the beast was slain, and the body thereof was destroyed, and given to the fire to be burnt; and that the power of the other beasts was taken away, and that times of life were appointed them for a time, and a time.

(1) Ten kingdoms, as in Apoc. 17: 12, among which the empire of the fourth beast shall be parcelled. Or ten kings of the number of the successors of Alexander, as figures of such as shall be about the time of Antichrist. (Bishop Challoner note).

(2) This is commonly understood of Antichrist. It may also be applied to that great persecutor Antiochus Epiphanes, figure of Antichrist. (Bishop Challoner note).

The Messianic Kingdom

"I beheld therefore in the vision of the night, and lo, one like the son of man came with the clouds of heaven, and he came even to the Ancient of days, and they presented him before him. And he gave him power, and glory, and a kingdom, and all peoples, tribes and tongues shall serve him. His power is an everlasting power that shall not be taken away, and his kingdom that shall not be destroyed.

"My spirit trembled: I Daniel was affrighted at these things, and the visions of my head troubled me. I went near to one of them that stood by, and asked the truth of him concerning all these things. And he told me the interpretation of the words, and instructed me: These four great beasts are four kingdoms, which shall arise out of the earth. But the saints of the most high God shall take the kingdom, and they shall possess the kingdom forever and ever.

"After this I would diligently learn concerning the fourth beast, which was very different from all, and exceedingly terrible. His teeth and claws were of iron: he devoured and broke in pieces, and the rest he stamped upon with his feet; and concerning the ten horns that he had on his head; and concerning the other that came up, before which three horns fell; and of that horn that had eyes, and a mouth speaking great things, and was greater than the rest. I beheld, and lo, that horn made war against the saints, and prevailed over them, till the Ancient of days came and gave judgment to the saints of the Most High, and the time came, and the saints obtained the kingdom.

"And thus he said: The fourth beast shall be the fourth kingdom upon earth, which shall be greater than all the kingdoms, and shall devour the whole earth, and shall tread it down, and break it in pieces. And the ten horns of the same kingdom, shall be ten kings. And another shall rise up after them, and he shall be mightier than the former, and he shall bring down three kings. And he shall speak words against the High One, and shall crush the saints of the Most High; and he shall think himself able to change times and laws, and they shall be delivered into his hand until a time, and times, and half a time. (1) And judgment shall sit, that his power may be taken away, and be broken in pieces, and perish even to the end, and that the kingdom, and power, and the greatness of the kingdom under the whole heaven, may be given to the people of the saints of the Most High, whose kingdom is an everlasting kingdom, and all kings shall serve him, and shall obey him.

"Hitherto is the end of the word. I Daniel was much troubled with my thoughts, and my countenance was changed in me, but I kept the word in my heart." (7: 3-28).

c. "And out of one of them came forth a little horn: and it became great against the south, and against the east, and against the strength. And it was magnified even unto the strength of heaven: and it threw down of the strength, and of the stars, and trod upon them. And it was magnified even to the prince of the strength: and it took away from him the continual sacrifice, and cast down the place of his sanctuary. And strength was given him against the continual sacrifice, because of sins: and truth shall be cast down to the ground, and he shall do and shall prosper. And I heard one of the saints speaking, and one saint said to another, I know not to whom that was speaking: How long shall be the vision, concerning the continual sacrifice, and the sin of desolation that is made: and the sanctuary, and the strength be trodden under foot? And he said to him: Unto evening and morning two thousand three hundred days: and the sanctuary shall be cleansed . . .

"And he said to me: I will show thee what things are to come to pass in the end of the malediction: for the time hath its end . . .

"When iniquities shall be grown up, there shall arise a king of a shameless face, and understanding dark sentences. And his power shall be strengthened, but not by his own force: and he shall lay all things waste and shall prosper, and do more than can be believed. And he shall destroy the mighty, and the people of the saints, According to his will,

---

(1) Three years and a half, which is supposed to be the length of the duration of the persecution of Antichrist. (Bishop Challoner note).

and craft shall be successful in his hand: and his heart shall be puffed up, and in the abundance of all things he shall kill many: and he shall rise up against the prince of princes, and shall be broken without hand. And the vision of the evening and the morning, which was told, is true: thou therefore seal up the vision, because it shall come to pass after many days" (8: 9-26).

d. "Seventy weeks (1) are shortened upon thy people and upon thy holy city, that transgression may be finished, and sin may have an end, and iniquity may be abolished, and everlasting justice may be brought, and vision and prophecy may be fulfilled, and the Saint of saints may be anointed. Know thou therefore, and take notice: that from the going forth of the word (2) to build up Jerusalem again, unto Christ the prince, there shall be seven weeks and sixty-two weeks; and the street shall be built again, and the walls in straitness of times. And after sixty-two weeks Christ shall be slain; and the people that shall deny him shall not be his, And a people with their leader (3) that shall come, shall destroy the city and the sanctuary; and the end thereof shall be' waste, and after the end of the war the appointed desolation. And he shall confirm the covenant with many in one week, and in the half of the week (4) the victim and the sacrifice shall fail, and there shall be in the temple the abomination of desolation. And the desolation shall continue even to the consummation, and to the end." (9: 24-27).

e. "And there shall stand up in his place one despised,

---

(1) That is, of years or seventy times seven, that is 490 years.

(2) That is from the twentieth year of King Artaxerxes, when by his commandment Nehemias rebuilt the walls of Jerusalem.

(3) The Romans under Titus.

(4) Because Christ preached three years and a half, and then by His sacrifice upon the Cross abolished all the sacrifices of the Law. The abomination of desolation: some understand this of the profanation of the temple by the crimes of the Jews, and by the bloody faction of the zealots; others think it refers to bringing the ensigns and standards of the pagan Romans to the temple. Others distinguish three different times of desolation: that under Antiochus, the destruction of the temple by the Romans, and the last near the end of the world under Antichrist. (Bishop Challoner note).

26

(1) and the kingly honor shall not be given him, and he shall come privately, and shall obtain the kingdom by fraud . . .

"The king shall do according to his will, and he shall be lifted up, and shall magnify himself against every god: and he shall speak great things against the God of gods, and shall prosper, till the wrath be accomplished. For the determination is made. And he shall make no account of the God of his fathers: and he shall follow the lust of women, and he shall not regard any gods: for he shall rise up against all things. But he shall worship the God Maozim in his place: and a god whom his fathers knew not, he shall worship with gold, and silver, and precious stones, and things of great price. And he shall do this to fortify Maozim with a strange god, whom he hath acknowledged, and he shall increase glory and shall give them power over many, and shall divide the land gratis.

"And at the time prefixed the king of the south shall fight against him, and the king of the north shall come against him like a tempest, with chariots, and with horsemen, and with a great navy, and he shall enter into the countries, and shall destroy, and pass through. And he shall enter into the glorious land, and many shall fall: and these only shall be saved out of his hand, Edom, and Moab, and the principality of the children of Ammon. And he shall lay his hand upon the lands: and the land of Egypt shall not escape. And he shall have power over the treasures of gold, and of silver, and all the precious things of Egypt: and he shall pass through Libya, and Ethiopia. And tidings out of the east, and out of the north shall trouble him: and he shall come with a great multitude to destroy and slay many. And he shall fix his tabernacle in Apadno between the seas, upon a glorious and holy mountain: and shall come even to the top thereof, and none shall help him" (11: 21, 36-45).

---

(1) Antiochus Epiphanes, who at first was despised and not received as king. What is here said of this prince, is regarded by St. Jerome and others to pre-figure Antichrist. (Bishop Challoner note).

f. "But (1) at that time shall Michael rise up, the great prince, who standeth for the children of thy people. And a time shall come such as never was from the time that nations began even until that time. And at that time shall thy people be saved, everyone that shall be found written in the book.

"And many of those that sleep in the dust of the earth, shall awake; some unto life everlasting, and others unto reproach, to see it always. But they that are learned shall shine as the brightness of the firmament, and they that instruct many to justice, as stars for all eternity.

"But·thou, O Daniel, shut up the words, and seal the book, even to the time appointed. Many shall pass over, and knowledge shall be manifold.

"And I Daniel looked, and behold as it were two others stood: one on this side upon the bank of the river, and another on that side, on the other bank of the river. And I said to the man that was clothed in linen, that stood upon the waters of the river: How long shall it be to the end of these wonders? And I heard the man that was clothed in linen, that stood upon the waters of the river, when he had lifted up his right hand, and his left hand to heaven, and had sworn, by him that liveth forever, that it should be unto a time, and times, and half a time. And when the scattering of the band cf the holy people shall be accomplished, all these things shall be finished. And I heard, and understood not. And I said: O my Lord, what shall be after these things? And he said: Go, Daniel, because the words are shut up, and sealed until the appointed time. Many shall be chosen, and made white, and shall be tried as fire; and the wicked shall deal wickedly, and none of the wicked shall understand, but the learned shall understand. And from the time when the continual sacrifice shall be taken away, and the abomination unto desolation shall be set up, there shall be a thousand two hundred ninety days. Blessed is he that waiteth, and cometh unto a thousand

_____

(1) Bishop Challoner heads this chapter of Daniel thus: (The Archangel) Michael shall stand up for the people of God: with other things relating to Antichrist, and the end of the world.

three hundred thirty-five days. But go thou thy ways until the time appointed, and thou shalt rest, and stand in thy lot unto the end of the days.' ' (12:1-13).

213-216. *The Minor Prophets*

In the former book will be found the relative prophesies from Joel (14), Amos (15), Micheas (16), and Zacharias (17). They deal with divine chastisements, false prophets and the reestablishment of Israel.

217. Malachias

"Behold I will send you Elias the prophet, before the coming of the great and dreadful day of the Lord. And he shall turn the heart of the fathers to the children, and the heart of the children to their fathers: lest I come, and strike the earth with anathema" (4: 5-6).

218. *I Machabees*

17. "Elias, while he was full of zeal for the law, was taken up into heaven" (1 Mac. 2: 58).

The New Testament

In quoting this part of the Bible we have as a rule used the most recent and to our mind the best English version, namely the **Confraternity** or version issued by the Catholic Bishops of the United States. We shall change the arrangement of the prophesies somewhat so that those which fit together may be more readily understood.

Henoch and Elias In The New Testament

We do not give here the texts concerning these two unless they have a prophetic content, e.g. **St. Luke, 4**: 25-26; **St. James 5**: 17-18; **Hebrews 11**: 5.

It will be noted that the **Gospels** identify St. John the Baptist with the Elias that was to precede the coming of Christ, but in that case St. John merely typified the Elias that is to appear before Christ's second coming.

219. "Suddenly he saw an angel of the Lord, standing at the right of the altar where incense was burnt. Zachary was bewildered at the sight, and overcome with fear; but the angel said, Zachary, do not be afraid; thy prayer has been

heard, and thy wife Elizabeth is to bear thee a son, to whom thou shalt give the name of John. Joy and gladness shall be thine, and many hearts shall rejoice over his birth, for he is to be high in the Lord's favour; he is to drink neither wine nor strong drink; and from the time when he is yet a child in his mother's womb he shall be filled with the Holy Ghost. He shall bring back many of the sons of Israel to the Lord their God, ushering in his advent in the spirit and power of an Elias. He shall unite the hearts of all, the fathers with the children, and teach the disobedient the wisdom that makes men just, preparing for the Lord a people fit to receive him" (Luke, 1: 5-17).

220a. "Whereas all the prophets and the law, before John's time, could only speak of things that were to come. And this I tell you, if you will make room for it in your minds, that he is that Elias whose coming was prophesied. Listen, you that have ears to hear with" (Matthew 11: 13-15).

b. "And his disciples asked him, Tell us, why is it that the scribes say Elias must come before Christ? He answered, Elias must needs come and restore all things as they were; but I tell you this, that Elias has come already, and they did not recognize him, but misused him at their pleasure, just as the Son of Man is to suffer at their hands. Then the disciples understood that he had been speaking to them of John the Baptist" (Mathew 17: 10-13).

221. "And they asked him, Tell us, why do the Pharisees and scribes say Elias must come before Christ? He answered them, Elias must needs come and restore all things as they were; and now, what is written of the Son of Man? That he must be much ill-used, and despised. Elias too, I tell you, has already come, and they have misused him at their pleasure, as the scriptures tell of him" (Mark 9: 10-12).

222. "Of these, (Godless men) among others, Henoch was speaking, Adam's descendant in the seventh degree, when he prophesied, Behold, the Lord came with his saints in their thousands, to carry out his sentence on all men, and to convict the godless. Godless and sinners, with how

many ungodly acts they have defied God, with how many rebellious words have they blasphemed him" (Jude 14-15).

223. "Then I was given a reed, shaped like a wand, and word came to me, Up, and measure God's temple, and the altar, and reckon up those who worship in it. But leave out of thy reckoning the court which is outside the temple; do not measure that, because it has been made over to the Gentiles, who will tread the holy city under foot for the space of forty-two months. Meanwhile I will give the power of prophecy to my two witnesses; for twelve hunderd and sixty days they shall prophecy, dressed in sackcloth; these are the two olive-trees, the two candlesticks thou knowest of, that stand before him who is Lord of the earth. Does anyone try to hurt them? Fire will come out from their mouths and devour such enemies of theirs; that will be the end of all who try to do them hurt. These two have it in their power to shut the doors of heaven, and let no rain fall during the days of their ministry; they can turn the waters into blood, and smite the earth with any other plague, whenever they will. Then, when they have borne me witness to the full, the beast which comes up out of the abyss will make war on them, and defeat and kill them. Their bodies will lie in the open street, in that great city which is called Sodom or Egypt in the language of the prophecy; there, too, their Lord was crucified. For three days and a half, men of every tribe and people and language and race will gaze at their bodies, those bodies to which they refuse burial; and all who dwell on earth will triumph over them, and take their ease, and send presents to one another; such a torment were these two prophets to all that dwell on the earth. Then, after three and a half days, by God's gift the breath of life entered into them, and they rose to their feet, while great dread fell on all who watched them. Then they heard a loud voice from heaven, Come up to my side; and, while their enemies watched them, they went up, amid the clouds, to heaven. At that hour there was a great earthquake, which overthrew a tenth of the city; the count of those who were killed by the earthquake was seven thous-

and, and the rest were filled with dread, and acknowledged the glory of God in heaven' (Apoc. 11: 1-13).

224. St. Mathew On The Latter Days

a. "Yes, and you will be brought before governors and kings on my account, so that you can bear witness before them, and before the Gentiles. Only, when they hand you over thus, do not consider anxiously what you are to say or how you are to say it: words will be given you when the time comes; it is not you who speak, it is the Spirit of your Father that speaks in you. Brothers will be given up to execution by their brothers, and children by their fathers; children will rise up against their parents and will compass their deaths, and you will be hated by all men because you bear my name; that man will be saved, who endures to the last. Only, if they persecute you in one city, take refuge in another; I promise you, the Son of Man will come before your task with the cities of Israel is ended" (10: 18-23).

b. "Afterwards, while he was sitting down on Mount Olivet, the disciples came to him privately, and said, "Tell us, when will this be? And what sign will be given of thy coming, and of the world being brought to an end? Jesus answered them, Take care that you do not allow anyone to deceive you. Many will come making use of my name; they will say, I am Christ, and many will be deceived by it . . .

"In those days, men will give you up to persecution, and will put you to death; all the world will be hating you because you bear my name; whereupon many will lose heart, will betray and hate one another. Many false prophets will arise, and many will be deceived by them; and the charity of most men will grow cold, as they see wickedness abound everywhere . . .

c. "And now, when you see that which the prophet Daniel called the abomination of desolation, set up in the holy place (let him who reads this, recognize what it means), then those who are in Judaea must take refuge in the mountains; not going down to carry away anything from the house, if they are on the housetop; not going back to pick up a cloak, if they are in the fields. It will go hard with women who are with child, or have children at the breast, in those days; and you must pray that your flight may not be in the winter, or on the sabbath day, for there will be distress then such as has not been since the beginning of the world, and can never be again. There would have been no hope left for any human creature, if the number of those days had not been cut short; but those days will be cut short, for the sake of the elect. At such time, if a man tells you, See, here is Christ, or, See he is there, do not believe him. There will be false Christs and false prophets, who will rise up and shew great signs and wonders, so that if it were possible, even the elect would be deceived . . .

"Immediately after the distress of those days, the sun will be darkened, and the moon will refuse her light, and the stars will fall from heaven, and the powers of heaven will rock . . .

"So you, when you see all this come about, are to know that it is near, at your very doors . . .

"And you too must stand ready; the Son of Man will come at an hour when you are not expecting him" (24: 3-44). cf. Mark 13:14; Luke 21:25 ff.

225. St. Luke On The Latter Days

a. "Henceforward five in the same house will be found at variance, three against two and two against three; the father will be at variance with his son, and the son with his father, the mother against her daughter, and the daughter against her mother, the mother-in-law against her daughter-in-law, and the daughter-in-law against her mother-in-law" (12: 52-53).

b. "And to his own disciples he said, The time will come when you will long to enjoy for a day, the Son of Man's presence, and it will not be granted you. Men will be saying to you, See, he is here, or See, he is there; do not turn aside and follow them; the Son of Man, when his time comes, will be like the lightning which lightens from one border of heaven to the other. But before that, he must undergo many sufferings, and be rejected by this generation. In the days when the Son of Man comes, all will be as it was in the days of Noe; they ate, they drank, they married and were given in marriage, until the day when Noe went into the ark, and the flood came and destroyed them all. So it was, too, in the days of Lot; they ate, they drank, they bought and sold, they planted and built; but on the day when Lot went out of Sodom, a rain of fire and brimstone came from heaven and destroyed them all. And so it will be, in the day when the Son of Man is revealed. In that day, if a man is on the house-top and his goods are in the house, let him not come down to take them with him; and if a man is in the fields, he too must beware of turning back. Remember Lot's wife. The man who tries to save his own life will lose it; it is the man who loses it that will keep it safe. I tell you, on that night, where two men are sleeping in one bed, one will be taken and the other left; where two women are grinding together, one will be taken and the other left. Then they answered him, Where, Lord? And he told them, It is where the body lies that the eagles gather" (17: 22-37). cf. Matt. 24: 37 ff.

c. "But ah, when the Son of Man comes, will he find faith left on the earth?" (18: 8).

d. "And they asked him, Master, when will this be? What sign will be given, when it is soon to be accomplished? Take care, he said, that you do not allow anyone to deceive you. Many will come making use of my name; they will say, Here I am, the time is close at hand; do not turn aside after them. And when you hear of wars and revolts, do not be alarmed by it; such things must happen first, but the end will not come all at once. Then he told them, Nation will rise in arms against nation, and kingdom against kingdom; there will be great earthquakes in this region or that, and plagues and famines; and sights of terror and great portents from heaven. Before all this, men will be laying hands on you and persecuting you; they will give you up to the synagogues, and to prison, and drag you into the presence of kings and governors on my account...

"And Jerusalem will be trodden under the feet of the Gentiles, until the time granted to the Gentile nations has run out" (21: 7-24).

e. "Behold, a time is coming when men will say, It is well for the barren, for the wombs that never bore children,

and the breasts that never suckled them. It is then that
they will begin to say to the mountains, Fall on us, and to
the hills, Cover us. If it goes so hard with the tree that is still
green, what will become of the tree that is already dried
up?" (23: 29-31).

226. St. John's Gosple

a. "I have come in my Father's name, and you give me
no welcome, although you will welcome some other, if he
comes in his own name. How should you learn to believe, you
who are content to receive honor from one another, and are
not ambitious for the honour which comes from him, who
alone is God?" (5: 43-44).

b. "They will forbid you the synagogue; nay, the time
is coming when anyone who puts you to death will claim that
he is performing an act of worship to God; such things they
will do to you, because they have no knowledge of the
Father, or of me, And I have told you this, so that when
the time comes for it to happen, you may remember that I
told you of it" (16: 2-4).

227. St. Paul's Epistles

a. "Do not allow anyone to cheat you with empty promises; these are the very things which bring down God's
anger on the unbelievers" (Eph. 5:6).

b. "You must not allow anyone to cheat you by insisting
on a false humility which addresses its worship to angels.
Such a man takes his stand upon false visions; his is the
ill-founded confidence that comes of human speculation"
(Col. 2: 18).

c. "But there is one entreaty we would make of you,
brethren, as you look forward to the time when our Lord
Jesus Christ will come, and gather us in to himself. Do not
be terrified out of your senses all at once, and thrown into
confusion, by any spiritual utterance, any message or letter
purporting to come from us, which suggests that the day
of the Lord is close at hand. Do not let anyone find the
means of leading you astray. The apostasy must come first;
the champion of wickedness must appear first, destined to
inherit perdition. This is the rebel who is to lift up his head

above every divine name, above all that men hold in reverence, till at last he enthrones himself in God's temple, and
proclaims himself as God. Do not you remember my telling
you of this, before I left your company? At present there
is a power (you know what I mean) which holds him in
check, so that he may not shew himself before the time
appointed to him; meanwhile, the conspiracy of revolt is
already at work; only, he who checks it now will be able to
check it, until he is removed from the enemy's path. Then
it is that the rebel will shew himself; and the Lord Jesus
will destroy him with the breath of his mouth, overwhelming him with the brightness of his presence. He will come,
when he comes, with all of Satan's influence to aid him;
there will be no lack of power, of counterfeit signs and
wonders; and his wickedness will deceive souls that are
doomed, to punish them for refusing that fellowship in the
truth which would have saved them. That is why God is
letting loose among them a deceiving influence, so that they
give credit to falsehood; he will single out for judgment
all those who refused credence to the truth, and took their
pleasure in wrongdoing" (2 Thes. 2: 1-11). cf. Eph. 6: 11 ff.

d. "We are expressly told by inspiration that, in later
days, there will be some who abandon the faith, listening
to false inspirations, and doctrines taught by the devils.
They will be deceived by the prentensions of impostors,
whose conscience is hardened as if by a searing-iron. Such
teachers bid them abstain from marriage, and from certain
kinds of food, although God has made these for the grate-
ful enjoyment of those whom faith has enabled to recognize the truth. All is good that God has made, nothing is
to be rejected; only we must be thankful to him when we
partake of it" (1 Tim. 4: 1-4).

e. "It is for thee, Timothy, to keep safe what has been
entrusted to thee, avoiding these new, intruding forms of
speech, this quibbling knowledge that is knowledge only in
name; there are those who profess them, and in professing
them have shot wide of the mark which faith sets us. Grace
be with thee, Amen" (1 Tim. 6: 20-21).

f. "Be sure of this, that in the world's last age there

are perilous times coming. Men will be in love with self, in love with money, boastful, proud, abusive; without reverence for their parents, without gratitude, without scruple, without love, without peace; slanderers, incontinent, strangers to pity and to kindness; treacherous, reckless, full of vain conceit, thinking rather of their pleasures than of God. They will preserve all the outward form of religion, although they have long been strangers to its meaning. From these, too, turn away. They count among their number the men that will make their way into house after house, captivating weak women whose consciences are burdened by sin" (2 Tim. 3: 1-6).

g. "And indeed, all those who are resolved to live a holy life in Christ Jesus will meet with persecution; while the rogues and the mountebanks go on from bad to worse, at once imposters and dupes" (2 Tim. 3: 12-13).

h. "The time will surely come, when men will grow tired of sound doctrine, always itching to hear something fresh; and so they will provide themselves with a continuous succession of new teachers, as the whim takes them, turning a deaf ear to the truth, bestowing their attention on fables instead" (Tim. 4:3-4).

i. "There are many rebellious spirits abroad, who talk of their own fantasies and lead men's minds astray; those especially who hold by circumcision; and they must be silenced. They will bring ruin on entire households by false teaching, with an eye to their own base profits. Why, one of themselves, a spokesman of their own, has told us, The men of Crete were ever liars, venomous creatures, all hungry belly and nothing besides; and that is a true account of them. Be strict, then, in taking them to task, so that they may be soundly established in the faith, instead of paying attention to these Jewish fables, these rules laid down for them by human teacher who will not look steadily at the truth" (Titus 1: 10-14).

228. St. Peter

"Remember always that in the last days mocking deceivers must needs come, following the rule of their own

37

appetites, who will ask, What has become of the promise that he would appear? Ever since the fathers went to their rest, all is as it was from the foundation of the world. They are fain to forget how, long ago, heaven stood there, and an earth which God's word had made with water for its origin, water for its frame; and those were the very means by which the world, as it then was, came to perish overwhelmed by water. That same word keeps heaven and earth, as they now are, stored up, ready to feed the fire on the day when the godless will be judged, and perish. But one thing, beloved, you must keep in mind, that with the Lord a day counts as a thousand years, and a thousand years count as a day. The Lord is not being dilatory over his promise, as some think; he is only giving you more time, because his will is that all of you should attain repentance, not that some should be lost" (2 Peter 3: 3-9).

229. St. John's Epistles

It is only in these two short missives that the name Antichrist appears in Biblical literature. Moreover these are the earliest works in which that name is found. The very words of St. John, however, indicate that the Apostle did not coin the expression nor originate the idea. He says that his readers have already been told that Antichrist will come. In these epistles too we find the first clear indication that we are to distinguish between Antichrists of minor stature and **the** Antichrist.

a. "Not all prophetic spirits, brethren, deserve your credence; you must put them to the test, to see whether they come from God. Many false prophets have made their appearance in the world. This is the test by which God's Spirit is to be recognized; every spirit which acknowledges Jesus Christ as having come to us in human flesh has God for its author; and no spirit which would disunite Jesus comes from God. This is the power of Antichrist, whose coming you have been told to expect; now you must know that he is here in the world already. You, little children, who take your origin from God, have gained the mastery over it; there is a stronger power at work in you, than in the world. Those other, belonging to the world, speak

38

the world's language, and the world listens to them; we belong to God, and a man must have knowledge of God if he is to listen to us; if he does not belong to God, he does not listen to us at all. That is the test by which we distinguish the true Spirit from the false spirit. Beloved, let us love one another; love springs from God; no one can love without being born of God, and knowing God. How can the man who has no love have any knowledge of God, since God is love? (1 John 4: 1-8).

b. "Many false teachers have appeared in the world, who will not acknowldege that Jesus Christ has come in human flesh; here is the deceiver you were warned against, here is Antichrist'' (2 John 7).

230. St. Jude

"What defilement there is in their banquets, as they fare sumptuously at your side, shepherds that feed themselves without scruple! They are clouds with no water in them, driven before the winds, autumn trees that bear no fruit, given over anew to death, plucked up by the roots; they are fierce waves of the sea, with shame for their crests, wandering stars, with eternal darkness and storm awaiting them. Of these, among others, Henoch was speaking, Adam's descendant in the seventh degree, when he prophesied, Behold, the Lord came with his saints in their thousands, to carry out his sentence on all men, and to convict the godless. Godless and sinners, with how many ungodly acts they have defied God, with how many rebellious words have they blasphemed him! Such men go about whispering and complaining, and live by the rule of their own appetites; meanwhile, their mouths are ready with fine phrases, to flatter the great when it serves their ends.

But as for you, beloved, keep in mind the warnings given you long since by the apostles of our Lord Jesus Christ; how they told you, that mocking spirits must needs appear in the last age, who would make their own ungodly appetites into a rule of life. Such are the men who now keep themselves apart; animal natures, without the life of the Spirit" (12-19).

231. *The Apocalypse*

As we have noted before the chief Biblical source of information on the reign of Antichrist is this last book by the Apostle St. John. In a way his work is a commentary on what the Old Testament, especially Daniel, has to say about the last days. But of course it is much more. It completes all the Biblical prophesies concerning events that had not yet happened when it was written, namely some sixty-five years after the death of Our Lord.

Many commentaries have been written on this last book of Sacred Scripture and it is without doubt the most difficult book to understand. This is quite natural. The prophet himself need not have understood and most likely did not understand anything more about the material than what he actually committed to writing. As a result there was very little that he could explain to his disciples by word of mouth so that they could form a traditional method of interpretation such as was the case with non-prophetic books.

This is about what one would expect. Most of the book had little or no message for the author or his contemporaries. It spoke to generations yet unborn just as had the Great Isaias, Jeremias and Daniel. When the generations for whom it was chiefly intended would come into being the true author of all true prophesy, the Holy Spirit, would in his own ways allow his elect to take from the text the knowledge that had from the beginning been concealed therein. In this then is to be found the reason why the **magisterium** of the Church which is based directly on tradition in all matters of doctrine and morals must depend largely on experience and the interpretation of signs when there is a question of unfulfilled or only partially fulfilled prophesy.

In choosing a commentary for reproduction in this book we have selected one written by a twentieth century personage, who seems to be a humble, realistic man and whose work is declared of Church Authority to contain nothing contrary to the Faith. It must, naturally, be remembered that most parts of his commentary, as well as those of other authors, are purely private opinions (1).

a. "Then, in my vision, he broke the sixth seal; and with that there was a great earthquake, and the sun grew dark as sackcloth, and the whole moon blood-red; the stars of heaven fell to earth, like unripe fruit shaken from a fig tree, when a high wind rocks it; the sky folded up like a scroll, and disappeared; no mountain, no island, but was removed from its place. The kings of the world with their noblemen and their captains, men of wealth and of strength, all alike, slaves and free men, took shelter in caves and rockfastnesses among the hills. Fall on us, they said to the hills and the rocks, and hide us from the presence of Him who sits on the throne, and from the vengeance of the Lamb. Which of us can stand his ground, now that the great day, the day of their vengeance, has come? (6: 12-17).

b. "And when the second angel sounded, it was as if a great mountain, all in flames, fell into the sea, turning a third part of the sea into blood, (cf. Ex. 7:20 ff) and killing a third of all the creatures that live in the sea, and wrecking a third of the ships. And when the third angel sounded, a great star fell from heaven, (cf. Is. 14-12) burning like a torch, fell upon a third part of the rivers, and on the springs of the water. The name of this star is Wormwood: (cf. Jer. 9:15) and it changed a third of the water into wormwood, till many died of drinking the water, so bitter had it become. And when the fourth angel sounded, a third of the sun and a third of the moon and a third of the stars were smitten with darkness, so that the day must go without light for a third of its length, and the night too. (cf. Ex. 10:21-23) And I heard, in my vision, words spoken by an eagle that flew across the middle part of heaven, crying aloud, Woe, woe, woe to all that dwell on earth, when those other calls are sounded by the three angels whose trumpets have yet to sound" (8:8-13).

---

(1) This commentary will be found below under prophesy number 359. It may be well to read it in conjunction with the Sacred text, that is to read after each section of the text the section of the commentary that relates to it.

41

c. "They were not to injure the grass on the land, the green things that grew there, or the trees; they were to attack men, such men as did not bear God's mark on their foreheads. These they had no power to kill, only to inflict pain on them during a space of five months; such pain as a man feels when he has been stung by a scorpion. (When those days come, men will be looking for the means of death, and there will be no finding it; longing to die, and death will always give them the slip). The semblance of these locusts was that of horses caparisoned for war; on their heads they wore a kind of circlet that shone like gold, and their faces were like human faces; they had their hair like women's hair, and teeth like lions' teeth. They wore breastplates that might have been of iron, and the noise of their wings was like the noise of chariots, drawn at full speed by many horses into battle. It was their tails and the stings in their tails that made them like scorpions, and with these they were empowered to do men hurt for a space of five months. And they fought under a king; their king was the angel of the abyss, whose name in Hebrew is Abaddon, in Greek Apollyon, that is, in Latin, the Exterminator. Of the three woes that were pronounced, one is now past; the two others are still to come.

And when the sixth angel sounded, I heard a voice that came from the four corners of the golden altar which stands in the presence of God. It said to the sixth angel, as he stood there with his trumpet, Release the four angels who are imprisoned by the great river, the river Euphrates. So these were released, four angels who were awaiting for the year, the month, the day, the hour, when they were to destroy a third part of mankind. And the muster of the armies that followed them on horseback (for I heard their muster called) was twenty thousand armies of ten thousand. This is what I saw in my vision of the horses and of their riders; the riders had breastplates of fiery red, and blue, and brimtone yellow, and the horses' heads seemed like the heads of lions, with fire and smoke and brimstone coming out of their mouths. This fire, this smoke, this brimstone that came out of their mouths were three plagues, from which a third

42

part of mankind perished. The power these horses have to do mischief lies in their mouths and in their tails; their tails are like serpents, with serpent's heads, and they use them to do hurt. The rest of mankind, that did not perish by these plagues, would not turn away from the things their own hands fashioned; still worshipped evil spirits, false gods of gold and silver and brass and stone and wood, that can neither see, nor hear, nor move. Nor would they repent of the murders, the sorceries, the fornications, and the thefts which they committed" (9:4-21).

d. "And now I saw a second angel of sovereign strength coming down from heaven, with a cloud for his vesture, and a rainbow about his head; with a face bright as the sun, and feet like pillars of fire. He carried in his hand an open book. Setting his right foot on the sea, and his left on the dry land, he cried with a loud voice, like the roaring of a lion; and as he cried, the seven thunders of heaven made their voices heard. And I, when the seven thunders had finished their utterance, was making as if to write it down, when I heard a voice say from heaven, Do not write down the message of the seven thunders, keep it sealed. Then that angel, whom I had already seen with his feet on the sea and on the dry land, lifted up his right hand towards heaven, and swore an oath by him who lives through endless ages, who made heaven and all that is in heaven, earth and all that is on earth, the sea and all that is in the sea. He swore that there should be no more waiting; when the time came for the seventh angel to make himself heard, as he stood ready to sound his trumpet, God's secret design, made known by his servants the prophets, would be accomplished. Then once more I heard the voice speaking to me from Heaven, thus: Go and take the open book from the hand of that angel, whose feet are on the sea and on the dry land. So I went to the angel, bidding him give me the book. Take it, he said, and eat it; it will turn thy belly sour, though in thy mouth it be as sweet as honey. So I took the book from the angel's hand and ate it; it was sweet as honey in my mouth, but my belly turned sour once I had eaten it" (10-1-10).

e. "Then, when they have borne me witness to the full,

43

the beast which comes up out of the abyss will make war on them, and defeat and kill them . . .

"At that hour there was a great earthquake, which overthrew a tenth of the city; the count of those who were killed by the earthquake was seven thousand, and the rest were filled with dread, and acknowledged the glory of God in heaven (11:7-13).

f. "And now, in heaven, a great portent appeared; a woman that wore the sun for her mantle, with the moon under her feet, and a crown of twelve stars about her head. She had a child in her womb and was crying out as she travailed, in great pain of her delivery. Then a second portent appeared in heaven; a great dragon was there, fiery red, with seven heads and ten horns, and on each of the seven heads a royal diadem; his tail dragged down a third part of the stars in heaven, and flung them to earth. And he stood fronting the woman who was in child-birth, ready to swallow up the child as soon as she bore it. She bore a son, the son who is to herd the nations like sheep with a crook of iron; and this child of hers was caught up to God, right up to his throne, while the mother fled into the wilderness, where God had prepared a place of refuge for her, and there, for twelve hundred and sixty days, she is to be kept safe.

"Fierce war broke out in heaven, where Michael and his angels fought against the dragon. The dragon and his angels fought on their part, but could not win the day, or stand their ground in heaven any longer; the great dragon, serpent of the primal age, was flung down to earth, and his angels with him" (12: 1-9).

g. "Rejoice over it, heaven, and all you that dwell in heaven; but woe to you, earth and sea, now that the devil has come down upon you, full of malice, because he knows how brief is the time given him. So the dragon, finding himself cast down to earth, went in pursuit of the woman, the boy's mother; but the woman was given two wings, such as the great eagle has, to speed her flight into the wilderness, to her place of refuge, where for a year, and two years, and half a year she will be kept hidden from the serpent's view. Thereupon the serpent sent a flood of water out of his mouth in pursuit of the woman, to carry her away on its tide; but the earth came to the woman's rescue. The earth gaped wide, and swallowed up this flood which the dragon had sent out of his mouth. So, in his spite against the woman, the dragon went elsewhere to make war on the rest of her children, the men who keep God's commandments, and hold fast to the truth concerning Jesus. And he stood there waiting on the sea beach" (12: 12-18).

h. "And out of the sea, in my vision, a beast came up to land, with ten horns and seven heads, and on each of its ten horns a royal diadem; and the names it bore on its heads were names of blasphemy. This beast which I saw was like a leopard, but it had bear's feet and a lion's mouth. To it the dragon gave the strength that was his, and great dominion. One of his heads, it seemed, had been mortally wounded, but this deadly wound had been healed. And now the whole world went after the beast in admiration, falling down and praising the dragon for giving the beast all this dominion; praising the beast too.

"Who is a match for the beast? they asked; Who is fit to make war upon him? And he was given power of speech, to boast and blaspheme with, and freedom to work his will for a space of forty-two months. So he began to utter blasphemy against God, blasphemy against his name, against his dwelling-place and all those who dwell in heaven. He was allowed, too, to levy war on the saints, and to triumph over them. The dominion given to him extended over all tribes and peoples and languages and races; all the dwellers on earth fell down in adoration of him, except those whose names the Lamb has written down in his book of life, the Lamb slain in sacrifice ever since the world was made.

"Listen to this, you that have ears to hear with. The captor will go into captivity; he who slays with the sword must himself be slain with the sword. Such good ground have the saints for their endurance. and for their faithfulness (13: 1-10).

i. "Then, from the land itself, I saw another beast come up; it had two horns like a lamb's horns, but it roared like a dragon. And it stood in the presence of the former beast, to carry out all that it was empowered to do, bidding the world and all its inhabitants worship the former beast, that beast whose deadly wound was healed. Such wonders could it accomplish, that it brought down fire, before men's eyes, from heaven to earth; and by these wonders, which it was enabled to do in its masters' presence, it deluded the inhabitants of the world, bidding those who dwell in it set up an image to that beast which was smitten with the sword, and lived. Further, it was able to put life into that beast's image, so that even the beast's image uttered speech; and if anyone refused to worship the image of the beast, it had him put to death. All alike, little and great, rich and poor, free men and slaves, must receive a mark from him on their right hands, or on their foreheads, and none might buy or sell, unless he carried this mark, which was the beast's name, or the number that stands for his name. Here is room for discernment; let the reader, if he has the skill, cast up the sum of the figures in the beast's name, after our human fashion, and the number will be six hundred and sixty-six" (13: 11-18).

j. "And these were followed by a third angel, who cried aloud, Whoever worships the beast and his image, or wears the beast's mark on forehead or hand, he too shall drink; but the wine he shall drink is God's anger, untempered wine poured out in the cup of his vengeance. Fire and brimstone shall be his torment, in the presence of the holy angels, in the presence of the Lamb. The smoke of their torment goes up for ever and ever; day and night no rest is theirs, who worshipped the beast and his image, who bore the mark of his name" (14: 9-11).

k. "Then, in my vision, a white cloud appeared; and on this cloud sat one who seemed like a son of man, with a crown of gold on his head, and a sharp sickle in his hand. And now, from the temple, came another angel, crying out to him who sat on the cloud, Put in thy sickle, and reap; the crop of earth is dry, and the time has come to reap it. So he who sat on the cloud put in his sickle, and earth's harvest was reaped. Then another angel came from the heavenly temple; he too had a sharp sickle. And from the altar came another angel, the same that had power over the fire on it, and cried out to the angel with the sharp sickle, Put in thy sharp sickle, and gather the grapes from the earth's vineyard; its clusters are ripe. So the angel put in his sickle over the earth, and gathered in earth's vintage, which he drew into the great winepress of God's anger; and when the winepress was trodden out, away from the city, blood came from the winepress, and reached as high as a horse's bridle, sixteen hundred furlongs off" (14: 14-20).

l. "The first angel went on his errand, pouring out his cup on to the earth; whereupon an ulcer broke out, malignant and troublesome, upon all the men who bore the beast's mark, and worshipped his image. And the second angel poured out his cup over the sea, where it turned into blood, as if murder had been done there, till every living creature in the sea was dead. And the third poured out his cup over the rivers and the springs of water where it turned into blood. Then I heard the angel of the waters cry out, Holy thou art, O Lord, and wast ever holy, and this is a just award of thine, blood to drink for those who have shed the blood of thy saints and prophets; it is their due" (16: 2-6).

m. "The fourth angel poured out his cup over the sun, which thereupon was given the power to afflict mankind with burning heat; and in the great heat which burned them, men blasphemed the name of God, who disposes of these plagues, instead of repenting and giving praise to him. And the fifth angel poured out his cup where the beast's throne was; and with that, all the beast's kingdom was turned into darkness, in which men sat biting their tongues in pain, finding cause to blaspheme the God of heaven in their pains and their ulcers, instead of finding cause for repentence in their ill deeds. And the sixth angel poured out his cup over the great river Euphrates, whose waters were dried up, to make a passage for the kings that march from the East.

"Then, in my vision, three unclean spirits appeared in the form of frogs; one from the mouth of the dragon, one from the mouth of the beast, and one from the mouth of the false prophet. These are the devilish spirits that can do miracles, and find access to all the kings of the world, bidding them meet in battle when the great day comes, the day of the almighty God. (Behold, I come as the thief comes; blessed is he that keeps watch, and is ready clad, so that he has no need to go naked, and be ashamed in men's sight) The place where they are bidden to meet is the place called in Hebrew, Armegedon." (16: 8-6).

n. "And the seventh angel poured out his cup over the air. Then a loud voice came out of the shrine, a voice which cried from the throne, It is over; and there were lightnings and mutterings and thunder, and a violent earthquake; since men came into the world there was never an earthquake so great and so violent as this. The great city broke in three pieces, while the cities of the heathen came down in ruins. And God did not forget to minister a draught of his wine, his avenging anger, to Babylon, the great city" (16: 17-19).

o. "And now one of the angels that bear the seven cups came and spoke to me. Come with me, he said, and I will show thee how judgment is pronounced on the great harlot, that sits by the meeting place of many rivers. The kings of the world have committed fornication with her; all the dwellers on earth have been drunk with the wine of her dalliance.

"Then, in a trance he carried me off into the wilderness, where I saw a woman riding on a scarlet beast, scrawled over with the names of blasphemy; it had seven heads and ten horns. The woman went clad in purple and scarlet, all hung about with gold and jewels and pearls, and held a golden cup in her hand, full to the brim with those abominations of hers, with the lewdness of her harlot's ways. There was a title written over her forehead, The mystic Babylon, great mother-city of all harlots, and all that is abominable on earth. I saw this woman drunk with the blood of saints, the blood of those who bore witness to Jesus; and I was filled with great wonder at the sight.

"But the angel said to me, Why dost thou find cause for wonder? I will disclose to thee the mystery of this woman, and of the beast she rides, with its seven heads and ten

48

horns. The beast thou sawest is that which lived once, and now is dead; soon it must rise from the abyss, and find its way to utter destruction. The sight of this beast which lived once, and now is dead, will strike awe into every dweller on earth, except those whose names have been written, before the world was, in the book of life. Here is need for a discerning mind. These seven heads are seven hills; upon these the woman sits enthroned. They are also seven kings; of these, five have fallen already, one is reigning now; the last has not yet come, but when he does, his reign will be a short one. And the beast which lived once and now is dead must be reckoned as the eighth, yet it is one of the seven; now it is to find its way to utter destruction.

"And the ten horns which thou sawest are ten kings, who have not yet received their royal title, but are to enjoy such power as kings have, for one hour, in succession to the beast. All of them have a single policy; they surrender to the beast the power and the dominion which is theirs. And they will fight against the Lamb, but the Lamb will have the mastery of them; he is Lord of all lords, King of all kings; whoever is called, is chosen, is faithful, will take his part.

"Then he told me, These waters in thy vision at whose meeting the harlot sits enthroned, are all her peoples, nations, and languages. And the ten horns, which the beast had in thy vision, will become the harlot's enemies; they will lay her waste, and strip her quite bare, eat her flesh away, and then burn what is left of her. God has put it into their hearts to carry out his design, and to give their dominion over to the beast, so that at last all the words of God may be fulfilled. And as for the woman of thy vision, she is that great city that bears rule over the rulers of the earth" (17: 1-18).

p. "After this I saw another angel, entrusted with great power, come down from heaven; earth shone with the glory of his presence. And he cried aloud, Babylon, great Babylon is fallen; she has become the abode of devils, the stronghold of all unclean spirits, the eyrie of all birds that are unclean and hateful to man. The whole world has drunk the maddening wine of her fornication; the kings of the earth have lived in dalliance with her, and its merchants have grown rich through her reckless pleasures. And now I heard another voice from heaven, say, Come out of her, my people, that you may not be involved in her guilt, nor share the plagues that fall upon her. Her guilt mounts up to heaven; the Lord has kept her sins in remembrance. Deal with her as she has dealt with you; repay her twice for all she has done amiss; brew double measure for her in the cup she has brewed for others; requite her with anguish and sorrow for all her pride and luxury. She tells herself, Here I sit enthroned like a queen, widowhood is not for me, I shall never know what it is to mourn; and all her plagues shall come upon her in one day, death and mourning and famine, and she will be burned to the ground; such power has the God who is her judge. How they will weep over her and beat their breasts, those kings of the earth who once lived in dalliance and took their pleasures with her, as they see the smoke rise where she burns! Standing at a distance, for fear of sharing her punishment, they will cry out, Alas, Babylon the great, alas, Babylon the strong, in one brief hour judgment has come upon thee!" (18: 1-10).

q. "After this I heard, as it seemed, the voices of countless multitudes crying out in heaven, Alleluia; salvation and glory and power belong to our God; his sentence is ever true and just, and now he has given sentence against the great harlot, who poisoned the earth with her harlot's ways; now he has called her to account for the blood of his servants. And again they cried, Alleluia, the smoke of her burning goes up everlastingly" (19: 1-3).

r. "And then I saw the beast and the kings of the earth muster their armies, to join battle with the rider on the white horse and the army which followed him. The beast was made prisoner and with it the false prophet that did miracles in its presence, deluding all those who bore the beast's mark and worshipped its image; and both were thrown alive into the fiery lake that burns with brimstone. All the rest were slain by the sword of that horseman, the sword that comes from his mouth; and all the birds feasted royally on their flesh" (19: 19-21).

CHAPTER II

EARLIEST PRIVATE PROPHESY

Introductory Remarks

In dividing the prophetic texts into Scriptural and non-Scriptural instead of Scriptural, Patristic and Private prophesies we have been influenced by the Theologians who claim that there are very few notions about Antichrist on which the Fathers of the Church agree. Since such is the case we must consider all that matter on which they disagree or seem to disagree as private interpretation of Scriptural prophesy and therefore as open to question.

The fact, however, that the sayings of the Fathers, which in fact have the value of Tradition, are found in this section is not to be taken to mean any disrespect on our part. We have chosen for the reason given above and for convenience to put all non-Scriptural prophesy in chronological order. Our readers will readily distinguish the ideas on which all agree from those which are controverted or at least expressed by only one or other prophet or commentator.

Likewise we have put all texts on one level, so to speak: Those who do not claim the gift of prophesy and those who do, those who most certainly merit our attention and those of quite doubtful nature. This too is necessitated not only by convenience but by the fact that our purpose is to give our readers all the texts we could lay our hands on so that within the compass of one book it would be possible for all to survey at first hand the thinking of the whole Christian world on the Antichrist through the ages. We have only this caution to add: Be very careful not to put great faith in statements of a private nature eminating from only one source unless you have the proper Ecclesiastical guarantee that the source in question merits special credence.

We have deliberately omitted the ravings of the 16th and 17th Century fanatics who wasted much good paper trying to absolve themselves by making the papacy Antichrist. Even all their own followers have long since repudiated their bigotry. And likewise we omit the rantings of certain sect leaders of our own day who try to revive the papal Antichrist legend by choosing some letters alleged to be on the tiara and omitting others. Let us take all or none.

We finally consign to the ash can the trash ground out on sectarian presses which chooses dates for the second coming of Christ and changes them as the fixed dates arrive. We even turn a deaf ear to sectarian speeches which put the Second Coming just around the corner and the preachers and their flock in white robes waiting with out-stretched arms while the rest of mankind are gathered up by the Avenger. The reason is evident: God has reserved for himself a knowledge of exact dates and we believe even of approximate times. Signs he tells us, he will give, Signs which the elect alone, but all the elect, high and low, will recognize. So let us be content to do exactly as He says "Watch and pray, for ye know not the day nor the hour."

Jewish Apocrapha

233. *Book of Enoch* (170 B.C.)

a. "The Lord said unto Michael: Go, bind Semjaza and his associates who have united themselves with women so as to have defiled themselves with them in all their unclean-ness. And when their sons have slain one another, and they have seen the destruction of their beloved ones, bind them fast for seventy generations in the valleys of the earth, till the day of their judgment and of their consummation, till the judgment that is forever and ever is consummated. In those days they shall be led to the abyss of fire: (and) to the torment and the prison in which they shall be confined forever. And whosoever shall be condemned and destroyed will from henceforth be bound together with them to the end of all generations. And destroy all the spirits of the reprobate and the children of the Watchers, because they have wronged mankind. Destroy all wrong from the face of the earth and let every evil work come to an end: and let the plant of righteousness and truth appear: and it shall prove a blessing; the works of righteousness and truth shall be planted in truth and joy for evermore (10: 11-16).

b. "Enoch was hidden, and no one of the children of men knew where he was hidden . . . His activities had to do with the Watchers and his days were with the holy ones . . ." (12: 1).

c. "And Enoch was raised aloft on the chariots of the spirit and his name vanished among them . . ." (70: 1, 2).

d. "When sin and righteousness, blasphemy and violence and all kind of deeds increase, and apostasy in transgression and uncleanness increase, a great chastisement shall come from heaven" (91: 7).

e. "I was born the seventh in the first week, while justice reigned yet upon the earth.

"And after me, in the second week will come a great evil (the deluge) and in that week the first consummation will take place. Then one man will be saved. And after this week, injustice will again grow.

"And then, in the third week, towards its end, a man shall be chosen, (Abraham) as a plant of just judgment, and he will then grow as a plant in justice for all eternity.

"Then, in the fourth week, towards its end, the visions of the holy and just will appear, and a law for all generations, and an ark (enclos?) shall be prepared for them.

"Then, in the fifth week, towards its end, a House of Glory and domination shall be built for eternity.

"Then, in the sixth week, those who live in that time shall be all blinded and their hearts shall fall into iniquity, far from wisdom, and then, a Man will ascend to Heaven; and at the end of this week the house of domination shall be destroyed by fire, and the race of the powerful root shall be dispersed.

"Then, in the seventh week, a perverse generation shall arise, — many will be their works, but all shall be works of abomination. And at the end of this week the just branches of the plant of just shall be chosen, for the end that the science of God's Creation shall be given them a hundred-fold — for who is the child of man who can hear the voice of the Holy One without being moved, and who can think His thoughts, and who can contemplate all the works of heaven? Who is he who can see the heavens, and who is he that may know the works' of heaven? And how could he see a soul or a spirit, and how could he speak of such, how could he rise to see their workings or act as they do? And who is the child of man who may know the length or the breadth of heaven, or upon what base it is founded, how great is the number of stars and where they rest, the lights of heaven.

"Then there will be another week, the eighth. This week shall be that of justice, and a sword shall be given (to justice?) that judgment may be accomplished and the oppressors and the sinners will be broken by the hands of the just, and towards the end of this week, the just shall acquire dwelling-places because of their justice, and a house shall be erected for the great King, of an eternal splendor.

"And after this, in the ninth week, the judgment of the just shall be unveiled to all men, throughout the universe, and all the works of the impious shall disappear from the earth and the number inscribed for perdition, and all men shall see the path of righteousness.

"And then, in the tenth week, at its seventh part, will take place the great eternal Judgment. He shall exercise judgment and vengeance amid the angels. And then the first heaven shall disappear and pass away, and a new heaven will appear, and all the powers of heaven shall shine eternally, seven times greater, and after this week shall come weeks, numerous weeks, which shall pass on, innumerable, and eternal, for kindness and justice, and from thence, sin will be no longer named forever." (93: 1-14; 91: 12-17).

f. "Woe to you, ye rich, for ye have trusted in your riches, and from your riches shall ye depart, because ye have not remembered the Most High in the days of your riches."

g. "Woe to you who work godlessness, and glory in lying and extol them: ye shall perish, and no happy life shall be yours. Woe to them who pervert the words of uprightness, and transgress the eternal law, and transform themselves into what they were not (into sinners): they shall be trodden under foot and upon the earth. In those days make ready, ye righteous, to raise your prayers as a memorial, and place them as a testimony before the angels, that they may place the sin of the sinners for a memorial before the Most High. In those days the nations shall be stirred up, and the families of the nations shall arise on the day of destruction. And in those days the destitute shall go forth and carry off their children, and they shall abandon them, so that their children shall perish through them: Yea, they shall abandon their children (that are still) sucklings, and not return to them, and shall have no pity on their beloved ones. And again I swear to you, ye sinners, that sin is prepared for a day of unceasing bloodshed. And they who worship stones, and grave images of gold and silver and wood (and stone) and clay, and those who worship impure spirits and demons and all kinds of idols not according to knowledge, shall get no manner of help from them. And they shall become godless by reason of the folly of their hearts, and their eyes shall be blinded through the fear of their hearts and through visions in their dreams. Through these they shall become godless and fearful; for they shall have wrought all their work in a lie, and shall have worshipped a stone: therefore in an instant shall they perish. But in those days blessed are all they who accept the words of wisdom, and understand them, and observe the paths of the Most High, and walk in the path of His righteousness, and become not godless with the godless; for they shall be saved. Woe to you who spread evil to your neighbors; for you shall be slain in Sheol. Woe to you who make deceitful and false measures, and (to them) who cause bitterness on the earth; for they shall thereby be utterly consumed. Woe to you who build your houses through the grievous toil of others, and all their building materials are the bricks and stones of sin; I tell you ye shall have no peace. Woe to them who reject the measure and eternal heritage of their fathers and whose souls follow after idols; for they shall have no rest. Woe to them who work unrighteousness and help oppresion, and slay their neighbors until the day of the great judgment. For He shall cast down your glory, and bring affliction on your hearts, and shall arouse His fierce indignation and destroy you all with the sword; and all the Holy and righteous shall remember your sins" (99: 1-16).

h.   "And in those days in one place the fathers together

with their sons shall be smitten and brothers one with another shall fall in death till the streams flow with their blood. For a man shall not withhold his hand from slaying his sons and his sons' sons, and the sinner shall not withhold his hand from his honoured brother; from dawn till sunset they shall slay one another. And the horse shall walk up to the breast in the blood of sinners, and the chariot shall be submerged to its height. In those days the angels shall descend into the secret places and gather together into one place all those who brought down sin, and the Most High will arise on that day of judgment to execute great judgment amongst sinners" (100:1-4).

i. "Sinners will alter and pervert the words of righteousness in many ways, and will speak wicked words, and lie, and practice great deceits, and write books concerning their words" (104: 10).

j. "Another book . . . Enoch wrote for his son Mathusala and for those who will come after him, and keep the law in the last days. Ye who have done good shall wait for those days till an end is made of those who work evil, and an end of the might of the transgressors. And wait ye indeed till sin has passed away, for their names shall be blotted out of the book of life and out of the holy books, and their seed shall be destroyed forever, and their spirits shall be slain, and they shall cry and make lamentation in a place that is a chaotic wilderness, and in the fire shall they burn; for there is no earth there" (108: 1-3).

234. Book of Jubilees (105 B.C.)

"And Enoch was the first among men that are born on earth who learnt writing and knowledge and wisdom and who wrote down the signs of heaven according to the order of their months in a book, that men might know the seasons of the years.

"And what was and what will be he saw in a vision of his sleep, as it will happen to the children of men throughout their generations until the day of judgment; he saw and understood everything, and wrote his testimony, and placed the testimony on earth for all the children of men . . .

"And he was taken from amongst the children of men, and we conducted him into the Garden of Eden in majesty and honour, and behold there he writes down the condemnation and judgment of the world, and all the wickedness of the children of men. And on account of it (God) brought the waters of the flood upon all the land of Eden; for there he was set as a sign and that he should testify against all the children of men, that he should recount all the deeds of the generations until the day of condemnation.

"Enoch's office was ordained for a testimony to the generations of the world, so that he should recount all the deeds of generation unto generation, till the day of judgment" (4: 17-24).

235. *Book of the Secrets of Enoch* (cir. 25 A.D.)

a. "It came to pass, when Enoch had told his sons, that the angels took him on to their wings and bore him up on to the first heaven and placed him on the clouds. And there I looked, and again I looked higher, and saw the ether, and they placed me on the first heaven and showed me a very great sea, greater than the earthly sea." (3: 1-3).

b. "And I fell prone and bowed down to the Lord, and the Lord with his lips said to me: 'Have courage, Enoch, do not fear, arise and stand before my face into eternity.' And the archistratege Michael lifted me up, and led me to before the Lord's face. And the Lord said to his servants tempting them: 'Let Enoch stand before my face into eternity,' and the glorious ones bowed down to the Lord, and said: 'Let Enoch go according to Thy word.' And the Lord said to Michael: 'Go and take Enoch from out his earthly garments, and anoint him with my sweet ointment, and put him into the garments of My glory.' And Michael did thus, as the Lord told him. He anointed me, and dressed me, and the appearance of that ointment is more than the great light, and his ointment is like sweet dew, and its smell mild, shining like the sun's ray, and I looked at myself, and was like one of his glorious ones. And the Lord summoned one of his archangels by name Pravuil, whose knowledge was quicker in wisdom than the other archangels, who wrote all the deeds of the Lord; and the Lord said to Pravuil: 'Bring out the books from my store-houses, and a reed of quick writing, and give it to Enoch, and deliver to him the choice and comforting books out of thy hand'." (22: 4-12).

c. "When Enoch had talked to the people, the Lord sent out darkness on to the earth, and there was darkness, and it covered those men standing and talking with Enoch, and they took Enoch up on to the highest heaven, where the Lord is; and he received him and placed him before his face, and the darkness went off from the earth, and light came again. And the people saw and understood not how Enoch had been taken, and glorified God, and found a roll in which was traced: 'the invisible God,' and all went to their homes . . . He was taken up to heaven on the first day of the month of Tsivan and remained in heaven sixty days. He wrote all these signs of all creation, which the Lord created, and wrote three hundred and sixty-six books, and handed them over to his sons and remained on earth thirty days, and was again taken up to heaven on the sixth day cf the month of Tsivan . . . All the sons of Enoch, made haste, and erected an altar at the place called Achuzan, whence and where Enoch had been taken up to heaven. And they took sacrificial oxen and summoned all people and sacrificed the sacrifice before the Lord's face. All people, the elders of the people and the whole assembly came to the feast and brought gifts to the sons of Enoch. And they made a great feast, rejoicing and making merry three days, praising God, who had given them such a sign through Enoch, who had found favour with him, and that they should hand it on to their sons from generation to generation, from age to age" (67: 1 — 68: 7).

236. *IV Esdras* (1st Century A.D.)

a. "The Day of Judgment is decisive, and displays unto all the seal of truth. None shall pray for another on that Day, neither shall one lay a burden on another; for then every one shall bear his own righteousness or unrighteousness. And I anwered and said: How is it that we now find that Elias prayed for those who recieved the rain, and for the dead, that he might live? And he answered me and said: The present age is not the End; the glory of God abides not therein continuously: therefore have the strong prayed for the weak. But the Day of Judgment shall be the end of this age and the beginning of the eternal age that is to come."

b. "Concerning the signs of the end: Behold, the days come when the inhabitants of the earth shall be seized with great panic, and the way of truth shall be hidden, and the land be barren of faith. And iniquity shall be increased above that which thou thyself now seest or that thou hast heard of long ago. And the land that thou seest now to bear rule shall be a pathless waste; and men shall see it forsaken: if the Most High grant thee to live, thou shalt see it after the third (period) in confusion. Then shall the sun suddenly shine forth by night and the moon by day; and blood shall trickle forth from wood, and the stone utter its voice: The peoples shall be in commotion, the movements (?) (of the stars) shall change, and one whom the dwellers upon earth do not look for shall wield sovereignty, and the birds shall take to general flight, and the sea shall cast forth its fish. And one whom the many do not know will make his voice heard by night; and all shall hear his voice. And the earth o'er wide regions shall open, and fire burst forth for a long period: The wild beasts shall desert their haunts, and women bear monsters. (And one-year old children shall speak with their voices; pregnant women shall bring forth untimely births at three or four months, and these shall live and dance. And suddenly shall the sown places appear unsown, and the full storehouse shall suddenly be found empty.) Salt waters shall be found in the sweet; friends shall attack one another suddenly. Then shall intelligence hide itself, and wisdom withdraw to its chamber — by many shall be sought and not found. And unrighteousness and incontinency shall be multiplied upon the earth. One land shall also ask another and say: Is Righteousness — that doeth the right — passed through thee? And it shall answer, No. And it shall be in that time men shall hope and not obtain, shall labour and not prosper" (5: 1-12).

c. "Behold the days come, and it shall be, when I am

about to draw nigh to visit the dwellers upon earth, and when I require from the doers of iniquity (the penalty of) their iniquity; (and when the humiliation of Sion shall be complete,) and when the Age which is about to pass away shall be sealed then (will I show these signs)" (6: 18-20).

d.   "Measure (the matter) carefully in thy mind, and when thou seest that a certain part of the predicted signs are past, then shalt thou understand that it is the very time when the Most High is about to visit the world which he has made. When in the world there shall appear quakings of places, tumult of peoples, scheming of nations, confusion of leaders, disquietude of princes, then shalt thou understand that it is of these things the Most High has spoken since the days that were aforetime from the beginning. For just as with respect to all that has happened in the world the beginning is obscure (?) but the end (issue) manifest, so also are the times of the Most High: the beginnings are (visible) in portents and secret signs, and the end in effects and marvels"

e.   "In the last days thereof the Most High will raise up three kings; and they shall change many things therein, and shall exercise lordship over the earth and over the dwellers therein with much oppression, above all those that were before them. Therefore are they called the heads of the eagle: for these are they that shall bring to a head his wickedness, and consummate his last end. And whereas thou didst see that the great head disappeared — one of them shall die upon his bead, but yet with pain. But as for the two who remain the sword shall devour them. For the sword of the one shall devour him that was with him; nevertheless this one also shall fall by the sword in the last days. And whereas thou didst see two under-wings passing over to the head that is upon the right side; this is the interpretation: These are they whom the Most High hath kept for his (i.e. the eagle's) end; and their rule shall be short and full of uproar, as thou hast seen. And as for the lion whom thou didst see roused from the wood and roaring, and speaking to the eagle and reproving him for his unrighteousness and all his deeds, as thou hast heard: This

60

is the Messiah whom the Most High hath kept unto the end (of the days, who shall spring from the seed of David, and shall come and speak) unto them; he shall reprove them for their ungodliness, rebuke them for their unrighteousness, reproach them to their faces with their treacheries. For at the first he shall set them alive for judgment; and when he hath rebuked them he shall destroy them" (12: 23-33).

f. "These are the interpretations of the vision: Whereas thou didst see a Man coming up from the heart of the Sea: this is he whom the Most High is keeping many ages (and) through whom he will deliver his creation and the same shall order the survivors. And whereas thou didst see that out of his mouth there came wind, and fire, and storm; and whereas he held neither spear, nor any warlike weapon, but destroyed the assault of that multitude which had come to fight against him — this is the interpretation: (Behold, the days come when the Most High is about to deliver them that are upon earth. And there shall come astonishment of mind upon the dwellers on earth: and they shall plan to war one against another, city against city, place against place, people against people, and kingdom against kingdom. And it shall be when these things shall come to pass, and the signs shall happen which I showed thee before, then shall my Son be revealed whom thou didst see as a Man ascending). It shall be, when all the nations hear His voice, every man shall leave his own land and the warfare which they have one against another; and an innumerable multitude shall be gathered together, as thou didst see, desiring to come and to fight against him. But he shall stand upon the summit of Mount Sion. (And Sion shall come and shall be made manifest to all men, prepared and builded, even as thou didst see the mountain cut without hands. But he, my Son, shall reprove the nations that are come for their ungodliness — which things (i.e., the rebukes) are like unto a storm—; and shall reproach them to their face with their evil thoughts and with the tortures with which they are destined to be tortured — which are compared unto a flame —; and then shall he destroy them without labour by the Law which is compared unto fire" (13:25-38).

g. "For still worse evils than those which thou hast seen happen shall yet take place. For the weaker the world grows through age, so much the more shall evils increase upon the dwellers on earth. Truth shall withdraw further off, and falsehood be right at hand: for already the Eagle is hastening to come whom thou sawest in vision" (14: 15-17).

237. *II Baruch* (1st Century A.D.)

a. "God answered and said unto me: 'Into twelve parts is that time (end) divided, and each one of them is reserved for that which is appointed for it . . . In the eighth part a multitude of spectres and attacks of Shedim.. And in the ninth part the fall of fire. And in the tenth part rapine and much oppression. And in the eleventh part wickedness and unchastity. And in the twelfth part confusion from the mingling together of all those things aforesaid. For these parts of that time are reserved, and shall be mingled one with another and minister one to another. For some shall leave out some of their own, and receive (in its stead) from others, and some complete their own and that of others, so that those may not understand who are upon the earth in those days that this is the consummation of the times" (27: 1-15).

b. "For that time shall arise which brings affliction; for it shall come and pass by with quick vehemence, and it shall be turbulent coming in the heat of indignation. And it shall come to pass in those days that all the inhabitants of the earth shall be moved one against another, because they know not that My judgment has drawn nigh. For there shall not be found many wise at that time, and the intelligent shall be but a few; Moreover, even those who know shall most of all be silent. And there shall be many rumours and tidings not a few, and the doings of phantasmata shall be manifest, and promises not a few be recounted, some of them shall prove idle, and some of them shall be confirmed. And honour shall be turned into shame, and strength humiliated into contempt, and probity destroyed, and beauty' shall become ugliness. And many shall say to many at that time: 'Where hath the multitude of intelligence hidden itself, and whither hath the multitude of wisdom removed itself?' And whilst they are meditating these things, then envy shall arise in those who had not thought aught of themselves and passion shall seize him that is peaceful, and many shall be stirred up in anger to injure many, and they shall rouse up armies in order to shed blood, and in the end they shall perish together with them. And it shall come to pass at the self-same time, that a change of times shall manifestly appear to every man, because in all those times they polluted themeselves and they practiced oppression, and walked every man in his own works, and remembered not the law of the Mighty One. Therefore a fire shall consume their thoughts, and in flame shall the meditations of their reins be tried: for the Judge shall come and will not tarry. Because each of the inhabitants of the earth knew when he was transgressing. But My law they knew not by reason their pride. But many shall then assuredly weep, Yea, over the living more than over the dead. And I answered and said: ' O Adam, what hast thou done to all those who are born from thee?' And what will be said to the first Eve who hearkened to the serpent? For all this multitude are going to corruption, nor is there any numbering of those whom the fire devours" (48: 31-43).

c. "Behold! the days come, and it shall be when the time of the age has ripened, and the harvest of its evil and good seeds has come, that the Mighty One will bring upon the earth and its inhabitants and upon its rulers perturbation of spirit and stupor of heart. And they shall hate one another, and provoke one another to fight" (2 Bar. 70: 2-3).

d. "And when those things which were predicted have come to pass, then shall confusion fall upon all men, and some of them shall fall in battle, and some of them shall perish in anguish, and some of them shall be destroyed by their own. Then the Most High will reveal those peoples whom He has prepared before, and they shall come and make war with the leaders that shall then be left. And it shall come to pass that whosoever gets safe out of the war shall die in the earthquake, and whosoever gets safe out of the earthquake shall be burned by the fire, and whosoever gets safe out of the fire shall be destroyed by famine . . . For all the earth shall devour its inhabitants" (70: 6-10).

238. *Martyrdom of Isaias* (1st Century A.D.)

"The angel of lawlessness, who is the ruler of this world, is Beliar, whose name is Matanbuchus. And he delighted in Jerusalem because of Manasseh, and he made him strong in apostatizing and in the lawlessness which was spread abroad in Jerusalem. And witchcraft and magic increased and divination and auguration, and fornication (and adultery), and the persecution of the righteous by Manassen and (Belachira, and) Tobia the Canaanite, and John of Anathoth, and by (Zadok) the chief of the works. And the rest of the acts, behold they are written in the book of the Kings of Judah and Israel. And when Isaiah the son of Amoz saw the lawlessness which was being perpetrated in Jerusalem and the worship of Satan and his wantonness, he withdrew from Jerusalem and settled in Bethlehem of Judah" (2:4b-6)

239. *Testament of Abraham* (1st Century A.D.)

"He that bears witness here is the teacher of heaven and earth, and the scribe of righteousness, Enoch, for the Lord sent him hither to write down the sins and righteousness of each one. Abraham said, And how can Enoch bear the weight of the souls, not having seen death? or how can he give sentence to all the souls? Michael said, If he gives sentence concerning the souls, it is not permitted; but Enoch himself does not give sentence, but it is the Lord who does so, and he has no more to do than only to write. For Enoch prayed to the Lord saying, I desire not, Lord, to give sentence on the souls, lest I be grievous to anyone; and the Lord said to Enoch, I shall command thee to write down the sins of the soul that makes atonement and it shall enter every breath and every creature. But the third time they shall be judged by the Lord God of all, and then, indeed, the end of that judgment is near, and the sentence terrible, and there is none to deliver"

240. Testament of Isaias (1st Century A.D.)

"In the last times your sons will forsake singleness and will cleave unto insatiable desires; and leaving guilelessness will draw near to malice; and forsaking the commandments of the Lord they will cleave unto beliar (Satan); and leaving husbandry they will follow after their own wicked devices" (6: 1 ss).

241. Revelation of Esdras (1st Century A.D.)

"God said: 'First I will make an earthquake for the fall of four-footed beasts and of men; and when you see that brother gives up brother to death, and that children shall rise up against their parents, and that a woman forsakes her own husband, and when nation shall rise up against nation in war, then you will know that the end is near. For then neither brother pities brother, nor man wife, nor children parents, nor friends friends, nor a slave his master, for he who is the adversary of men shall come up from Tartarus (Hell), and shall show men many things."

Christian Apocrapha

The books quoted here date from the second and third centuries after Christ. None of them has any other value than to illustrate the notions of Antichrist which were current in some Christian circles during these centuries.

242. History of Joseph

a. "I say to you, O my brethren, that they also, Enoch and Elias, must towards the end of time return into the world and die — in the day, namely, of commotion, of terror, of perplexity, and affliction. For Antichrist will slay four bodies, and will pour out their blood like water, because of the reproach to which they shall expose him, and the ignomy with which they, in their lifetime, shall brand him when they reveal his impiety. And we said: O our Lord, our God and Saviour, who are those four whom Thou hast said Antichrist will cut off from the reproach they bring upon him? The Lord answered: They are Enoch, Elias, Schila, and Tabitha. When we heard this from our Saviour, we rejoiced and exulted; and we offered all glory and thanksgiving to the Lord God, and our Saviour Jesus Christ. He it is to whom is due glory, honour, dignity, dominion, power, and praise, as well as to the good Father with Him, and to the Holy Spirit that giveth life, henceforth and in all time for evermore"

b. "We asked why Joseph should not have been exempted from death like Enoch and Elias. Jesus speaks of the inevitableness of death, and tells how Enoch and Elias still have to die, and are in trouble until their death is over. Antichrist will shed the blood of two men like a cup of water, because of the reproaches they will heap upon him. We asked: Who are the two whom he will slay? Answer: Enoch and Elias"

243. *Acts of Pilate*

a. "And the apostles have told you with an oath, saying: We saw Jesus upon the Mount Mamilch with his disciples and that he taught them all things that ye heard of them, and, say they, we saw him taken up into heaven. And no man asked them in what manner he was taken up. For like as the book of the holy scriptures hath taught us that Elias also was taken up into heaven, and Eliseus cried out with a loud voice, and Elias cast his hairy cloak upon Eliseus, and Eliseus cast the cloak upon Jordan and passed over and went unto Jericho. And the sons of the prophets met him and said: Eliseus, where is thy lord Elias? And he said that he was taken up into heaven"

b. "But the Lord holding the hand of Adam delivered him unto Michael the archangel, and all the saints followed Michael the archangel, and he brought them all into the glory and beauty (grace) of paradise. And there met with them two men, ancients of days, and when they were asked of the saints: Who are ye that have not yet been dead in hell with us and are set in paradise in the body? then one of them answering, said: I am Enoch which was translated hither by the word of the Lord, and this that is with me is Elias the Thesbite which was taken up in a chariot of fire: and up to this day we have not tasted death, but we are received unto the coming of Antichrist to fight against him with signs and wonders of God, and to be slain of him in Jerusalem, and after three days and a half to be taken up again alive on the clouds" ("hell" here means "abode of the dead").

244. Book of Bartholomew

"The angels cried unto the powers, saying: Remove your gates, ye princes, remove the everlasting doors, for behold the King of glory cometh down. Hades said: Who is the King of Glory, that cometh down from heaven unto us?

"The devil said unto Hades: Why affrightest thou me, Hades? it is a prophet, and he hath made himself like unto God: this prophet will we take and bring him hither unto those that think to ascend into heaven. And Hades said: Which of the prophets is it? Show me: Is it Enoch the scribe of righteousness? But God hath not suffered him to come down upon the earth before the end of the six thousand years. Sayest thou that it is Elias, the avenger? But before the end he cometh not down. What shall I do, whereas the destruction is of God: for surely our end is at hand? For I have the number of the years in mine hands."

245. Book of John the Evangelist

a. "I asked the Lord and said: What shall be in that time? And he said to me: From the time when the devil fell from the glory of the Father and lost his own glory, he sat upon the clouds, and sent his ministers, even angels flaming with fire, unto men from Adam even unto Henoch his servant. And he raised up Henoch upon the firmament and showed him his godhead, and commanded pen and ink to be given him: and he sat down and wrote threescore and seven books. And he commanded that he should take them to the earth and deliver them unto his sons, and began to teach them to perform the custom of sacrifice, and unrighteous mysteries, and so did he hide the kingdom of heaven from men. And he said unto them: Behold that I am your god and beside me is none other god. And therefore did my Father send me into the world that I might make it known unto men, that they might know the evil device of the devil."

b. "I asked the Lord concerning the day of judgment: What shall be the sign of thy coming? And he answered and said unto me: When the numbers of the righteous shall be accomplished, that is, the number of the righteous that are crowned, then shall Satan be loosed out of his prison, having great wrath, and shall make war with the righteous, and they shall cry unto the Lord with a loud voice. And immediately the Lord shall command an angel to blow with the trumpet, and the voice of the archangel shall be heard in the trumpet from heaven even unto hell. And then shall the sun be darkened and the moon shall not give her light, and the stars shall fall, and the four winds shall be loosed from their foundations, and shall cause the earth and the sea and the mountains to quake together. And the heaven shall immediately shake and the sun shall be darkened, and it shall shine even to the fourth hour"

246. *Apocalypse of Peter*

a. "Hast thou not understood that the fig-tree is the house of Israel? Verily I say unto thee, when the twigs thereof have sprouted forth in the last days, then shall feigned Christs come and awake expectation, saying: I am the Christ, that am now into the world. And when they (Israel) shall perceive the wickedness of their deeds they shall turn away after them and deny him (whom our fathers did praise), even the first Christ whom they crucified and therein sinned a great sin. But this deceiver is not the Christ. And when they reject him he shall slay with the sword, and there shall be many martyrs. Then shall the twigs of the fig-tree, that is, the house of Israel, shoot forth: many shall become martyrs at his hand. Enoch and Elias shall be sent to teach them that this is the deceiver which must come into the world and do signs and wonders to deceive. And therefore shall they that die by his hand be martyrs, and shall be reckoned among the good and righteous martyrs who have pleased God in their life."

b. "Many of them shall be false prophets, and shall teach ways and diverse doctrines of perdition. And they shall become sons of perdition. And then shall God come unto my faithful ones that hunger and thirst and are afflicted and prove their souls in this life, and shall judge the sons of iniquity. Take heed that no man deceive you, and you be not doubters and servers of other gods. Many shall come in My name, saying: I am the Christ: believe them not, neither draw near unto them. . . .

"And this shall come at the day of judgment upon them that have fallen away from faith in God and that have committed sin: Floods (cataracts) of fire shall be let loose; and darkness and obscurity shall come and clothe and veil the whole world; and the waters shall be changed and turned into coals of fire, and all that is in them shall burn, and the sea shall become fire. Under the heaven shall be a sharp fire that cannot be quenched, and floweth to fulfill the judgment of wrath. And the stars shall fly in pieces by flames of fire, as if they had not been created, and the powers (firmaments) of the heaven shall pass away for lack of water and shall be as though they had not been.

"Woe unto all them that are found great with child in that day, and to them that give suck to infant children, and to them that dwell by the sea (the waves). Woe to them that shall behold that day. For a dark mist shall cover the boundless world, of the east and west, the south and north."

247. Apocalypse of Paul

"Straightway the gate was opened, and there came forth a hoary-headed man to meet us; and he said to me: Welcome, Paul, beloved of God! and, with a joyful countenance, he kissed me with tears. And I said to him: Father, why weepest thou? And he said to me: Because God hath prepared many good things for men, and they do not His will in order that they may enjoy them. And I asked the angel: My Lord, who is this? And he said to me: This is Enoch, the witness of the last day.

"Looking away, I saw other two from afar off. And I asked the angel: Who are these, my Lord? And he said to me: These are Enoch and Elias. And they came and saluted me, saying: Welcome, Paul, beloved of God! And I said to them: Who are you? And Elias the prophet answered and said to me: I am Elias the prophet, who prayed to God, and He caused that no rain should come down upon the earth for three years and six months, on account of the unrighteousness of the sons of men. For often, of a truth, even the angel besought God on account of the rain; and I heard, be patient until Elias my beloved shall pray, and I send rain upon the earth."

248. *Revelation of John*

"Then shall appear the denier, and he who is set apart in the darkness, who is called Antichrist. And again I said: Lord, reveal to me what he is like. And I heard a voice saying to me: The appearance of his face is dusky; the hairs of his head are sharp like darts; his eyebrows like a wild beast's; his right eye like the star which rises in the morning, and the other like a lion's; his mouth about one cubit; his teeth a span long; his fingers like scythes; the print of his feet of two spans; and on his face an inscription, Antichrist; he holds in his hand a cup of death; and all that worship him drink of it. His right eye is like the morning star, and his left like a lion's; because he was taken prisoner by the archangel Michael, and he took his godhead from him. And I was sent from the bosom of my Father, and I drew up the head of the polluted one, and his eye was consumed. And when they worship him, he writes on their right hands, that they may sit with him in the outer fire; and for all who have not been baptized, and have not believed, have been reserved all anger and wrath. And I said: My Lord, and what miracles does he do? Hear righteous John: He shall remove mountains and hills, and he shall beckon with his polluted hand, Come all to me; and through his displays and deceits they will be brought together to his own place. He will raise the dead, and show in everything like God. He shall be exalted even to heaven, and shall be cast down even to Hades, making false displays. And then will I make the heaven brazen, so that it shall not give moisture upon the earth; and I will hide the clouds in secret places, so that they shall not bring moisture upon the earth; and I will command the horns of the wind, so that the wind shall not blow upon the earth.

"And again I said: Lord, and how many years will he do this upon the earth? And I heard a voice saying to me: Hear, righteous John. Three years shall those times be; and I will make the three years like three months, and the three months like three weeks, and the three weeks like three days, and the three days like three hours, and the three hours like three seconds, as said the prophet David, His throne hast Thou broken down to the ground; Thou hast shortened the days of his time; Thou hast poured shame upon him. And then I shall send forth Enoch and Elias to convict him; and they shall show him to be a liar and a deceiver and he shall kill them at the altar, as said the prophet, Then shall they offer calves upon Thine altar."

249. Epistle of Barnabas

"And God made in six days the works of his hands; and he finished them on the seventh day, and he rested the seventh day, and sanctified it. Consider, my children, what that signifies, he finished them in six days. The meaning of it is this; that in six thousand years the Lord God will bring all things to an end. For with him one day is a thousand years; as himself testifieth, saying, Behold this day shall be as a thousand years. Therefore, children, in six days, that is, in six thousand years, shall all things be accomplished. And what is that he saith, And he rested the seventh day: he meaneth this; that when his Son shall come, and abolish the season of the Wicked One, and judge the ungodly; and shall change the sun and moon, and the stars; then he shall gloriously rest in that seventh day."

250. Epistle of the Apostles (Ethiopic Text)

"Take heed that no man deceive you, and that ye be not doubters and serve other gods. Many shall come in My name, saying: I am the Christ. Believe them not, neither draw near unto them . . . Verily I say unto thee, when the twigs of the fig tree have sprouted forth in the last days (the fig tree is the House of Israel) then shall feigned

71

Christs awake expectations, saying: I am the Christ that
am now come into the world."

251. *Epistle of the Apostles*

"In the last days the kinsman shall show no favor to
his kinsman, nor any man to his neighbor. And they that
were overthrown shall rise up and behold them that overthrew them; and men shall take from one and give to another . . . But they that are deceivers in the world and
enemies of righteousness, upon them shall come the fulfillment of the prophecy of David, who said: Their feet
are swift to shed blood, their tongue uttereth slander, ad-
ders' poison is under their lips. I behold thee companying
with theives, and partaking with adulterers, thou continuest
speaking against thy brother and puttest stumbling-blocks
before thine own mother's son . . . And there shall be many
that believe on my name and yet follow after evil and
spread vain doctrine. And men shall follow after them and
their riches, and be subject unto their pride, and lust for
drink, and bribery, and there shall be respect of persons
among them . . . There shall come forth another doctrine,
and because they shall strive after their own advancement,
they shall bring forth an unprofitable doctrine. And therein
shall be a deadly corruption (of uncleanness), and they
shall teach it, and shall turn away them from eternal life.
But woe unto them that falsify this my word and commandment, and draw away them that hearken to the commandment of life; for together with them they shall come into
everlasting judgment."

252. *Epistle of James*

"There shall be wonders and strange appearances in
heaven and on earth before the end of the world come. 'Tell
us now, how shall we perceive it?' And he answered us: 'I
will teach it to you; and not that which believe, as well as
them who shall hear that man and believe in me. In those
years and days shall it come to pass.'

"The sun and moon fighting one with the other, a continual rolling and noise of thunders and lightnings, thunder
and earthquakes; cities falling and men perishing in their

over-throw, a continual drouth for lack of rain, a terrible pestilence and great mortality, mighty and untimely, so they that die lack burial: and the bearing forth of brethren and sisters and kinsfolk shall be upon one bier. The kinsman shall show no favour to his kinsman, nor any man to his neighbor. And they that were overthrown shall rise up and behold them that overthrew them, that they lack burial, for the pestilence shall be full of hatred and pain and envy: and man shall take from one and give to another, and thereafter shall it wax yet worse than before. Then shall my Father be wroth at the wickedness of men, for many are their transgressions and the abominations of their uncleannes weighth heavy upon them in the corruption of their life.

"Lord will not then the nations say: 'Where is their God?' And he answered and said unto us: 'Thereby shall the elect be known, that they, being plagued with such afflictions, come forth.' We said: 'Will then their departure out of the world be by a pestilence which giveth them pain?' He answered us: 'Nay, but if they suffer much affliction, it will be a proving of them.'

"In those years and days shall war be kindled upon war, the four ends of the earth shall be in commotion and fight against each other. Thereafter shall be quakings of clouds, darkness, and drouth and persecutions of them that believe in me and against the elect. Thereupon shall come doubt and strife and transgressions against one another."

253. Gospel of Bartholomew
"Antichrist said: I will tell thee. And a wheel came up out of the abyss, having seven fiery knives. The first knife hath twelve pipes. Antichrist answered: The pipe of fire in the first knife, in it are put the casters of lots and diviners and enchanters, and they that believe in them or have sought them, because in the iniquity of their heart they have invented false divinations. In the second pipe of fire are first the blasphemers . . suicides . . idolaters . . In the rest are the first perjurers. And Bartholomew said: Dost thou then do these things by thyself alone? And Satan said: If I were

able to go forth by myself, I would have destroyed the whole
world in three days: but neither I nor any of the six hundred
go forth. For we have other swift ministers whom we command, and we furnish them with an hook of many points
and send them forth to hunt, and they catch for us souls of
men, enticing them with sweetness of divers baits, that is
by drunkenness and laughter, by backbiting, hypocrisy,
pleasures, fornication, and the rest of the trifles that come
out of their treasures."

254. *Apoclypse of Thomas*

"Hear thou, Thomas, the things which must come to pass
in the last times: there shall be famine and war and earthquakes in divers places, snow and ice and great drought shall
there be, and many dissensions among the peoples, blasphemy, iniquity, envy and villainy, indolence, pride and
intemperance, so that every man shall speak that which
pleaseth him. And my priests shall not have peace among
themselves, but shall sacrifice unto me with deceitful mind;
therefore will I not look upon them. Then shall the priests
behold the people departing from the House of the Lord
and turning unto the world, as well as transgressing in the
House of God . . . The House of the Lord shall be desolate
and her altars be abhorred . . . The place of holiness shall be
corrupted, the priesthood polluted, distress shall increase,
virtues shall be overcome (i.e., vices made to appear as
virtues?), joy perish, and gladness depart (i.e., without
holiness there can be no peace — without peace no real happiness) . . . In those days evils shall abound: there shall be
respectors of persons, hymns shall cease out of the House
of the Lord, truth shall be no more, covetousness shall
abound among the priests; an upright man shall not be
found. And they shall vindicate for themselves many things.

"At that time shall be very great rising of the sea, (common people?) so that no man shall tell news to any man. The
kings of the earth and the princes and the captains shall be
troubled, and no man shall speak freely. Grey hairs shall be
seen upon boys, and the young shall not give place unto the
aged. After that shall arise another king, a crafty man,

74

who shall hold rule for a short space: in whose days there shall be all manner of evils, even the death of the race of men from the east even unto Babylon. And thereafter death and famine and sword in the land of Chanaan even unto Rome. Then shall all the fountains of waters and wells boil over and be turned into blood (or into dust and blood). The heaven shall be moved, the stars shall fall upon the earth, the sun shall be cut in half like the moon, and the moon shall not give her light. There shall be great signs and wonders in those days when Antichrist draweth near. These are the signs unto them them that dwell in the earth. In those days the pains of great travail shall come upon them. Woe unto them that build, for they shall not inhabit. Woe unto them that break up the fallow, for they shall labour without cause. Woe unto them that make marriages, for unto famine and need shall they beget sons. Woe unto them that join house to house or field to field, for all things shall be consumed with fire. Woe unto them that look not unto themselves while time alloweth, for hereafter shall they be condemned for ever. Woe unto them that turn away from the poor when he asketh.

"And on the third day of judgment, about the second hour, shall be a voice from the four corners of the world. The first heaven shall be rolled up like a book and shall straightaway vanish. And because of the smoke and stench of the brimstone of the abyss the days shall be darkened unto the tenth hour. Then shall all men say: I think that the end draweth near, that we shall perish. These are the signs of the third day.

"And on the fourth day at the first hour, the earth of the east shall speak, the abyss shall roar: then shall all the earth be moved by the strength of an earthquake. In that day shall all the idols of the heathen fall, and all the buildings of the earth. These are the signs of the fourth day.

"And on the fifth day, at the sixth hour, there shall be great thunderings suddenly in the heaven, and the powers of light and the wheel of the sun shall be caught away, and there shall be great darkness over the world until evening, and the stars shall be turned away from their ministry.

In that day all nations shall hate the world and despise the life of this world. These are the signs of the fifth day.

"After a little space there shall arise a king out of the east, a lover of the law, who shall cause all good things and necessary to abound in the house of the Lord: he shall show mercy unto the widows and to the needy, and command a royal gift to be given unto the priests: in his days shall be abundance of all things"

Other Ancient Oracles

255. Sibyline Oracle

"In a ring around the city the accursed kings shall place each one his throne with his infidel people by him. And then with a mighty voice God shall speak unto all the undisciplined empty-minded people, and judgment shall come upon them from the mighty God, and all shall perish at the hand of the Eternal. From heaven shall fall fiery swords down to the earth: lights shall come bright and great, flashing into the midst of men. And earth, the universal Mother, shall shake in those days at the hand of the Eternal, and the fishes in the sea, and all the beasts of the earth and the countless tribes of flying things, and all souls of men and every sea shall shudder at the presence of the Eternal and there shall be panic. And the towering mountain peaks and the hills of the giants He shall rend, and the murky abyss shall be visible to all. And the high-hung ravines in the lofty mountains shall be full of dead bodies: the rocks shall flow with blood, and each torrent shall flood the plain. The well-built walls of the disaffected men shall all fall to the ground, because they knew not the law nor the judgment of the Mighty God, but with witless mind with one united onslaught ye cast your spears against the Holy One. And God shall judge all with war and sword, and with fire and cataclysms of rain. And there shall be brimstone from heaven, yea stones and hail incessant and grievous: and death shall be upon the fourfooted beasts. And then shall they know the Immortal God, who ordains these things. Wailing and lamenting through the length and breadth of the land shall come with the perishing of men: and all the shameless shall

76

be washed with blood. Yea, the land itself shall drink of the blood of the perishing: the beasts shall eat their fill of flesh." (cf also Prophesy 63).

256. Sibylla Tiburtina

"A prince of iniquity shall come forth from the tribe of Dan, who will be called Antichrist. Child of perdition, full of arrogance, and of an insane malice, he shall work upon earth a number of prodigies in order to support his erroneous doctrines. Through his magical arts he will surprise the good faith of many persons. At his command fire shall come from above.

"At that time the years shall be shortened as well as the months, the weeks, and the days and hours. God will shorten, not the measure or duration, but the number of those terrible days.

"For the sake of God's elect, Antichrist shall be killed upon Mount Olivet by Michael (the Archangel). Then the dead shall rise." (cf Prophesy 36)

CHAPTER III

EARLY PATRISTIC WRITERS

257. St. Clement (d. 97)

a. "Let us be imitators also of those who in goatskins and sheepskins went about proclaiming the coming of Christ; I mean Elijah, Elisha, and Ezekiel among the prophets."

"But that He might show that these things were done on account of the ungrateful, He translated to immortality a certain one of the first race of men, because He saw that he was not unmindful of His grace, and because he hoped to call on the name of God; while the rest who were so ungrateful that they could not be amended and corrected even by labours and tribulations, were condemned to a terrible death."

b. "Let us steadfastly contemplate those who have perfectly ministered to God's excellent glory. Let us take (for instance) Enoch, who, being found righteous in obedience, was translated, and death was never known to happen to him."

258. *Didache* (90-100)

"In the last days false prophets and corrupters shall be multiplied and the sheep shall be turned into wolves and love into hate. When their iniquity shall have increased they shall hate each other and persecute and betray; and then shall appear the deceiver of the world as the son of God. And he shall do signs and wonders and the earth shall be given into his hands and he shall do evil such as has not been done through the ages. Then shall come the creature of men in fire of probation and many shall be scandalized (meaning led into evil doing) and they shall perish.

"He however who shall have persevered in his faith shall be saved from that accursed one. And then shall appear the signs of truth: first the sign of the heavens opened, secondly the sign of the trumpet, and third the resurrection of the dead; but by no means the resurrection of all, but as is said, 'The Lord shall come and all the saints with Him. Then the world shall see the Lord coming upon the clouds of heaven'."

The above quotation from the Didache is found incorporated in the Seventh Book of the so-called CONSTITUTIONS OF THE TWELVE APOSTLES (cir. 325 A. D., section XXXII) but so embellished that it departs considerably from the sense of the original. As an example of the interpretation of the redactor, I quote the changed parts, "and then shall appear the enemy of truth, the prince of lies (2 Thes. 2) whom the Lord Jesus shall destroy with the spirit of his mouth, who takes away the wicked with His lips; and many shall be offended at Him. But they that endure to the end, the same shall be saved. And then shall appear the sign of the son of man in heaven (Isa. 9: 4; Matt. 24); and afterwards shall be the voice of a trumpet by the archangel (1 Thes. 4: 16) and in that interval shall be the revival of those that were asleep. And then shall the Lord come, and all his saints with Him, with a great concussion above the clouds, with the angels of His power (Matt. 16: 27) in the throne of his kingdom, to condemn the devil, the deceiver of the world, and to render to everyone according to his deeds." (Note: as is evident this commentator shies from the idea of a "first resurrection" as given in the Didache).

259. *Pastor of Hermes* (2nd Century)
"When these things thus come to pass then He who is Lord, looking upon what is done and opposing His own will to the disorder, He cleanses the wickedness, partly by inundating the world with much water, and partly by burning it with most rapid fire, and sometimes pressing it with wars and pestilences, He will bring His world to its ancient state." (cf also Prophesy 34)

260. St. Irenaeus (130-200)
a. "By means of the events which shall occur in the time of Antichrist it is shown that he, being an apostate and a robber, is anxious to be adored as God; and that although a mere slave, he wishes himself to be proclaimed as a king. For he (Antichrist) being endued with all the power of the devil, shall come, not as a righteous king, nor as a legitimate king, (i.e. one) in subjection to God, but an im-

pious, unjust, and lawless one; as an apostate, iniquitous and murderous; as a robber, concentrating in himself (all) satanic apostasy, and setting aside idols to persuade (men) that he himself is God, raising up himself as the only idol, having in himself the multifarious errors of the other idols. This he does, in order that they who do (now) worship the devil by means of many abominations, may serve himself by this one idol, of whom the apostle thus speaks in the second Epistle to the Thessalonians: "Unless there shall come a falling away first, and the man of sin shall be revealed, the son of perdition who opposeth and exalteth himself above all that is called God, or that is worshipped; so that he sitteth in the temple of God, showing himself as if he were God." The apostle therefore clearly points out his apostasy, and that he is lifted up above all that is called God, or that is worshipped — that is, above every idol — for these are indeed so called by men, but are not (really) gods; and that he will endeavour in a tyrannical manner to set himself forth as God."

b. "Daniel, looking forward to the end of the last kingdom, i.e., the ten last kings, amongst whom the kingdom of those men shall be partitioned, and upon whom the son of perdition shall come, declares that ten horns shall spring from the beast, and that another little horn shall arise in the midst of them, and that three of the former shall be rooted up before his face. He says: 'And, behold, eyes were in this horn as the eyes of a man, and a mouth speaking great things, and his look was more stout than his fellows. I was looking, and this horn made war against the saints, and prevailed against them, until the Ancient of days came and gave judgment to the saints of the most high God, and the time came, and the saints obtained the kingdom.' Then, further on, in the interpretation of the vision, there was said to him: 'The fourth beast shall be the fourth kingdom upon earth, which shall excell all other kingdoms, and devour the whole earth, and tread it down, and cut it in pieces. And its ten horns are ten kings which shall arise, and after them shall arise another, who shall surpass in evil deeds all that were before him, and shall overthrow three

80

kings; and he shall speak words against the most high God, and wear out the saints of the most high God, and shall purpose to change times and laws; and (everything) shall be given into his hand until a time, times and a half time, that is, for three years and six months, during which time, when he comes, he shall reign over the earth. Of whom also the Apostle Paul again, speaking in the second Epistle to the Thessalonians, and at the same time proclaiming the cause of his advent, thus says: 'And then shall the wicked one be revealed, whom the Lord Jesus shall slay with the spirit of His mouth, and destroy by the presence of His coming; whose coming (i.e., the wicked one's) is after the working of Satan, in all power, and signs, and portents of lies, and with all deceivableness of wickedness for those who perish; because they did not receive the love of the truth, that they might be saved. And therefore God will send them the working of error, that they may believe a lie; that they all may be judged who did not believe the truth, but gave consent to iniquity'."

c. "The Lord also spoke as follows to those who did not believe in Him: 'I have come in my Father's name, and ye have not received Me: when another shall come in his own name, him ye will receive,' calling Antichrist **the other**, because he is alienated from the Lord. This is also the unjust judge, whom the Lord mentioned as one 'who feared not God, neither regarded man,' to whom the widow fled in her forgetfulness of God, — that is, the earthly Jerusalem, — to be avenged for her adversary. Which also he shall do in the time of his kingdom: he shall remove his kingdom into that (city), and shall sit in the temple of God, leading astray those who worship him, as if he were Christ. To this purpose Daniel says again: 'And he shall desolate the holy place; and sin has been given for a sacrifice, and righteousness been cast away in the earth, and he has been active and gone on prosperously.' And the angel Gabriel, when explaining his vision, states with regard to this person: 'And towards the end of their kingdom a king of a most fierce countenance shall arise, one understanding (dark) questions, and exceedingly powerful, full of wonders; and he shall corrupt, direct, influence, and put strong men down, the holy people likewise; and his yoke shall be directed as a wreath (round their neck); deceit shall be in his hand, and he shall be lifted up in his heart: he shall also ruin many by deceit, and lead many to perdition, bruising them in his hand like eggs.' And then he points out the time that his tyranny shall last, during which the saints shall be put to flight, they who offer a pure sacrifice unto God: 'And in the midst of the week,' he says, 'the sacrifice and the libation shall be taken away, and the abomination of desolation (shall be brought) into the temple: even unto the consummation of the time shall the desolation be complete.' Now three years and six months constitute the half-week."

d. "In a still clearer light has John, in the Apocalypse, indicated to the Lord's disciples what shall happen in the last times, and concerning the ten kings who shall then arise, among whom the empire which now rules (the earth) shall be partitioned. He teaches us what the ten horns shall be which were seen by Daniel, telling us that thus it had been said to him: 'And the ten horns which thou sawest are ten kings, who have received no kingdom as yet, but shall receive power as if kings one hour with the beast. These have one mind, and give their strength and power to the beast. These shall make war with the Lamb, and the Lamb shall overcome them, because He is the Lord of lords and the King of kings.' It is manifest, therefore, that of these (potentates), he who is to come shall slay three, and subject the remainder to his power, and that he shall be himself the eighth among them. And they shall lay Babylon waste and burn her with fire, and shall give their kingdom to the beast, and put the Church to flight. After that they shall be destroyed by the coming of our Lord. For that kingdom must be divided, and thus come to ruin, the Lord (declares when he) says:, 'Every kingdom divided against itself shall not stand'."

e. "It must be therefore, that the kingdom, the city, and the house be divided into ten; and for this reason He has already foreshadowed the partition and division (which shall take place). Daniel also says particularly, that the end of the kingdom consists in the toes of the image seen by Nebuchadnezzar, upon which came the stone cut out without hands; and as he does himself say: 'The feet were indeed the one part iron, the other part clay, until the stone was cut without hands, and struck the image upon the iron and clay feet, and dashed them into pieces, even to the end.' Then afterwards, when interpreting this, he says: 'And as thou sawest the feet and the toes, partly indeed of clay, and partly of iron, the kingdom shall be divided, and there shall be in it a root of iron, as thou sawest the iron mixed with baked clay. And the toes were indeed the one part iron, but the other part clay.' The ten toes, therefore, are these ten kings, among whom the kingdom shall be partitioned, of whom some indeed shall be strong and active, or energetic; others, again, shall be sluggish and useless, and shall not agree; as also Daniel says: 'Some part of the kingdom shall be strong, and part shall be broken from it. As thou sawest the iron mixed with the baked clay, there shall be minglings among the human race, but no cohesion one with the other, just as iron cannot be welded on to pottery ware.' And since an end shall take place, he says: "And in the days of these kings shall the God of heaven raise up a kingdom which shall never decay, and His kingdom shall not be left to another people. It shall break in pieces and shatter all kingdoms, and shall itself be exalted for ever. As thou sawest that the stone was cut without hands from the mountain, and brake in pieces the baked clay, the iron, the brass, the silver, and the gold, God has pointed out to the king what shall come to pass after these things; and the dream is true, and the interpretation trustworthy."

f. "The apostle John says: 'Because they received not the love of God, that they might be saved, therefore God shall also send them the operation of error, that they may believe a lie, that they all may be judged who have not believed the truth, but consented to unrighteousness.' For when he (Antichrist) is come, and of his own accord concentrates in his own person the apostasy, and accomplishes whatever he shall do according to his own will and choice, sitting also in the temple of God, so that his dupes may adore him as the Christ; wherefore also shall he deservedly 'be cast into the lake of fire:' (this will happen according to divine appointment), God by his prescience foreseeing all this, and at the proper time sending such a man, 'that they may believe a lie, that they all may be judged who did not believe the truth, but consented to unrighteousness;' whose coming John has thus described in the Apocalypse:

g. "And the beast which I had seen was like unto a leopard, and his feet as of a bear, and his mouth as the mouth of a lion; and the dragon conferred his own power upon him, and his throne, and great might. And one of his heads was as it were slain unto death; and his deadly wound was healed, and all the world wondered after the beast. And they worshipped the dragon because he gave power to the beast; and they worshipped the beast, saying, Who is like unto this beast, and who is able to make war with him? And there was given unto him a mouth speaking great things, and blasphemy and power was given to him during forty and two months. And he opened his mouth for blasphemy against God, to blaspheme His name and His tabernacle, and those who dwell in heaven. And power was given him over every tribe, and people, and tongue, and nation. And all who dwell upon the earth worshipped him, (every one) whose name was not written in the book of the Lamb slain from the foundation of the world. If any one have ears, let him hear. If any one shall lead into captivity, he shall go into captivity. If any shall slay with the sword, he must be slain with the sword. Here is the endurance and the faith of the saints.

"After this he likewise describes his armour-bearer, whom he also terms a false prophet: 'He spake as a dragon, and exercised all the power of the first beast in his sight, and caused the earth, and those that dwell therein, to adore the first beast, whose deadly wound was healed. And he shall perform great wonders, so that he can even cause fire to descend from heaven upon the earth in the sight of men, and he shall lead the inhabitants of the earth astray.' Let no one imagine that he performs these wonders by divine power, but by the working of magic. And we must not be surprised if, since the demons and apostate spirits are at his service, he through their means performs wonders, by which he leads the inhabitants of the earth astray. John says further: 'And he shall order an image of the beast to be made, and he shall give breath to the image, so that the image shall speak; and he shall cause those to be slain who will not adore it.' He says also: 'And he will cause a mark (to be put) in the forehead and in the right hand, that no one may be able to buy or sell, unless he who has the mark of the name of the beast or the number of his name; and the number is six hundred and sixty-six,' that is, six times a hundred, six times ten, and six units. (He gives this) as a summing up of the whole of that apostasy which has taken place during six thousand years.

h. "In the end the Church shall be suddenly caught up from this, it is said, 'There shall be tribulation such as has not been since the beginning, neither shall be.' For this is the last contest of the righteous, in which, when they overcome, they are crowned with incorruption.

i. "And there is therefore in this beast, when he comes, a recapitulation made of all sorts of iniquity and of every deceit, in order that all apostate power, flowing into and being shut up in him, may be sent into the furnace of fire. Fittingly, therefore, shall his name possess the number six hundred and sixty-six, since he sums up in his own person all the comixture of wickedness which took place previous to the deluge, due to the apostasy of the angels. For Noah was six hundred years old when the deluge came upon the earth, sweeping away the rebellious world, for the sake of that most infamous generation which lived in the times of Noah. And (Antichrist) also sums up every error of devised idols since the flood, together with the slaying of the prophets and the cutting off of the just. For that image which was set up by Nebuchadnezzar had indeed a height of sixty cubits, while the breadth was six cubits; on account of which Ananias, Azarias, and Misael, when they did not worship it, were cast into a furnace of fire, pointing out prophetically, by what happened to them, the wrath against the righteous which shall rise towards the (time of the)

85

end. For that image, taken as a whole, was a prefiguring of this man's coming, decreeing that he should undoubtedly himself alone be worshipped by all men. Thus, then, the six hundred years of Noah, in whose time the deluge occurred because of the apostasy, and the number of cubits of the image for which these just men were sent into the fiery furnace, do indicate the number of the name of that man in whom is concentrated the whole apostasy of six thousand years, and unrighteousness, and wickedness, and false prophecy, and deception, for which things' sake a cataclysm of fire shall also come (upon the earth).

j. "Such, then, being the state of the case, and this number being found in all the most approved and ancient copies (of the Apocalypse), and those men who saw John face to face bearing their testimony (to it); while reason also leads us to conclude that the number of the name of the beast, (if reckoned), according to the Greek mode of calculation by the (value of) the letters contained in it, will amount to six hundred and sixty and six; that, the number of tens shall be equal to that of the hundreds, and the number of hundreds equal to that of the units for that number which (expresses) the digit six being adhered to throughout, indicates the recapitulations of that apostasy, taken in its full extent which occurred at the beginning, during the intermediate periods, and which shall take place at the end, — I do not know how it is that some have erred following the ordinary mode of speech, and have vitiated the middle number in the name, deducting the amount of fifty from it, so that instead of the six decads they will have it that there is but one. (I am inclined to think that this occurred through the fault of the copyists, as is wont to happen, since numbers also are expressed by letters; so that the Greek letter which expresses the number sixty was easily expanded into the letter Iota of the Greeks.) Others then received this reading without examination; some in their simplicity, and upon their own responsibility, making use of this number expressing one decad; while some, in their inexperience, have ventured to seek out a name which should contain the erroneous and spurious number. Now, as regards those who have done this in simplicity, and without evil intent, we are at liberty to assume that pardon will be granted them by God. But as for those, who for the sake of vainglory, lay it down for certain that names containing the spurious number are to be accepted, and affirm that this name, hit upon by themselves, is that of him who is to come; such persons shall not come forth without loss, because they have led into error both themselves and those who have confided in them. Now, in the first place, it is loss to wander from the truth, and to imagine that as being the case which is not; then again, as there shall be no light punishment (inflicted) upon him who either adds or subtracts anything from the Scripture, under that such a person must necessarily fall. Moreover, another danger, by no means trifling, shall overtake those who, falsely presume that they know the name of Antichrist. For if these men assume one (number), when this (Antichrist) shall come having another, they will be easily led away by him, as supposing him not to be the expected one, who must be guarded against.

k. "These men, therefore, ought to learn (what really is the state of the case), and go back to the true number of the name, that they be not reckoned among false prophets. But, knowing the sure number declared by Scripture, that is, six hundred sixty and six, let them await, in the first place, the division of the kingdom into ten; then, in the next place, when these kings are reigning, and beginning to set their affairs in order, and advance their kingdom, (let them learn) to acknowledge that he who shall come claiming the kingdom for himself, and shall terrify those men of whom we have been speaking, having a name containing the aforesaid number, is truly the abomination of desolation. This, too, the apostle affirms: 'When they shall say, Peace and safety, then sudden destruction shall come upon them.' And Jeremiah does not merely point out his sudden coming, but he even indicates the tribe from which he shall come, where he says, 'We shall hear the voice of his swift horses from Dan; the whole earth shall be moved by the voice of the neighing of his galloping horses:

he shall also come and devour the earth, and the fulness thereof, the city also, and they that dwell therein.' This, too, is the reason that this tribe is not reckoned in the Apocalypse along with those which are saved.

l. "It is therefore more certain, and less hazardous, to await the fulfillment of the prophecy, than to be making surmises, and casting about for any names that may present themselves, inasmuch as many names can be found possessing the number mentioned; and the same question will, after all, remain unsolved. For if there are many names found possessing this number, it will be asked which among them shall the coming man bear. It is not through a want of names containing the number of that name that I say for the truth: for the name Evanthas contains the number, but I make no allegation regarding it. Then also Lateinos has the number six hundred and sixty-six; and it is very probable (solution), this being the name of the last kingdom (of the four seen by Daniel). For the Latins are they who at present bear rule: I will not, however, make any boast over this (coincidence). Teitan too, among all the names which are found among us, is rather worthy of credit. For it has in itself the predicted number, and is composed of six letters, each syllable containing three letters; and (the word itself) is ancient, and removed from ordinary use; for among our kings we find none bearing this name Titan, nor have any of the idols which are worshipped in public among the Greeks and barbarians this appellation. Among many persons, too, this name is accounted divine, so that even the sun is termed "Titan" by those who do now possess (the rule). This word, too, contains a certain outward appearance of vengeance, and of one inflicting merited punishment because he (Antichrist) pretends that he vindicates the oppressed. And besides this, it is an ancient name, one worthy of credit, of royal dignity, and still further, a name belonging to a tyrant. Inasmuch, then, as this name "Titan" has so much to recommend it, there is a strong degree of probability, that from among the many (names suggested), we infer, that perchance he who is to come shall be called "Titan." We will not, however, incur the risk of pronouncing positively as to the name of Antichrist; for if it were necessary that his name should be distinctly revealed in this present time, it would have been announced by him who beheld the apocalyptic vision. For that was seen no very long time since, but almost in our day, towards the end of Domitian's reign.

m. "But he indicates the number of the name now, that when this man comes we may avoid him, being aware who he is: the name, however, is suppressed, because it is not worthy cf being proclaimed by the Holy Spirit. For if it had been declared by Him, he (Antichrist) might perhaps continue for a long period. But now as 'he was, and is not, and shall ascend out of the abyss, and goes into perdition,' as one who has no existence; so neither has his name been declared, for the name of that which does not exist is not proclaimed. But when this Antichrist shall have devastated all things in this world he will reign for three years and six months, and sit in the temple at Jerusalem; and then the Lord will come from heaven in the clouds, in the glory of the Father, sending this man and those who follow him into the lake of fire; but bringing in for the righteous the times of the kingdom, that is, the rest, the hallowed seventh day; and restoring to Abraham the promised inheritance, in which kingdom the Lord declared, that 'many coming from the east and from the west should sit down with Abraham, Issac, and Jacob'."

261. St. Justin (d. 165)

"And Trypho said, 'Those who affirm him to have been a man, and to have been anointed by election, and then to have become Christ, appear to me to speak more plausibly than you who hold those opinions which you express. For we all expect that Christ will be a man (born) of men, and that Elijah when he comes will anoint him. But if this man appear to be Christ, he must certainly be known as man (born) cf men; but from the circumstance that Elijah has not yet come, I infer that this man is not He (the Christ).' Then I inquired of him, 'Does not Scripture, in the book of Zechariah, say that Elijah shall come before the great and terrible day of the Lord?' And he answered, 'Certainly.' 'If therefore Scripture compels you to admit that two advents of Christ were predicted to take place, — one in which He would appear suffering, and dishonoured, and without comeliness; but the other in which He would come glorious, and Judge of all, as has been made manifest in many of the forecited passages, — shall we not suppose that the word of God has proclaimed that Elijah shall be the precursor of the great and terrible day, that is, of His second advent?' 'Certainly,' he answered.

'And, accordingly, our Lord in his teaching,' I continued, 'proclaimed that this very thing would take place, saying that Elijah would also come. And we know that this shall take place when our Lord Jesus Christ shall come in glory from heaven; whose first manifestation the Spirit of God who was in Elijah preceded as herald in (the person of) John, a prophet among your nation; after whom no other prophet appeared among you. He cried, as he sat by the river Jordan: 'I baptize you with water to repentance; but He that is stronger than I shall come, whose shoes I am not worthy to bear: He shall baptize you with the Holy Ghost and with fire: whose fan is in His hand, and He will thoroughly purge His floor, and will gather the wheat into the barn; but the chaff He will burn up with unquenchable fire.' And this very prophet your king Herod had shut up in prison; and when his birthday was celebrated, and the niece of the same Herod by her dancing had pleased him, he told her to ask the head of John, who was in prison; and having asked it, (Herod) sent and ordered the head of John to be brought in on a charger. Wherefore also our Christ said, (when He was on earth) to those who were affirming that Elijah must come before Christ: 'Elijah shall come, and restore all things: but I say unto you, that Elijah has already come, and they knew him not, but have done to him whatsoever they chose.' And it is written, 'Then the disciples understood that He spake to them about John the Baptist.'

And Trypho said, 'This statement also seems to me paradoxical; namely, that the prophetic Spirit of God, who was in Elijah, was also in John.' To this I replied, 'Do you not think that the same thing happened in the case of Joshua the son of Nave (Nun), who succeeded to the command of the people after Moses, when Moses was commanded to lay his hands on Joshua, and God said to him, 'I will take of the spirit which is in thee, and put it on him?' And he said, 'Certainly.'

'As therefore,' I say, 'while Moses was still among men, God took of the spirit which was in Moses and put it on Joshua, even so God was able to cause (the spirit) of Elijah to come upon John; in order that, as Christ at His first coming appeared inglorious, even so the first coming of the spirit, which remained always pure in Elijah like that of Christ, might be perceived to be inglorious. For the Lord said He would wage war against Amalek with concealed hand; and you will not deny that Amalek fell. But if it is said that only in the glorious advent of Christ war will be waged with Amalek, how great will the fulfillment of Scripture be which says, 'God will wage war against Amalek with concealed hand!' You can perceive that the concealed power of God was in Christ the crucified, before whom demons, and all the principalities and powers of the earth, tremble."

262. St. Clement of Alexandria (d. 215)

"Enoch, too, pleasing God, without circumcision, discharged the office of God's legate to the angels although he was a man, and was translated, and is preserved until now as a witness of the just judgment of God, because the angels when they had transgressed fell to the earth for judgment, but the man who pleased (God) was translated for salvation.

"In order to learn that bodies did continue in existence for a lengthened period, as long as it was God's good pleasure that they should flourish let these heretics read the Scriptures, and they will find that our predecessors advanced beyond seven hundred, eight hundred, and nine hundred years of age; and that their bodies kept pace with the protracted length of their days, and participated in life as long as God willed that they should live. But why do I refer to these men? For Enoch, when he pleased God, was translated in the same body in which he did please Him, thus pointing out by anticipation the translation of the just. Elijah, too, was caught up when he was yet in the substance of the natural form; thus exhibiting in prophecy the assumption of those who are spiritual, and that nothing stood in the way of their body being translated and caught up. For by means of the very same hands through which they were moulded at the beginning, did they receive this translation and assumption. For in Adam the hands of God had become accustomed to set in order, to rule, and to sustain His own workmanship, and to bring it and place it where they pleased. Where, then, was the first man placed? In paradise certainly, as the Scripture declares: 'And God planted a garden (paradisum) eastward in Eden, and there He placed the man whom he had formed.' And then afterwards, when man proved disobedient, he was cast out thence into this world. Wherefore also the elders who were disciples of the apostles tell us that those who were translated were transferred to that place (for paradise has been prepared for righteous men, such as have the Spirit); in which place also Paul the apostle, when he was caught up, heard words which are unspeakable as regards us in our present condition, and that there shall they who have been translated remain until the consummation of all things, as a prelude to immortality.

"If, however, anyone imagine it impossible that men should survive for such a length of time, and that Elias was not caught up in the flesh, but that his flesh was consumed in the fiery chariot, let him consider that Jonah, when he had been cast into the deep, and swallowed down into the whale's belly, was by the command of God again thrown out safe upon the land.

"Look, for instance, to Elias the Thesbite, in whom we have a beautiful example of frugality, when he sat down beneath the thorn, and the angel brought him food. 'It was a cake of barley and a jar of water.' Such the Lord sent as the best for him."

263. Tertullian (d. 220)

a. "Enoch had preceded, predicting that 'the demons, and the spirits of the angelic apostates, would turn into idolatry all the elements, all the garniture of the universe, all things contained in the heaven, in the sea, in the earth, that they might be consecrated as god, in opposition to God.' All things, therefore, does human error worship, except the Founder of all Himself. The images of those things are idols, the consecration of the images is idolatry. Whatever guilt idolatry incurs, must necessarily be imputed to every artificer of every idol. In short, the same Enoch forecondemns in general menace both idol-worshipers and idol-makers together. And again: 'I swear to you, sinners, that against the day of perdition of blood repentance is being prepared. Ye who serve stones, and ye who make images of gold, and silver, and wood, and stones and clay, and serve phantoms, and demons, and spirits in fanes, and all errors not according to knowledge, shall find no help from them.'

b. "Enoch and Elias were transported hence without suffering death, which was only postponed. The day will come when they will actually die that they may extinguish Antichrist with their blood." (On the Soul, 51: 5)

264. St. Hippolytus (d. 235)

a. "But since the Saviour was the beginning of the resurrection of all men, it was meet that the Lord alone should rise from the dead, by whom too the judgment is to enter for the whole world, that they who have wrestled worthily may be also crowned worthily by Him, by the illustrious Arbiter, to wit, who Himself first accomplished the course, and was received into the heavens, and was set down on the right hand of God the Father, and is to be manifested again at the end of the world as Judge. It is a matter of course that His forerunners must appear first, as He says by Malachi and the angel, 'I will send you Elias the Tishbite before the day of the Lord, the great and notable day, comes; and he shall turn the hearts of the fathers to the children, and the disobedient to the wisdom of the just, lest I come and smite the earth utterly.' These, then, shall come and proclaim the manifestation of Christ that is to be from heaven; and they shall also perform signs and wonders, in order that men may be put to shame and turned to repentance for their surpassing wickedness and impiety.

"For John says, 'And I will give power unto my two witnesses, and they shall prophecy a thousand and two hundred and threescore days, clothed in sackcloth.' That is the half of the week whereof Daniel spake. 'These are the two olive trees and the two candlesticks standing before the Lord of the earth. And if any man will hurt them, fire will proceed out of their mouth and devour their enemies; and if any man will hurt them, he must in this manner be killed. These have power to shut heaven, that it rain not in the days of their prophecy; and have power over waters, to turn them to blood, and to smite the earth with all plagues as often as they will. And when they shall have finished their course and their testimony,' what saith the prophet? 'The beast that ascendeth out of the bottomless pit shall make war against them, and shall overcome them, and kill them,' because they will not give glory to Antichrist. For this is meant by the little horn that grows up. He, being now elated in heart, begins to exalt himself, and to glorify himself as God, persecuting the saints and blaspheming Christ.

"For this is what the prophets Enoch and Elias will preach: Believe not the enemy who is to come and be seen; for he is an adversary and corrupter and son of perdition, and deceives you; and for this reason he will kill you, and smite them with the sword."

   b. "'And I inquired about the fourth beast. It is to the fourth kingdom, of which we have already spoken, that he here refers; that kingdom, than which no greater kingdom of like nature has arisen upon the earth; from which also ten horns are to spring, and to be apportioned among ten crowns. And amid these another little horn shall rise, which is that of Antichrist. And it shall pluck by the roots the three others before it; that is to say, he shall subvert the three kings of Egypt, Libya, and Ethiopia, with the view of acquiring for himself universal dominion. And after conquering the remaining seven horns, he will at last begin, inflated by a strange and wicked spirit, to stir up war against the saints, and to persecute all everywhere, with the aim of being glorified by all, and being worshipped as god. (Antichrist)

c. "'There shall be a time of trouble.' For at that time there shall be great trouble, such as has not been from the foundation of the world, when some in one way, and others in another, shall be sent through every city and country to destroy the faithful; and the saints shall travel from the west to the east, and shall be driven in persecution from the east to the south, while others shall conceal themselves in the mountains and caves; and the abomination shall war against them everywhere, and shall cut them off by sea and by land by his decree, and shall endeavour by every means to destroy them out of the world; and they shall not be able any longer to sell their own property, nor to buy from strangers, unless one keeps and carries with him the name of the beast, or bears its mark upon his forehead. For then they shall be driven out from every place, and dragged from their own homes and haled into prison, and punished with all manner of punishment, and cast out from the whole world.

"'These shall awake to everlasting life.' That is, those who have believed in the true life, and who have their names written in the book of life. 'And these to shame.' That is, those who are attached to Antichrist, and who are cast with him into everlasting punishment.

e. "'And they that be wise shall shine.' And the Lord has said the same thing in the Gospel: 'Then shall the righteous shine forth as the sun.'

f. "'For a time, times, and an half.' By this he indicated the three and half years of Antichrist. For by a time he means a year; and by times, two years; and by an half time, half a year. These are the "one thousand two hundred and ninety days" of which Daniel prophesied.

g. "'The abomination of desolation shall be given (set up).' Daniel speaks, therefore, of two abominations: the one of destruction, which Antiochus set up in its appointed time, and which bears a relation to that of desolation, and the other universal, when Antichrist shall come. For, as Daniel says, he too, shall be set up for the destruction of many. When the iron legs that now hold the sovereignty have given place to the feet and the toes, in accordance with the representation of the terrible beast, as has also been signified in the former times, then from heaven will come the stone that smites the image, and breaks it; and it will subvert all the kingdoms, and give the kingdom to the saints of the Most High.

h. "Now, as our Lord Jesus Christ, who is also God, was prophesied of under the figure of a lion, on account of his royalty and glory, in the same way have the Scriptures also aforetime spoken of Antichrist as a lion, on account of his tyranny and violence. For the deceiver seeks to liken himself in all things to the Son of God. . . .

i. "Thus did the Scriptures preach before time of this lion and lion's whelp. And in like manner also we find it written regarding Antichrist. For Moses speaks thus: 'Dan is a lion's whelp, and he shall leap from Bashan.' But that no one may err by supposing that this is said of the Saviour, let him attend carefully to the matter. 'Dan,' he says, 'is a lion's whelp;' and in naming the tribe of Dan, he declared clearly the tribe from which Antichrist is destined to spring. For as Christ springs from the tribe of Judah, so Antichrist is to spring from the tribe of Dan. And that the case stands thus, we see also from the words of Jacob: 'Let Dan be a serpent, lying upon the ground, biting the horse's heel.' What, then, is meant by the serpent but Antichrist, that deceiver who is mentioned in Genesis, who deceived Eve and supplanted Adam.

j. "These words then being thus presented, let us observe somewhat in detail what Daniel says in his visions. For in distinguishing the kingdoms that are to rise after these things, he showed also the coming of Antichrist in the last times, and the consummation of the whole world.

k. "Now since these things, spoken as they are with a mystical meaning, may seem to some hard to understand, we shall keep back nothing fitted to impart an intelligent apprehension of them to those who are possessed of a sound mind.

l. "The golden head of the image and the lioness denoted the Babylonians; the shoulders and arms of silver, and the bear, represented the Persians and Medes; the belly and thighs of brass, and the leopard, meant the Greeks, who held the sovereignty from Alexander's time; the legs of iron, and the beast dreadful and terrible, expressed the Romans, who hold the sovereignty at present; the toes of the feet which were part clay and part iron, and the ten horns, were emblems of the kingdoms that are yet to rise; the other little horn that grows up among them meant the Antichrist in their midst; the stone that smites the earth and brings judgment upon the world was Christ.

m. "Daniel says: 'And one week will make a covenant with many, and it shall be that in the midst (half) of the week my sacrifice and oblation shall cease.' By one week, therefore, he meant the last week which is to be at the end of the whole world; of which week the two prophets Enoch and Elias will take up the half. For they will preach 1,260 days clothed in sackcloth, proclaiming repentance to the people and to all the nations.

n. "Here is wisdom. Let him that hath understanding count the number of the beast; for it is the number of a man, and his number is six hundred threescore and six.

o. "By the beast, then, coming up out of the earth, he (John) means the kingdom of Antichrist and by the two horns he means him and the false prophet with him. And in speaking of 'the horns being like a lamb,' he means that he will make himself like the Son of God, and set himself forward as king. And the terms, 'he spake like a dragon,' mean that he is a deceiver, and not truthful. And the words, 'he exercised the power of the beast before him, and caused the earth and them which dwell threin to worship the first beast, whose deadly wound was healed,' signify that, after the manner of the law of Augustus, by whom the empire of Rome was established, he too will rule and govern, sanctioning everything by it, and taking greater glory to himself. For this is the, fourth beast, whose head was wounded and healed again, in its being broken up or even dishonoured, and partitioned into four crowns; and he then (Antichrist) shall with knavish skill heal it, as it were, and restore it. For this is what is meant by the prophet when he says, 'He will give life unto the image, and the image of the beast will speak.' For he will act with vigour again, and prove strong by reason of the laws established by him; and he will cause all those who will not worship the image of the beast to be put to death.

p. "For, being full of guile, and exalting himself against the servants of God, with the wish to afflict them and persecute them out of the world, because they give not glory to him, he will order incense-pans to be set up by all everywhere, that no man among the saints may be able to buy or sell without first sacrificing; for this is what is meant by the mark received upon the right hand. And the word — 'in their forehead' — indicates that all are crowned, and put on a crown of fire, and not of life, but of death.

q. "With respect to his name, it is not in our power to explain it exactly, as the blessed John understood it and was instructed about it, but only to give a conjectural account of it; for when he appears, the blessed one will show us what we seek to know. Yet as far as our doubtful apprehension of the matter goes, we may speak. Many names indeed we find, the letters of which are the equivalent of this number: such as, for instance, the word Titan, an ancient and notable name; or Evanthas, for it too makes up the same number; and many others which might be found. But, as we have already said, the wound of the first beast was healed, and he (the second beast) was to make the image speak, that is to say, he should be powerful; and it is manifest to all that those who at present still hold the power are Latins. If, then, we take the name as the name of a single man, it becomes Latinus. Wherefore we ought neither to give it out as if this were certainly his name, nor again ignore the fact that he may not be otherwise designated. But having the mystery of God in our heart, we ought in fear to keep faithfully what has been told us by the blessed prophets, in order that when those things come to pass, we may be prepared for them, and not deceived. For when the times advance, he too, of whom these things are said, will be manifested.

r. "In those times, then, he shall arise and meet them. And when he has overmastered three horns out of the ten in the array of war, and has rooted these out, viz., Egypt, and Libya, and Ethiopia, and has got their spoils and trappings, and has brought the remaining horns which suffer into subjection, he will begin to be lifted up in heart, and to exalt himself against God as master of the whole world. And his first expedition will be against Tyre and Berytus, and the circumjacent territory. For by storming these cities first he will strike terror into the others.

s. "These things, then, shall be in the future, beloved; and when the three horns are cut off, he will begin to show himself as God.

t. "He will call together all the people to himself, out of every country of the dispersion, making them his own, as though they were his own children, and promising to restore their country and establish again their kingdom and nation, in order that he may be worshipped by them as God.

u. "He will allure mankind to himself, wishing to gain possession of those who are not his own, and promising deliverance to all, while he is unable to save himself. He then, having gathered to himself the unbelieving everywhere throughout the world, comes at their call to persecute the saints, their enemies and antagonists, as the apostle and evangelist says: 'There was in a city a judge, which feared not God, neither regarded man: and there was a widow in that city, who came unto him, saying, Avenge me of mine adversary. And he would not for a while: but afterwards he said within himself, Though I fear not God, nor regard man; yet because this widow troubleth me, I will avenge her.' (cf. Luke 18: 2-5)

v. "By the unrighteous judge, who fears not God, neither regards man, he means without doubt Antichrist, as he is a son of the devil and a vessel of Satan. For when he has the power, he will begin to exalt himself against God, neither in truth fearing God, nor regarding the Son of God, who is

99

the Judge of all. And in saying that there was a widow in the city, he refers to Jerusalem itself, which is a widow indeed, forsaken of her perfect, heavenly spouse, God. She calls Him her adversary, and not her Saviour.

w. "And he, being puffed up with pride by their subserviency, will begin to despatch missives against the saints, commanding to cut them all off everywhere, on the ground of their refusal to reverence and worship him as God.

x. "Concerning the tribulation of the persecution which is to fall upon the Church from the adversary, John also speaks. (cf. Apoc. 12: 1 ff)

y. "By the 'woman clothed with the sun,' he meant most manifestly the Church, endued with the Father's word, whose brightness is above the sun. And by 'the moon under her feet' he referred to her being adorned, like the moon, with heavenly glory. And the words, 'upon her head a crown of twelve stars,' refer to the twelve apostles by whom the Church was founded. And those, 'she, being with child, cries, travailing in birth, and pained to be delivered,' mean that the Church will not cease to bear from her heart the Word that is persecuted by the unbelieving in the world. 'And she brought forth,' he says, 'a man-child, who is to rule all the nations;' by which is meant that the Church, always bringing forth Christ, the perfect man-child of God, who is declared to be God and man, becomes the instructor of all the nations. And the words, 'her child was caught up unto God and to His throne,' signify that he who is always born of her is a heavenly king, and not an earthly one.

z. "'And the dragon,' he says, 'saw and persecuted the woman which brought forth the man-child. And to the woman were given two wings of the great eagle, that she might fly into the wilderness, where she is nourished for a time, and times, and half a time, from the face of the serpent.' That refers to the one thousand two hundred and threescore days (the half of the week) during which the tyrant is to reign and persecute the Church, which flees from city to city, and seeks concealment in the wilderness among the mountains, possessed of no other defense than the two wings of the great eagle, that is to say, the faith of

Jesus Christ, who, in stretching forth His holy hands on the holy tree, unfolded two wings, the right and the left, and called to Him all who believed upon Him, and covered them as a hen her chickens.

aa. "In every respect that deceiver seeks to make himself appear like the Son of God. Christ is a lion, and Antichrist is a lion. Christ is King of things celestial and things terrestrial, and Antichrist will be king upon earth. The Saviour was manifested as a lamb; and he, too, will appear as a lamb, while he is a wolf within. The Saviour was circumcised, and he in like manner will appear in circumcision. The Saviour sent the apostles unto all the nations, and he in like manner will send false apostles. Christ gathered together the dispersed sheep, and he in like manner will gather together the dispersed people of the Hebrews. Christ gave to those who believed in Him the honourable and life giving cross, and he in like manner will give his own sign. Christ appeared in the form of man, and he in like manner will come forth in the form of man. Christ arose from among the Hebrews, and he will spring from among the Jews. Christ displayed His flesh like a temple, and raised it up on the third day; and he too will raise up again the temple of stone in Jerusalem. And these deceits fabricated by him will become quite intelligible to those who listen to us attentively, from what shall be set forth next in order.

bb. "When Daniel says, 'I shall make my covenant for one week,' he indicated even years; and the one half of the week is for the preaching of the prophets, and for the other half of the week — that is to say, for three years and a half — Antichrist will reign upon the earth. And after this his kingdom and his glory shall be taken away. Behold, ye who love God, what manner of tribulation there shall rise in those days, such as has not been from the foundation of the world, no, nor ever shall be, except in those days alone. Then the lawless one, being lifted up in heart, will gather together his demons in man's form, and will abominate those who call him to the kingdom, and will pollute many souls.

cc. "For he will appoint princes over them from among the demons. And he will no longer seem to be pious, but

101

altogether and in all things he will be harsh, severe, passionate, wrathful, terrible, inconstant, dread, morose, hateful, abominable, savage, vengeful, iniquitous. And, bent on casting the whole race of men into the pit of perdition, he will multiply false signs. For when all the people greet him with the acclamations at his displays, he will shout with a strong voice, so that the place shall be shaken in which the multitudes stand by him: 'Ye peoples, and tribes, and nations, acquaint yourselves with my mighty authority and power, and the strength of my kingdom. What prince is there so great as I am? What great God is there but I? Who will stand up against my authority?' Under the eye of the spectators he will remove mountains from their places, he will walk on the sea with dry feet, he will bring down fire from heaven, he will turn the day into darkness and the night into day, he will turn the sun about wheresoever he pleases; and, in short, in the presence of those who behold him, he will show all the elements of earth and sea to be subject to him in the power of his specious manifestation. For if, while as yet he does not exhibit himself as the son of perdition, he raises and excites against us open war even to battles and slaughters, at that time when he shall come in his own proper person, and men shall see him as he is in reality, what machinations and deceits and delusions will he not bring into play, with the purpose of seducing all men, and leading them off from the way of truth, and from the gate of the kingdom?

dd. "Then, after all these things, the heavens will not give their dew, the clouds will not give their rain, the earth will refuse to yield its fruits; the sea will be filled with stench, the rivers shall be dried up, the fish of the sea shall die, men shall perish of hunger and thirst; and father embracing son, and mother embracing daughter, will die together, and there will be none to bury them. But the whole earth will be filled with the stench arising from the dead bodies cast forth. And the sea, not receiving the floods of the rivers, will become like mire, and will be filled with an unlimited smell and stench. Then there will be a mighty pestilence upon the whole earth, and then, too, inconsolable lamentation, and measureless weeping, and unceasing mourning. Then men will deem those happy who are dead before them, and will say to them, 'Open your sepulchres, and take us miserable beings in; open your receptacles for the reception of your wretched kinsmen and acquaintances. Happy are ye, in that ye have not seen our days. Happy are ye, in that ye have not had to witness this painful life of ours, nor this irremediable pestilence, nor these straits that possess our souls.'

ee. "Then that abominable one will send his commands throughout every government by the hand at once of demons and of visible men, who shall say, 'A mighty king has arisen upon the earth; come ye all to worship him; come ye all to see the strength of his kingdom; for, behold, he will give you corn; and he will bestow upon you wine, and great riches, and lofty honours. For the whole earth and sea obeys his command. Come ye all to him.' And by reason of the scarcity of food, all will go to him and worship him; and he will put his mark on their right hand on his forehead, that no one may put the sign of the honourable cross upon his forehead with his right hand; but his hand is bound. And from that time he shall not have power to seal any one of his members, but he shall be attached to the deceiver, and shall serve him; and in him there is no repentance. But such an one is lost at once to God and to men, and the deceiver will give them scanty food by reason of his abominable seal. And his seal upon the forehead and upon the right hand is the number, 'Six hundred threescore and six.' And I have an opionion as to this number, though I do not know the matter for certain; for many names have been found in this number when it is expressed in writing. Still we say that perhaps the scription of this same seal will give us the word **I deny**. For even in recent days, by means of his ministers — that is to say, the idolaters — that bitter adversary took up the word deny, when the lawless pressed upon the witnesses of Christ, with the adjuration, 'Deny thy God, the crucified One.'

ff. "Of such kind, in the time of that hater of all good, will be the seal, the tenor of which will be this: I deny the

Maker of heaven and earth, I deny the baptism, I deny my (former) service, and attach myself to thee, and I believe in thee.

gg. "Behold the deceit of the enemy, know the machinations of the beguiler, how he seeks to darken the mind of men utterly. For he will show forth his demons brilliant like angels, and he will bring in hosts of the incorporeal without number. And in the presence of all he exhibits himself as taken up into heaven with trumpets and sounds, and the mighty shouting of those who hail him with indescribable hymns; the heir of darkness himself shining like light, and at one time soaring to the heavens, and at another descending to the earth with great glory, and again charging the demons, like angels, to execute his behests with much fear and trembling. Then he will send the cohorts of the demons among mountains, and caves and dens of the earth, to track out those who have been concealed from his eyes, and to bring them forward to worship him. And those who yield to him he will seal with his seal; but those who refuse to submit to him he will consume with incomparable pains and bitterest torments and machinations, such as never have been, nor have reached the ear of man, nor have been seen by the eye of mortals.

hh. "Blessed shall they be who overcome the tyrant then. For they shall be set forth as more illustrious and loftier than the first witnesses; for the former witnesses overcame his minions only, but these overthrow and conquer the accuser himself, the son of perdition. With what eulogies and crowns, therefore, will they not be adorned by our King, Jesus Christ!

ii. "But let us revert to the matter in hand. When men have received the seal, then, and find neither food nor water, they will approach him with a voice of anguish, saying, Give us to eat and drink, for we all faint with hunger and all manner of straits; and bid the heavens yield us water, and drive off from us the beasts that devour men. Then will that crafty one make answer, mocking them with absolute inhumanity, and saying, The heavens refuse to give rain, the earth yields not again its fruits; whence then can I give you food? Then on hearing the words of this deceiver, these miserable men will perceive that this is the wicked accuser, and will mourn in anguish, and weep vehemently, and beat their face with their hands, and tear their hair, and lacerate their cheeks with their nails, while they say to each other: Woe for the calamity! woe for the bitter contract! woe for the deceitful covenant! woe for the mighty mischance! How have we been beguiled by the deceiver! how have we been joined to him! How have we been caught in his toils! how have we been taken in his abominable net! how have we heard the Scriptures, and understood them not! For truly, those who are engrossed with the affairs of life, and with the lust of this world, will be easily brought over to the accuser then, and sealed by him.

jj. "But many who are hearers of the divine Scriptures, and have them in their hand, and keep them in mind with understanding, will escape his imposture. For they will see clearly through his insidious appearance and his deceitful imposture, and will flee from his hands, and betake themselves to the mountains, and hide themselves in the caves of the earth; and they will seek after the Friend of man with tears and a contrite heart; and He will deliver them out of his toils, and with His right hand He will save those from his snares who in a worthy and righteous manner make their supplication to Him.

kk. "You see in what manner of fasting and prayer the saints will exercise themselves at that time. Observe, also, how hard the season and the times will be that are to come upon those in city and country alike. At that time they will be brought from the east even unto the west; and they will come up from the west even unto the east, and will weep greatly and wail vehemently. And when the day begins to dawn they will long for the night, in order that they may find rest from their labours; and when the night descends upon them, by reason of the continuous earthquakes and the tempests in the air, they will desire even to behold the light of the day, and will seek how they may hereafter meet a bitter death. At that time the whole earth will bewail the life of anguish, and the sea and the air in like manner will bewail it; and the sun, too, will wail; and the wild beasts, together with the fowls will wail; mountains and hills, and the trees of the plain, will wail on account of the race of man, because all have turned aside from the holy God, and obeyed the deceiver, and received the mark of that abominable one, the enemy of God, instead of the quickening cross of the Saviour.

ll. "And the churches, too, will wail with a mighty lamentation, because neither 'oblation nor incense' is attended to, nor a service acceptable to God; but the sanctuaries of the churches will become like a garden-watcher's hut, and the holy body and blood of Christ will not be shown in those days. The public service of God shall be extinguished, psalmody shall cease, the reading of the Scriptures shall not be heard; but for men there shall be darkness, and lamentation on lamentation, and woe on woe. At that time silver and gold shall be cast out in the streets, and none shall gather them; but all things shall be held an offence. For all shall be eager to escape and to hide themselves, and they shall not be able anywhere to find concealment from the woes of the adversary; but as they carry his mark about them, they shall be readily recognized and declared to be his. Without there shall be fear, and within trembling, both by night and by day. In the street and in the houses there shall be the dead; in the streets and in the houses there shall be hunger and thirst; in the streets there shall be tumults, and in the houses lamentations. And beauty of countenance shall be withered, for their forms shall be like those of the dead; and the beauty of women shall fade, and the desire of all men shall vanish.

mm. "Notwithstanding, not even then will the merciful and benignant God leave the race of men without all comfort; but He will shorten even those days and the period of three years and a half, and He will curtail those times on account of the remnant of those who hide themselves in the mountains and the caves, that the phalanx of all those saints fail not utterly. But these days shall run their course rapidly; and the kingdom of the deceiver and Antichrist shall be speedily removed. And then, in fine, in the glance of an cye shall the fashion of this world pass away, and the power of men shall be brought to nought, and all these visible things shall be destroyed."

265. Origen (d. 254)

After quoting St. Paul (2 Thes. 2: 1-12), Origen continues:

a. "To explain each particular here referred to does not belong to our present purpose. The prophecy also regarding Antichrist is stated in the book of Daniel, and is fitted to make an intelligent and candid reader admire the words as truly divine and prophetic; for in them are mentioned the things relating to the coming kingdom, beginning with the times cf Daniel, and continuing to the destruction of the world. Any one who chooses may read it. Observe, however, whether the prophecy regarding Antichrist be not as follows: 'And at the latter time of their kingdom, when their sins are coming to the full, there shall arise a king, bold in countenance, and understanding riddles. And his power shall be great, and he shall destroy mighty men, and the holy people. And the yoke of his chain shall prosper: there is craft in his hand, and he shall magnify himself in his heart, and by craft shall destroy many; and he shall stand up for the destruction of many, and shall crush them as eggs in his hand.' What is stated by Paul in the words quoted from him, where he says, 'so that he sitteth in the temple of God, showing himself that he is God,' is in Daniel referred to in the following fashion: 'And on the temple shall be the abomination of desolations, and at the end of the time an end shall be put to the desolation.' So many, out of a greater number of passages, have I thought it right to adduce, that the hearer may understand in some slight degree the meaning of holy Scripture, when it gives us information concerning the devil and Antichrist.

b. "When the close of the times draws nigh, a great prophet (Elias) shall be sent from God to turn men to the knowledge of God, and he shall receive the power of doing wonderful things. Wherever men shall not hear him, he will shut up the heavens, and cause it to withhold its rains;

he will turn their water into blood, and torment them with thirst and hunger; and if any one shall endeavour to injure him, fire shall come forth out of his mouth, and shall burn that man. By these prodigies and powers he shall turn many to the worship of God; and when his works shall be accomplished, another king shall arise out of Syria, born from an evil spirit, the overthrower and destroyer of the human race, (Antichrist) who shall destroy that which is left by the former evil, together with himself. He shall fight against the prophet of God, and shall overcome, and slay him, and shall suffer him to lie unburied; but after the third day he shall come to life again; and while all look on and wonder, he shall be caught up into heaven. But that king will not only be most disgraceful of himself, but will also be a prophet of lies; and he will constitute and call himself God, and will order himself to be worshipped as the Son of God; and power will be given him to do signs and wonders, by the sight of which he may entice men to adore him. He will command fire to come down from heaven, and the sun to stand and leave his course, and an image to speak; and these things shall be done at his word, — by which miracles many even of the wise shall be enticed by him. Then he will attempt to destroy the temple of God, and persecute the righteous people; and there will be distress and tribulation, such as there never has been from the beginning of the world.

c. "As many as shall believe him and unite themselves to him, shall be marked by him as sheep; but they who shall refuse his mark will either flee to the mountains, or, being seized, will be slain with studied tortures. He will also enwrap righteous men with books of the prophets, and thus burn them; and power will be given him to desolate the whole earth for forty-two months. That will be the time in which righteousness shall be cast out, and innocence be hated; in which the wicked shall prey upon the good as enemies; neither law, nor order, nor military discipline shall be preserved; no one shall reverence hoary locks, nor recognize the duty of piety, nor pity sex or infancy; all things shall be confounded and mixed together against right, and against the laws of nature. Thus the earth shall be laid waste, as though by one common robbery. When these things shall so happen, then the righteous and the followers of truth shall separate themselves from the wicked, and flee into solitude. And when he hears of this, the impious king, inflamed with anger, will come with a great army, and bringing up all his forces, will surround all the mountains in which the right- eous shall be situated, that he may seize them. But they, when they shall see themselves to be shut in on all sides and besieged, will call upon God with a loud voice, and im- plore the aid of heaven; and God shall hear them, and send from heaven a great king to rescue and free them, and destroy all the wicked with fire and sword."

266. St. Cyprian (d. 258)

a. "Nor let any one of you, beloved brethren, be so terri- fied by the fear of future persecution, or the coming of the threatening Antichrist, as not to be found armed for all things by the evangelical exhortations and precepts, and by the heavenly warnings. Antichrist is coming, but above him comes Christ also. The enemy goeth about and rageth, but immediately the Lord follows to avenge our sufferings and our wounds. The adversary is enraged and threatens, but there is One who can deliver us from his hands.

b. "For even Antichrist, when he shall begin to come, shall not enter into the Church because he threatens; neither shall we yield to his arms and violence, because he declares that he will destroy us if we resist. Heretics arm us when they think that we are terrified by their threaten- ings."

267. Commodianus (d. 260)

a. "The wicked king who possesses her, (Church) when he hears, flies into the parts of the north, and collects all his followers. Moreover, when the tyrant shall dash him- self against the army of God, his soldiery are overthrown by the celestial terror; the false prophet is seized with the wicked one, by the decree of the Lord; they are handed over alive to Gehenna. From him chiefs and leaders are bid- den to obey; then will the holy ones enter into the breasts of their ancient mother, that moreover, they also may be refreshed whom he has evil persuaded. With various punishments he will torment those who trust in him; they come to the end, whereby offences are taken away from the world. The Lord will begin to give judgment by fire.

b. "The trumpet gives the sign in heaven, the lion being taken away, and suddenly there is darkness with the din of heaven. The Lord casts down His eyes, so that the earth trembles. He cries out, so that all may hear throughout the world: Behold, long have I been silent while I bore your doings in such a time. They cry out together, complaining and groaning too late. They howl, they bewail; nor is there room found for the wicked. What shall the mother do for the sucking child, when she herself is burnt up? In the flame of fire the Lord will judge the wicked. But the fire shall not touch the just."

268. St. Zenobius (d. 285)

a. "Antichrist, the son of perdition, will be born in Corozain, will be brought up in Bethsaida, and shall begin to reign in Capharnaum, according to what our Lord Jesus Christ said in the gospel. 'Woe to thee Corozain . . . Woe to thee Bethsaida . . . and thou Capharnaum, that are exalted up to heaven, thou shalt be thrust down to hell. (cf. Luke 10: 13)

b. "Antichrist shall work a thousand prodigies on earth. He will make the blind see, the deaf hear, the lame walk, the dead rise, so that even the elect, if possible, shall be deceived by his magical arts. Swollen with pride, Antichrist shall enter in triumph the city of Jerusalem, and will sit on a throne in the temple to be adored as if he were the Son of God. His heart being intoxicated with arrogance, he will forget his being mere man, and the son of a woman of the tribe of Dan. He shall seduce many credulous persons through his deceitful errors . . ."

c. "Elias and Henoch will attack him bodily in the presence of the people, and shall convict him of imposture and lies. Then the Jews of all the tribes of Israel will be converted to the faith of Jesus Christ, and shall suffer

110

martyrdom for his sake. In consequence of this Antichrist shall be seized with rage, and will put to death the two saints of God, and all those who have believed them.

"Then the Son of God, our Lord Jesus Christ, shall come in person. He shall appear on the clouds of heaven surrounded by legions of angels, and shining with glory He will put to death Antichrist, the beast, the enemy, the seducer, and all his followers. This shall be the end of time and the beginning of the general judgment."

269. St. Victorinus (d. 303)

a. "They shall tread the holy city down for forty and two months; and I will give to my two witnesses, and they shall predict a thousand two hundred and threescore days clothed in sackcloth." That is, three years and six months: these make forty-two months. Therefore their preaching is three years and six months, and the kingdom of Antichrist as much again.

"If any many will hurt them, fire proceedeth out of their mouth, and devoureth their enemies." That fire proceedeth out of the mouth of those prophets against the adversaries, bespeaks the power of the world. For all afflictions, however, many there are, shall be sent by their messengers in their word. Many think that there is Elisha, or Moses, with Elijah; but both of these died; while the death of Elijah is not heard of, with whom all our ancients have believed that it was Jeremiah. For even the very word spoken to him testifies to him, saying: "Before I formed thee in the belly I knew thee; and before thou camest forth out of the womb I sanctified thee, and I ordained thee a prophet unto the nations." But he was not a prophet unto the nations; and thus the truthful word of God makes it necessary, which it has promised to set forth, that he should be a prophet to the nations.

"These are the two candlesticks standing before the Lord of the earth." These two candlesticks and two olive trees He has to this end spoken of, and admonished you that if, when you have read of them elsewhere, you have not understood, you may understand here. For in Zechariah, one of the twelve prophets, it is thus written: "These are the two olive trees and two candlesticks which stand in the presence of the Lord of the earth;" that is, they are in paradise. Also, in another sense, standing in the presence of the lord of the earth, that is, in the presence of Antichrist. Therefore they must be slain by Antichrist."

b. "'And I saw a beast rising up from the sea, like unto a leopard.' This signifies the kingdom of that time of Antichrist, and the people mingled with the variety of nations. 'His feet were as the feet of a bear.' A strong and most unclean beast, the feet are to be understood as his leaders. 'And his mouth as the mouth of a lion.' That is, his mouth armed for blood is his bidding, and tongue which will proceed to nothing else than to the shedding of blood.

c. "'His number is the name of a man, and his number is six hundred three score and six.' As they have it reckoned from the Greek characters, they thus find it among many to be. In Latin DICLUX, which letters are reckoned in this manner: since D figures five hundred, I one, C a hundred, L fifty, V five, X ten, — which by the reckoning up of the letters makes six hundred and sixty-six, by which name, we understand Antichrist, who although he be cut off from the supernal light, and deprived thereof, yet transforms himself into an angel of light, daring to call himself light.

d. "'And I saw another beast coming up out of the earth.' He is speaking of the great and false prophet who is to do signs, and portents, and falsehoods before him in the presence of men.

e. "'And he had two horns like a lamb, that is, the appearance within of a man — and he spoke like a dragon.' But the devil speaks full of malice; for he shall do these things in the presence of men, so that even the dead appear to rise again.

f. "'And he shall make fire come down from heaven in the sight of men.' Yes, (as I also have said), in the sight of men. Magicians do these things, by the aid of the apostate angels, even to this day. He shall cause also that a golden image of Antichrist shall be placed in the temple at Jerusalem, and that the apostate angel should enter, and thence utter voices and oracles. Moreover, he himself shall contrive that his servants and children should receive as a mark on their foreheads, or on their right hands, the number of his name, lest any one should buy or sell them."

270. Lactantius (cir. 310)

a. "Nero would again reappear on earth as 'a messenger and forerunner of the Evil One, coming for the devastation of the earth and the overturning of the human race.'

b. "There will arise an impious king, hostile not only to mankind, but also to God. He will trample upon, torment, harass and put to death those who have been spared by that former tyrant. Then there will be ever-flowing tears, perpetual wailings and lamentations, and useless prayers to God; there will be no rest from fear, no sleep for a respite. The day will always increase disaster, the night alarm. Thus the world will be reduced almost to solitude, certainly to fewness of men. Then also the impious man will persecute the just and those who are dedicated to God, and will give orders that he himself shall be worshipped as God. For he will say that he is Christ, though he will be His adversary. That he may be believed, he will receive the power of doing wonders, so that fire may descend from heaven, the sun retire from his course, and the image which he shall have set up may speak. And by these prodigies he shall entice many to worship him, and to receive his sign in their hand or forehead. And he who shall not worship him and receive his sign will die with refined tortures. Thus he will destroy nearly two parts, the third will flee into desolate solitudes. But he, frantic and raging with implacable anger, will lead an army and besiege the mountain to which the righteous shall have fled. And when they shall see themselves besieged, they will implore the aid of God with a loud voice, and God shall hear them, and shall send to them a deliverer . . .
(cf. also prophesy 38)

271. St. Hilary (d. 367)

"Antichrist will teach that Christ was an imposter and not the real Son of God."

272. St. Ephrem (d. 375)

"When Antichrist begins to rave the Jews will doubt if he is really the Messiah. He will then remove the Jews from office and treat many of them worse even than the Christians. Antichrist will use worldly goods as bait. He will entice many Christians with money and goods to apostasize. He will give them free land, riches, honor and power. The devil will help him find all the hidden treasures of the world, even those at the bottom of the oceans. With those treasures he will attain greater success for the reign of Satan than at any time in past centuries. The waters will be firm as a rock under his feet and apparently at his command rivers and creeks will change their course so that the water will for a time, flow up instead of down stream."

273. St. Cyril of Jerusalem (d. 386)

"Antichrist will exceed in malice, perversity, lust, wickedness, impiety, and heartless cruelty and barbarity all men that have ever disgraced human nature. Hence St. Paul emphatically calls him 'the man of sin, the son of perdition, the wicked one, whose birth and coming is through the operation of Satan, in all manner of seduction of iniquity.' (2 Thess. 2) He shall through his great power, deceit, and malice succeed in decoying or forcing to his worship two-thirds of mankind; the remaining third part of men will most steadfastly continue true to the faith and worship of Jesus Christ. But in his satanic rage and fury, Antichrist will persecute these brave and devout Christians during three years and a half, and torture them with such an extremity of barbarity, with all the old and his newly invented instruments of pain, as to exceed all past persecutors of the Church combined. He will oblige all his followers to bear impressed upon their foreheads or right hands the mark of the beast, and will starve to death all those who refuse to receive it." (Apoc. 13: 16)

274. Sulpicius Severus (396) *Life of St. Martin of Tours.*

Various features about St. Martin's teaching concerning the end of the world (as Sulpicius reported Gallus stating it) were condemned by St. Jerome and by the so-called **Gelasian**

Decree. But this section of the works of Sulpicius has been consistently read by responsible Catholics. As is evident, we are not the first generation to fear that Antichrist was very near.

a. "In Spain . . . a young man who had made a name for himself through many signs and wonders . . . gave himself out to be Elias . . . He (then) went further and said that he was Christ . . . Again, many . . . reported to us that . . . in the East someone boasted that he was John. From the appearance of pseudo-prophets of this kind, we can conjecture that the coming of Antichrist is imminent, those persons serving as advance agents for him of the Mystery of Iniquity". (Ch. 14, **Life of St. Martin**)

b. "One day we asked Martin about the end of the world. He said that Nero and the Antichrist would come first. Nero would subdue ten Kings and rule in the regions of the West. A persecution he was to impose would go so far as to require the worship of heathen idols.

"The Antichrist would first seize the empire of the East; he would have Jerusalem as his seat and imperial Capital. Both the city and its temple were to be rebuilt by him. His persecution would require the denial of Christ's divinity (he himself pretending to be Christ) and would by law impose circumcision on all. Finally, Nero himself was to perish at the hands of the Antichrist. In this way the whole world and all its people would be brought under the latter's yoke, until, at Christ's coming, the impious imposter would be overcome.

"There was no doubt (in Martin's mind) that Antichrist, begotten by the Evil Spirit, was already born and had now come to the years of boyhood, awaiting the legal age to assume his empire. This we heard Martin say eight years ago (i. e. in A. D. 396). It is for you to judge how near to us now are those fearful events to come". (Ch. 14, **Second Dialogue**)

275. St. John Chrysostom (d. 407)

a. "The world will be faithless and degenerate after the birth of Antichrist."

b. "Antichrist will be possessed by Satan and be the illegitimate son of a Jewish woman from the East."

276. St. Jerome (d. 420)

"Antichrist will be born near Babylon. He will gain the support of many with gifts and money. He will sell himself to the devil and thereafter will have no guardian angel or conscience."

277. St. Augustine (d. 430)

a. "For to this beast belong not only the avowed enemies of the name of Christ and His most glorious city, but also the tares which are to be gathered out of His kingdom, the Church, in the end of the world.

b. "And when the thousand years are finished, Satan shall be loosed from his prison, and shall go out to seduce the nations which are in the four corners of the earth, Gog and Magog, and shall draw them to battle, whose number is as the sand of the sea. This, then, is his purpose in seducing them, to draw them to this battle. For even before this he was wont to use as many and various seductions as he could continue. And the words 'he shall go out' mean, he shall burst forth from lurking hatred into open persecution. For this persecution, occurring while the final judgment is imminent, shall be the last which shall be endured by the holy Church, throughout the world, the whole city of Christ being assailed by the whole city of the devil, as each exists on earth. For these nations which he names Gog and Magog are not to be understood of some barbarous nations in some part of the world.

c. "For John marks that they are spread over the whole earth, when he says, 'The nations which are in the four corners of the earth,' and he added that these are Gog and Magog. The meaning of these names we find to be, Gog, 'a roof,' Magog, 'from a roof,' — a house, as it were, and he who comes out of the house. They are therefore the nations in which we found that the devil was shut up as in an abyss, and the devil himself coming out from them and going forth, so that they are the roof, he from the roof. Or if we refer both words to the nations, not one to them and one to the devil, then they are both the roof, because in them the old enemy is at present shut up, and as it were roofed in; and they shall be from the roof when they break forth from concealed to open hatred. The words, 'And they went up on the breadth of the earth, and encompassed the camp of the saints and the beloved city,' do not mean that they have come, or shall come, to one place, as if the camp of the saints and the beloved city should be in some one place; for this camp is nothing else than the Church of Christ extending over the whole world. And consequently wherever the Church shall be,—and it shall be in all nations, as is signified by 'the breadth of the earth,'—there also shall be the camp of the saints and the beloved city, and there it shall be encompassed by the saints, wherewith they refuse to yield obedience to those who rage against them. For the firmament is 'heaven,' by whose firmness these assailants shall be pained with blazing zeal, for they shall be impotent to draw away the saints to the party of Antichrist. This is the fire which shall devour them, and this is 'from God;' for it is by God's grace the saints become unconquerable, and so torment their enemies.

e. " 'And now,' that is to say, not the fire of the last judgment. Or if by this fire coming down out of heaven and consuming them, John meant that blow wherewith Christ in his coming is to strike those persecutors of the Church whom He shall then find alive upon earth, when He shall kill Antichrist with the breath of His mouth, then even this is not the last judgment of the wicked.

f. "After this mention of the closing persecution, he summarily indicates all that the devil, and the city of which he is the prince, shall suffer in the last judgment. For he says, 'And the devil who seduced them is cast into the lake of fire and brimstone, in which are the beast and the false prophet, and they shall be tormented day and night for ever and ever.' We have already said that by the beast is well understood the wicked city. His false prophet is either Antichrist or that image or figment of which we have spoken in the same place.

g. "Truly Jesus Himself shall extinguish by His presence

117

that last persecution which is to be made by Antichrist. For so it is written, that 'He shall slay him with the breath of His mouth, and empty him with the brightness of His presence.'

h. "I can on no account omit what the Apostle Paul says, in writing, to the Thessalonians, 'We beseech you, brethren, by the coming of our Lord Jesus Christ,' etc.

i. "No one can doubt that he wrote this of Antichrist and of the day of judgment, which he here calls the day of the Lord, nor that he declared that this day should not come unless he first came who is called the apostate—apostate, to wit, from the Lord God.

j. "For when he fell from heaven as fire, and at a stroke swept away from the holy Job his numerous household and his vast flocks, and then as a whirlwind rushed upon and smote the house and killed his children, these were not deceitful appearances, and yet they were the work of Satan to whom God had given this power.

k. "Daniel prophesies of the last judgment in such a way as to indicate that Antichrist shall first come, and to carry on his description to the eternal reign of the saints. For when in prophetic vision he had seen four beasts, signifying four kingdoms, and the fourth conquered by a certain king, who is recognized as Antichrist, and after this the eternal kingdom of the Son of man, that is to say, of Christ. Some have interpreted these four kingdoms as signifying those of the Assyrians, Persians, Macedonians, and Romans. They who desire to understand the fitness of this interpretation may read Jerome's book on Daniel, which is written with a sufficiency of care and erudition. But he who reads this passage, even half asleep, cannot fail to see that the kingdom of Antichrist shall fiercely, though, for a short time, assail the Church before the last judgment of God shall introduce the eternal reign of saints. For it is patent from the context that the time, times, and half a time, means a year, and two years, and half a year, that is to say, three years and a half. Sometimes in Scripture the same thing is indicated by months. For though the word times seems to be used here in the Latin indefinitely, that is only because the Latins have no dual, as the Greeks have, and as the Hebrews also are said to have. Times, therefore, is used for two times."

1. "It is a familiar theme in the conversation and heart of the faithful, that in the last days before the judgment the Jews shall believe in the true Christ, that is, our Christ, by means of this great admirable prophet Elias who shall expound the law to them.

"For not without reason do we hope that before the coming of our Judge and Saviour Elias shall come, because we have good reason to believe that he is now alive; for as Scripture most distinctly informs us, he was taken up from this life in a chariot of fire. When, therefore, he is come, he shall give a spiritual explanation of the law which the Jews at present understand carnally, and shall thus "turn the heart of the father to the son," that is, the heart of fathers to their children; for the Septuagint translators have frequently put the singular for the plural number. And the meaning is, that the sons, that is, the Jews, shall understand the law as the fathers, that is, the prophets, and among them Moses himself, understood it. For the heart of the fathers shall be turned to their children when the children shall be turned to their fathers when they have the same sentiments as the fathers.

"The Septuagint used the expression, 'and the heart of a man to his next of kin,' because fathers and children are eminently neighbours to one another. Another and a preferable sense can be found in the words of the Septuagint translators, who have translated Scripture with an eye to prophecy, the sense, viz., that Elias shall turn the heart of God the Father to the Son, not certainly as if he should bring about this love of the Father for the Son, but meaning that he should make it known, and that the Jews also, who had previously hated, should then love the Son who is our Christ. For so far as regards the Jews, God has His heart turned away from our Christ, this being their conception about God and Christ. But in their case the heart of God shall be turned to the Son when they themselves shall turn in heart, and learn the love of the Father towards the Son.

"The words following, 'and the heart of a man to his next of kin,'—that is, Elias shall also turn the heart of a man to his next of kin,—how can we understand this better than as the heart of a man to the man Christ? For though in the form of God He is our God, yet, taking the form of a servant, He condescended to become also our next of kin. It is this, then, which Elias will do, 'lest,' he says, 'I come and smite the earth utterly.' For they who mind earthly things are the earth. Such are the carnal Jews until this day; and hence these murmers of theirs against God, 'The wicked are pleasing to Him,' and 'It is a vain thing to serve God' ".

278. St. Benedict (d. 543)

a. "During the three and one-half years reign of Antichrist, God will send Henoch and Elias to help the Christians."

b. "In the last times, the Benedictines will render the Church the truest service and fortify many in the faith."

279. St. Caesarius of Arles (d. 543) see prophesy 67.

CHAPTER IV

MEDIAEVAL PROPHESY

280. The prophesies of several Irish saints are given under numbers 69 (Senanus), 70 (Columbkille), 74 (Mael-tamhlacht), 82 (Malachy). The only additional text we have is attributed to St. Patrick (d. 493) "The ocean shall inun-date Ireland seven years before the end so that the devil may not rule over that people". St. Columbkille says: "Seven years before the last day the sea shall submerge Ireland in one inundation"; St. Nennius: "The sea will come over Ireland seven years before the Day of Judgment"; Leabhar Breac: "The sea shall overwhelm Ireland seven years before the Judgment."

281. For the following predictions see the prophesies in the former book: Premol (65), Merlin (72b), St. Odile (76), Leo the Philosopher (78), Thomas a Becket (83). Then there are several old national predictions which we do not repeat here: Irish 75, Welsh 73a, English 85, Scotch 86b, German, 87, 88b, Italian 92, 93b. To these we add the following:

282. *Old German*

a. "In the truth you will rejoice, after darkness you will see light, because before the beginning of 2000, the Beast and the Whore will be thrown headlong into the abyss. They will never come forth again, the Sign of the Cross will be resplendent in the glory of light, with faith and law—one flock and one shepherd."

b. "Woe! Woe! Where Rhine and Moselle meet a battle shall be fought against Turks and Russians so bloody that the Rhine shall be dyed red for twenty-five leagues."

283. *Old French*

"After the triumph of the Church under the Great Monarch and Pastor Angelicus many will revert to a sinful life and hate Christ."

284. *Old Irish*

a.   They will tax the pigs and goats
     They will tax the ducks and hens

They would tax the very Deal (devil)
Should he come out of Heal (Hell)

b. The rise of Antichrist shall be as a black pig in the north and he shall race to the south.

285. St. Gregory the Great (d. 604)

"In those days, near the end, hardly a Bishop, but an army of priests and two-thirds of the Christians will join the Schism."

286. St. John Damascene (d. 770)

a. "Everybody who denies the incarnation of the Son of God, and that Jesus Christ is true God and perfect man, such person is Antichrist. But in a more special and principal manner he will be known as Antichrist who shall come about the end of the world.

b. "His mother will proclaim she gave birth to him while remaining a virgin. He will reign from ocean to ocean.

c. "Antichrist shall be an illegitimate child under the complete power of Satan; and God, knowing his incredible future perversity, will allow the devil to take a full and perpetual possession of him from his very sinful conception.

d. St. John Damascene (with St. Cyril of Jerusalem) affirms that "though Antichrist will from his childhood have the most wicked and cruel disposition, yet, inspired by a preternatural precocious malice, he will practice the most consummate hypocrisy, deceiving the Jews and all his followers. In proportion as he shall advance in age, knowledge, vice, and power, his ambitions will become excessive. He will not only strive for universal dominion over men upon earth, but, as St. Paul teaches, 'he will oppose and be lifted up above all that is called God, or that is worshipped; namely, Antichrist will oppose all that is duly or unduly worshipped, and be lifted up by his satanic pride and ambition above all that is called God, not allowing men to worship any other being but himself, as if he were the only God. 'So that he sitteth in the temple of God, showing himself as if he were God.' (2 Thess. 2) 'He shall speak words against the High One, and he shall crush the saints of the Most High, and shall think himself able to change times and laws.' (Daniel 7:25)"

287. Rabanus Maurus (d. 856)

a. "Our principal doctors agree in announcing to us, that towards the end of time one of the descendants of the kings of France shall reign over all the Roman Empire; and that he shall be the greatest of the Empire; and that he shall be the greatest of the French monarchs, and the last of his race.

b. "After having most happily governed his kingdom, he will go to Jerusalem, and depose on Mount Olivet his sceptre and crown. This shall be the end and conclusion of the Roman and Christian Empire.

c. "Antichrist will heal the sick, raise the dead, restore sight to the blind, hearing to the deaf, speech to the dumb, raise storms and calm them, re-name mountains, make trees flourish and wither at a word, rebuild the temple of Jerusalem, and make Jerusalem the capital of the world with the vast wealth from hidden treasure."

288. St. Methodius (d. 885)

a. "A time will come when the enemies of Christ will boast: 'We have subjected the earth and all its inhabitants, and the Christians cannot escape our hands.' Then a Roman emperor will rise in great fury against them . . . Drawing his sword, he will fall upon the foes of Christianity and crush them. Then peace and quiet will reign on earth, and the priests will be relieved of all their anxieties.

b. "In the last period Christians will not appreciate the great grace of God who provided a Great Monarch, a long duration of peace, a splendid fertility of the earth. They will be very ungrateful, lead a sinful life, in pride, vanity, unchastity, frivolity, hatred, avarice, gluttony and many other vices that the sins of men will stink more than a pestilence before God. Many men will doubt whether the Catholic faith is the true and only saving one and whether the Jews are perhaps correct when they still expect the Messias. Many will be the false teachings and resultant bewilderment. The just God will in consequence give Lucifer and all his devils power to come on earth and tempt his godless creatures."

289. Adso the Monk (d. 992)

It would seem that the interpretation of the name "Antichrist" as given by the Monk Adso was most common, although many characterizations of Antichrist are seemingly based rather on the concept of "one resembling Christ in appearance and power." In keeping with his interpretation, he lists a few traits of Antichrist which are contrary to the character of Christ: Christ was humble; Antichrist will be proud. Christ came to raise the lowly and redeem sinners; Antichrist will reject the humble and glorify sinners and teach the vices which are contrary to the Christian virtues. He will condemn evangelical law, seek his own glory, and will call himself the omnipotent God. Antichrist will be born of Jewish parents, of the tribe of Dan, but his mother will not be a virgin, as many believe. As the Holy Ghost came into the heart of Mary, so will the devil enter into the mother of Antichrist, and his diabolical power will always support Antichrist. Babylon will be his birthplace, but he will be reared and instructed in Bethsaida and Corzaim. After his education at the hands of malignant spirits he will go to Jerusalem and place his seat in the Temple which he will have restored. He will submit to the rite of circumcision, proclaiming that he is the son of the omnipotent God. His first converts will be kings and princes. His influence will be extended from sea to sea, largely through force and persuasive eloquence. He will perform many signs and great miracles. Those who believe in him will be marked on the forehead with a sign. For three and one half years he will hold sway, and, at the end of that period, he will destroy Henoch and Elias, who will have previously opposed him by preaching the true faith. Shortly afterwards Christ will appear, and Antichrist will be killed by the Archangel Michael.

290. St. Anselm (d. 1109)

"Antichrist will rule the world from Jerusalem, which he will make into a magnificent city."

291. *Legenda Aurea (12th Centrury)*

"Advent or the coming of the Lord is celebrated during four weeks in order to signify that this coming is of four kinds, namely: in the flesh, in the spirit, in death, and at the Last Judgment. The last week remains uncompleted, to signify that the glory of the elect, such as the last coming of the Lord will bestow upon them, will be without end. But although this coming is, in reality, fourfold, the Church is especially concerned with two of its forms, namely: the coming in the flesh and the coming of the Last Judgment . . . The circumstances which will precede the Last Judgment are of three sorts: terrible signs, the imposture of Antichrist, and an immense conflagration."

b. " . . . the Last Judgment will be preceded by the impostor Antichrist, who will try to deceive men in four ways:

1. By a false exposition of the Scriptures, wherein he will try to prove that he is the Messias, promised by the Law.

2. By accomplishing miracles.

3. By the distribution of gifts.

4. By the infliction of punishments.

292. St. Hildegard (d. 1179)

a. "Henoch and Elias are being instructed by God in a mysterious manner in paradise. God shows them the works of men as though they could see these with natural eyes. The two men are, therefore, much wiser than all wise men put together. The same force which removed Henoch and Elias from the earth will bring them back in a storm wind at the time when the Antichrist will spread his false doctrine. As long as they will dwell amongst men they will always be refreshed after 40 days. They have the mission from God to resist the Antichrist and lead the erring back to the road of salvation. Both men, distinguished by age and stature, will speak to men: 'This accursed one is sent by the devil in order to lead men into error. We have been preserved by God at a secreted place, where we did not experience the suffering of men. We are now sent by God in order to oppose the heresy of this destroyer. Look, if we resemble you in stature and age.' And because the testimony of both

125

shall agree they will be believed. All will follow these two aged men and abandon heresy. They will visit all cities and towns, where previously the Antichrist had sown his heresy, and through the power of the Holy Ghost will work genuine miracles. All the people will be greatly astonished at them. Henoch and Elias will confuse the followers of Satan with thunder strokes, and destroy them and fortify the Christian in faith. Therefore, the Christians will hurry to martyrdom, which the son of evil will prepare for them, like to a banquet, so that the murderers will grow tired of counting the dead on account of their great numbers; for their blood will run like rivers."

b. "Henoch and Elias have been taught much wisdom and knowledge in Paradise while awaiting their return to earth. God will instruct them every forty days while they are on earth. They will receive exceptional graces and powers from God to use against Antichrist."

c. "When the fear of God has been disregarded everywhere violent and furious wars will take place. A multitude of people will be slaughtered and many cities will be transformed into heaps of rubbish. A few uncommonly cruel people will play their game at the expense of the peace and tranquility of the others. As it has been from the beginning of the world, God will deliver the rod of correction to his enemies for the extirpation of evil . . .

d. "The apostasy' or 'falling away' spoken of in the Bible as preceding the reign of Antichrist is interpreted by St. Hildegard as meaning—'ab impero', 'a sede apostolico', 'a fide', i.e. 'from royalty', 'from the Pope', and 'from the faith' of Christ itself.

e. "The Son of Corruption and Ruin will appear and reign only for a short time, towards the end of the days of the world's duration; the period which corresponds to the moment when the sun has disappeared beyond the horizon; that is to say, he shall come at the last days of the world. He will not be Satan himself, but a human being equaling and resembling him in atrocious hideousness. His mother, a depraved woman, possessed by the devil, will live as a prostitute in the desert. She will declare that she is ignorant as to the identity of his father, and will maintain that her son was presented to her by God in a supernatural manner, as was the Child of the Blessed Virgin. She will then be venerated as a saint by deceived people.

f. "Antichrist will come from a land that lies between two seas, and will practice his tyranny in the East. After his birth false teachers and doctrines will appear, followed by wars, famines, and pestilence.

g. "His mother will seldom let any one see him, and yet by magic art, she will manage to gain the love of the people for him. He will be raised at different secret places and will be kept in seclusion until full grown. When he has grown to full manhood he will publicly announce a hostile doctrine on religion. He will lure and attract the people to himself by granting them complete exemption from the observance of all divine and ecclesiastical commandments, by forgiving them their sins and requiring of them only their belief in his divinity. He will spurn and reject baptism and the gospel. He will open his mouth to preach contradiction. He will say, 'Jesus of Nazareth is not the son of God, only a deceiver who gave himself out as God and the Church instituted by him is only superstition'. The true Christ has come in his person. He will say, 'I am the Saviour of the world'. Especially will he try to convince the Jews that he is the Messiah sent by God, and the Jews will accept him as such. His doctrine of faith will be taken from the Jewish religion and seemingly will not differ much from the fundamental doctrine of Christianity, for he will teach that there is one God who created the world, who is omniscient and knows the thoughts of man and is just, who rewards the obeyers of his commands and the trespassers he chastises, who will raise all from the dead in due time. This God has spoken through Moses and the Prophets, therefore the precepts of the Mosaic laws are to be kept, especially circumcision and keeping the Sabbath, yet by his moral laws he will try to reverse all order on earth. Therefore he is called in Holy Writ the 'Lawless One'. · He will think that he can change time and laws. He will discard all laws, morals and religious principles, to draw the world to himself. He will grant entire freedom from the commandments of God and the Church and permit everyone to live as his passions dictate. By doing so he hopes to be acknowledged by the people as deliverer from the yoke, and as the cause of prosperity in the world. Religion he will endeavor to make convenient. He will say that you need not fast and embitter your life by renunciation, as the people of former times did when they had no sense of God's goodness. It will suffice to love God. He will let the people feast to their heart's content so that they will pity the unfortunate people of former centuries. He will preach free love and tear asunder family ties. He will scorn everything holy, and he will ridicule all graces of the Church with devilish mockery. He will condemn humility and foster proud and gruesome dogmas. He will tear down that which God has taught in the Old and New Testament and maintain sin and vice are not sin and vice. Briefly he will declare the road to Hell is the way to Heaven.

h. "A great enemy of the Church, a precursor of Antichrist, will take the title of Saviour. Heretics will join this precursor of Antichrist and persecute the true Church of Christ. Their cunning will be great, so great in fact that they will be able to draw many righteous men to their side. The Bishops in general will remain faithful, but all will, on account of their courage and faithfulness to the Church, suffer much, yet many Protestants will console the children of God by their conversion to the Catholic Church. Immediately preceding Antichrist there will be starvation and earthquakes. (It will be remembered that Protestants did not yet exist at the date assigned this oracle).

i. "When the great ruler exterminates the Turks almost entirely, one of the remaining Mohammadens will be converted, become a priest, bishop and cardinal, and when the new Pope is elected (immediately before Antichrist) this cardinal will kill the pope before he is crowned, through jealousy, he wishing to be pope himself; then when the other cardinals elect the next pope this cardinal will proclaim himself Anti-Pope, and two-thirds of the Christians will go with him. He, as well as Antichrist, are descendents of the Tribe of Dan. (Some say that the Turks are of the Tribe of Dan).

128

j. "The mark (of Antichrist) will be a hellish symbol of Baptism, because thereby a person will be stamped as an adherent of Antichrist and also of the Devil in that he thereby gives himself over to the influence of Satan. Whoever will not have this mark of Antichrist can neither buy nor sell anything and will be beheaded.

k. "He will win over to himself the rulers, the mighty and the wealthy, will bring about the destruction of those who do not accept his faith and, finally, will subjugate the entire earth.

l. "The streets of Jerusalem, will then shine in the brightest gold with the blood of Christians which will flow like water. Simultaneously Antichrist will try to increase his wonders. His executioners will work such miracles when they torment the Christians that the people will think Antichrist is the true God. The executioners will not permit the Christians to win the martyrs' crown easily for they will endeavor to prolong their pain until they renounce their faith. Yet some will receive a special grace from God to die during the torments.

m. "Antichrist will make the earth move, level mountains, dry up rivers, produce thunder and lightning and hail, remove the leaves from the trees and return them again to the trees, make men sick and cure them, exorcise devils, raise the dead to life (1). He will appear to be crucified and rise from the dead. All in all Christians will be astounded and in grievous doubts while Antichrist will be confirmed in their false faith.

n. "Finally, when he shall have converted all his plans into action, he will gather his worshippers about him and tell them that he will presently ascend toward heaven. However, at the moment of the ascension a bolt of lightning will overwhelm and annihilate him. The planned ascent into heaven will have been prepared by the artful employment of ingenious devices, and the moment at which the event was to

---

1. Only God can raise the dead, only He will cast out devils. This we know from the Gospels. A copyist probably left out the words "seem to."

2. 'and which' is probably a copyists error for 'than'.

have taken place, leading to his destruction, will produce a cloud that will spread an unbearable odor. Through this many people will again come to their senses and to understanding.

o. "Then the people should prepare for the last judgment, the day of which is indeed veiled in secrecy and obscurity, but not far distant.

p. "A longer time of peace is to follow the desolation and wars, and which (2) will precede the second coming of Christ. During this time God will pour out His richest blessing. During these blessed days fertility and blissful prosperity will spread over the earth. As the clouds fertilize the earth, so shall the Holy Spirit enrich the nations with the dew of His Grace. A real summer of spiritual life will come. During this time also the holy angels, who formerly were held back from human society by the vapor of sin, will associate intimately with men, because they are delighted with the renewal and holiness of their lives. Many pagans will also be converted during this time, be baptized and acknowledge Christ with praise. Many converted Jews and heretics will also increase the glory of the Church, much to the surprise of mankind. Many wise men with the gift of prophecy will unfold the secrets and meaning of Holy Scripture."

q. See also Prophesy 84.

293. Bl. Joachim (d. 1202)
"Towards the end of the world, Antichrist will overthrow the pope and usurp his see." See also prophesy 97.

294. St. Francis of Assisi (d. 1226)
"There will be an uncanonically elected pope who will cause a great Schism, there will be divers thoughts preached which will cause many, even those in the different orders to doubt, yea, even agree with those heretics which will cause my Order to divide, then will there be such universal dissensions and persecutions that if those days were not shortened even the elect would be lost."

295. St. Anthony (d. 1231)
"After Antichrist sells himself to the devil he will no longer have a guardian angel or a conscience."

296. St. Cyril of Constantinople (d. 1235)
"Foretells the fall of the Church and Papal throne."

297. Sister Ludmilla of Prague (cir. 1250)
"Hardly three generations will pass after the world war, when one will also endeavor to prevent the Pope from exercising his sacred office, which will be a sign that the fall of Rome and the end of the world is near."

298. St. Thomas Aquinas (d. 1274)
a. "Antichrist will pervert some in his day by exterior persuasion . . . He is the head of all the wicked because in him wickedness is perfect . . . As in Christ dwells the fulness of the Godhead so in Antichrist the fulness of all wickedness. Not indeed in the sense that his humanity is to be assumed by the devil into unity of person . . ., but that the devil by suggestion infuses his wickedness more copiously into him than into all others. In this way all the wicked that have gone before are signs of Antichrist." (Summa III:8:8)

b. "Infidels and even Antichrist are not deprived . . . of the guardianship of angels. Although this help . . . does not result in . . . eternal life by good works, it does none the less . . . protect them from certain evils which would hurt themselves and others. Even the demons are checked by good angels lest they harm as much as they would. In like manner Antichrist will not do as much harm as he would wish." (Summa I:113:4)

c. "The works of Antichrist may be called lying wonders either because he will deceive men's senses by means of phantoms, so that he will not really do what he seems to do; or because if he works real prodigies they will lead those into falsehood who believe in Him." (Summa I:114:4)

d. "(His miracles may be) said to be real just as Pharaoh's magicians made real frogs, but they will not be real miracles because they will be done by the power of natural causes." (Summa II-II:178:1)

e. "Although men be terrified by the signs appearing about the judgment day yet before those signs begin to appear the wicked will think themselves to be in peace and security after the death of Antichrist and before the coming of Christ seeing that the world is not at once destroyed as they thought hitherto." (**Summa,** Sup. 73:1)

f. "Some say that Enoch and Elias still dwell in paradise (Eden)." (**Summa** I:102:2)

g. "Elias was taken up into the atmospheric but not the empyrean heaven . . . and likewise Enoch was translated into the earthly paradise, where he is believed to live with Elias until the coming of Antichrist." (**Summa** III:49:5)

h. "There are two things: The revolt which preceeds Antichrist and the coming of Antichrist. The faith must first be receved in all the world and afterwards many are to abandon it. Others speak of a revolt against the Roman Empire to which all the world was subjected; but the nations rejected the empire and Antichrist has not come. Others have it that the Roman Empire did not really cease but merely changed from a temporal into a spiritual kingdom. In this sense the predicted revolt must be against the Catholic Faith of the Roman Church. This is logical enough. Christ came when all were subject to Rome; therefore, a proper sign of the coming of Antichrist is the revolt against Rome.

"As to Antichrist himself, as Christ abounded in a plenitude of virtue Antichrist will abound in a multitude of all sins and as Christ is better than all holy persons so Antichrist is to be worse than all evil men. For this reason he is called Man of Sin. He is called, too, Son of Perdition, meaning that he is destined to the extreme of perdition. As all the good and the virtues of the holy ones who preceeded Christ were figures of Christ so in all the persecutions of the Church the tyrants were and shall be figures of Antichrist and all the malice which lay hidden in them will be revealed at that time.

i. "The crime of Antichrist is duplex: He is against God and he puts himself before Christ. In opposing God, he puts himself above the true God, in place of all false gods and even denies the participation of humans in the Godhead. The pride of Antichrist surpassed that of all his predecessors and like Caesar and the King of Tyre, he will say he is God and man and so represented he will sit in the temple.

j. "Some say Antichrist is of the tribe of Dan and that, therefore, the Jews will first receive him and will rebuild the temple of Jerusalem and it will be in this temple that he will sit. Others, however, maintain that never will Jerusalem or the temple be rebuilt and that he will sit in the Church in the sense that many from the Church will receive him. St. Augustine says that he with his adherents will form a Church just as Christ and his followers are a Church.

k. "Antichrist will come in God's good time. Those who now work evil pretending it is good do the work of Antichrist. The devil, in whose power Antichrist comes, already in the time of St. Paul was working his iniquity in a hidden manner through tyrants and seducers because the persecutions of times past are figures of that ultimate persecution against all good persons and are imperfect when compared to it.

l. "Antichrist will be destroyed by the spirit of the mouth of Christ. That is, by the Holy Ghost or by Christ's command in that Michael will kill him on Mt. Olivet whence Christ ascended into Heaven just as Julian (the Apostate) was extinguished by the divine hand.

m. "Antichrist will enjoy the use of free will on which the devil will operate as it was said of Judas: 'Satan entered into him,' that is, by instigating him. He shall deceive both by worldly power and the operation of miracles. In the matter of worldly power, St. John (Apoc. XIII) says, 'He will control the treasures of gold and silver and all the precious things of Egypt.' The power of miracles will be simulated. 'He will do wondrous signs and even make fire come upon the earth' (Dan. XI) and thus, he will 'lead many into error even, were it possible, the elect' (Math. 24).

n. "But his miracles will be lies (as explained above in c and d). No one can perform a true miracle against the faith, because God is not a witness of falsity. Hence, no one preaching a false doctrine can work Miracles, whereas one leading a bad life could." (**Comment. in II Thess. II, Lec. 1-III**).

299. St. Mechtilda (d. 1299)

a. "Antichrist will, through base and false strategem, and with presents of gold and gems, attain influence over the worldly princes. These will look up to him as their Lord and God.

b. "During the time of Antichrist an Order of Preachers will unfold its activities; before this its members will be active for 30 years in peace. They will have no home of their own but will be guests everywhere. They will carry a staff before them whereupon the sufferings of Christ and His ascension is pictured. Many heathens and Jews will receive Baptism from these Brothers. Antichrist will pierce these men and capture all their followers.

c. "After the two prophets (Henoch and Elias) are killed, the greatest power on earth will be given to Antichrist. Then they will set up caldrons on the streets with boiling contents, and drive the men who are known as Christians, and their wives and children, there, to choose either to profess in the Deity of Antichrist and thereby keep their family and be rewarded with riches and a home, or to profess the Christian faith, and thereby, death in the boiling caldron. Thereupon the women and their children, who will choose to die, for love of Jesus, will be thrown into a pit of fire, covered with wood and straw and burnt."

d. "Both men are in Paradise, living in bliss and eating the same foods which once Adam had eaten. They, too, must shun, in obedience to God, the same tree from which Adam and Eve were not to eat. This tree is not large; its fruit looks very nice and lovely like a rose, in the interior, however, it is sour by nature whereby is indicated the bitter evil of sin. God has forbidden this fruit because it is very harmful to men and is even now regarded as poison. An angel will accompany Henoch and Elias from paradise. The clearness and bliss which surrounded their bodies will then disappear and they will receive again the terrestial appearance and will become mortal beings. As soon as they will see the earth they will be frightened like people who see the ocean and do not know how they can cross it. They will eat honey and figs and drink water mixed with wine, while their spirit will be nourished by God. They will appear as preachers in the last time of misery when most of the good men have already died as martyrs, and they will console the people for a long time yet. Henoch and Elias will close in on the Antichrist; they will tell the people who he is, by whose power he works miracles, in which way he came into the world and what will be his end. Then many a man and woman will be converted."

"Henoch and Elias will expose the devilish trickery of Antichrist to the people. As a consequence he will put them to death. For three and one-half days their bodies will be exposed to insults and the followers of Antichrist will presume that all danger is now past, but suddenly the bodies of the two prophets will move, rise and gaze on the crowd and begin to praise God. A great earthquake, similar to that at Christ's resurrection, will take place: Jerusalem will be partially destroyed and thousands killed. Then a voice from heaven will call out "Ascend!" whereupon the prophets will ascend into heaven, resulting in the conversion of many. Antichrist will reign thirty days after their ascension."

300. For other 12th Century oracles see prophesies 99, 100, 101 and 103.

301. John of the Cleft Rock (1340)

a. "Man will often think he recognizes this or that in an individual indicating that he is Antichrist, since the persecutors of the Lamb are all similar. All evil doers of importance are precursors of Antichrist.

b. "This Prince of Liars will swear by the Bible and pose as the arm of the Almighty, chastising a corrupt age.

c. "He will be a one-armed man with innumerable soldiers resembling the legions of Hell whose motto will be: 'God with us.' (In World War I this was said to refer to the Kaiser)

d. "In the beginning he will work by cunning and crime. His spies will infest the whole world and he will become master of the secrets of the mighty. He will pay theologians to show that his mission is from God.

e. "A war will give him the opportunity to assume his true role—this war will not be the one he will wage against a French sovereign (Great Monarch?) but one which will within a fortnight involve the whole world and will be easily recognized by his mark. (on his followers?)

f. "The Angels will enlighten men and in the third week they will wonder if this is truly the Antichrist, and realizing that it is, they will either have to fight to overthrow him or become his slaves.

g. "Antichrist will be recognized by various tokens: in especial he will massacre the priests, the monks, the women, the children, and the aged. He will show no mercy, but will pass torch in hand, like the barbarians, yet invoking Christ! His words of imposture will resemble those of Christians, but his actions will be those of Nero and of the Roman persecutors. He will have an eagle in his coat of arms as also will his lieutenant, the other wicked ruler—this latter will be a Christian who will die when cursed by the Pope, who will be elected at the beginning of the reign of Antichrist.

h. "Priests and monks will no longer be seen hearing confessions and absolving the combatants: partly because they will be fighting alongside other Christians and partly because the Pope having cursed Antichrist will proclaim that all who fight against him are in the State of Grace and if they die they will go to Heaven as martyrs (1). The Bull, proclaiming these things will re-inkindle the courage of the faint hearted and will cause the death of the monarch allied with Antichirst. Before Antichrist is overthrown, however, more men will have been killed than were ever within the walls of Rome.

i. "Never will humanity have been faced with such a peril, because the triumph of Antichrist would be that of the demon, who will have taken possession of his personality. For it has been said that, twenty centuries after the Incarnation of the Word, the Beast will be incarnate in his turn, and will menace the earth with as many evils as the Divine Incarnation has brought it graces.

j. "Towards the year 2000 Antichrist will be made manifest. His army will surpass in number anything that can be imagined. There will be Christians among his cohorts, and there will be Mohammedan and heathen soldiers among the defenders of the Lamb.

------

(1) The part about "State of Grace" is apparently copied or translated wrong.

k. "For the first time the Lamb will be all red. There will not be in the whole Christian world a single spot which is not red; and red also will be heaven, and earth, and water, and even the air; for blood will flow in the domain of the four elements at once.

l. "The battles fought up to that time will be as nothing compared with those which will take place in the country of Luther (2) ; for the seven angels will simultaneously pour out the fire of their censers upon the impious land. In other words, the Lamb ordains the extermination of the race of Antichrist.

m. "That which makes the decree of the Lamb so implacable, is that Antichrist has dared to claim to be a Christian and to act in the name of Christ, and if he did not perish, the fruit of the Redemption would be lost, and the gates of Hell would prevail against the Saviour.

n. "Then will commence an era of peace and prosperity for the universe, and there will be no war. Each nation will be governed according to its own heart and live in accordance with justice.

o. "There will be no longer Lutherans (1) or Schismatics. The Lamb will reign and the happiness of humanity will begin. Happy will be those who, escaping the perils of this marvelous time, are able to taste of its fruit. This will be the reign of the Spirit and the sanctification of humanity, which could not come to pass until after the defeat of Antichrist.

p. See also prophesy 104

302. Richard Rolle of Hampole (d. 1349)

a. "The greatest opposition to Antichrist will come from the preaching of Henoch and Elias whom he will destroy after 1260 days. They will rise again after three and one half days and ascend into heaven. Antichrist will then reign for three and one half years. The first fifteen days will be a reign of terror. At the age of thirty-two and one-half years he will be slain on Mt. Olivet, probably by St. Michael. The jubilation of his followers will be suddenly cut short by a

_____

(1) There is something amiss here. Luther was unknown at the dates ascribed to this oracle.

general slaughter. Forty-five days for repentance will intervene before the Last Judgment."

b. "After the destruction of Rome, Antichrist will appear and exalt himself above pagan deities and the Trinity. His name signifies one who is against Christ. Begotten of a sinful man and of a woman into whom the devil has entered, Antichrist will be born of the tribe of Dan in the city of Corozaim. The good angel assigned to him at his birth will be obliged to leave him as witches, necromancers and other disreputable characters take charge of his education in Bethsaida. Coming to Jerusalem, he will proclaim himself Christ and at first feign to be holy. He will succeed through false preaching, miracles, gifts, terror, aided throughout by the devil. An evil spirit will come out of the air and descend upon his followers. He shall feign a resurrection from the dead, cause rain to fall, stone images to speak, and perform other wonders, all through the power of the devil. The recalling of the dead to life will be only apparent; devils entering the dead bodies will cause the illusion. Antichrist will be the greatest tyrant of all time. His adherents will be marked with his sign. Devils shall be let loose from hell. The Jews will welcome him."

c. See also prophesy 105.

303. St. Bridget of Sweeden (d. 1373)

a. "The time of Antichrist will be near when the measure of injustice will overflow and when wickedness has grown to immense proportions, when the Christians love heresies and the unjust trample underfoot the servants of God.

b. "At the end of this age, the Antichrist will be born. As Christ was born from the highest type of womanhood (Virgin), so Antichrist will be born from the lowest (prostitute). He will be a child-wonder at birth. His mother will be an accursed woman, who will pretend to be well informed in spiritual things, and his father an accursed man, from the seed of whom the Devil shall form his work. The time of this Antichrist, well known to Me, will come when iniquity and impiety shall above measure abound, when injustice shall have filled the measure to overflowing, and wickedness shall have grown to immeasurable proportions. It is not in the time described by the brother whose books thou hast seen. Before, however, Antichrist arrives, the gate of Faith will be opened to some nations, and the Scripture shall be verified. People without intelligence shall glorify Me, and deserts shall be inhabited. Hence, when many Christians will be lovers of heresies, and wicked men will persecute the clergy and trample spirituality and justice under foot, this should be the sign that Antichrist shall come without delay.

c. "Lastly, he shall arrive, the most wicked of men, and, helped by the Jews, he will fight against the whole world; he will reign during three years, and shall have dominion over the whole earth; he will make every effort to abolish from the earth the Christian name, and very many Christians shall be killed.

d. "In the year 1980 the wicked shall prevail; they will profane and sacreligiously defile the churches, by erecting in them altars to idols and to Antichrist, whom they will worship, and will attempt to force others to do the same.

e. "Rome will be visited by sword and fire and plowed under." (St. Frances of Rome also foretells this catastrophe, as well as many other prophets, however, St. Benedict of Nursia says that Rome will not be destroyed by outside powers, but will die from within, by natural causes such as storms, whirlwinds, and earthquakes.)

f. See also prophesy 106.

304. Prophesy of Orval

a. "God alone is great. Much good has been accomplished. The saints are about to suffer. The man of sin arrives. He (Antichrist) is born from two bloods. The white flower becomes obscured during ten times six moons, and six times twenty moons (during about one hundred and eighty months), and it disappears, nevermore to be seen.

b. "In that time much evil will be done; little good. Many flourishing cities will perish through fire. Israel, with good heart, comes to Christ-God. The accursed sects and the faithful believers shall form two distinct parties.

139

c. "All is over. God alone shall be believed. A third part of the Gauls (France), and again a third part and half, shall have no more faith. The same shall be with other nations. And, behold, already six times three moons, and four times five moons, (thirty eight months) which are separated, and the age of the end is begun.

d. "After a number of moons not full (those evil days shall be shortened, as promised by our Divine Saviour, because of the elect. Matt. 24: 22). God fights through his two just ones (Henoch and Elias), and the man of sin (Antichrist) will get the upper hand (he will kill them.) But all is not finished. (The apparent temporary success of the wicked is ever the most certain sign of their impending defeat; and this defeat is always more complete in proportion to their success).

e. "The high God sets a wall of fire that obscures my understanding. I can see no more. May He be forever praised."

f. See also prophesy 102.

305. Monk Kosmos
"When ye shall see many ships assemble on the coast of Greece, women, children and old men will be forced to flee to the mountains to escape the sword of Antichrist."

306. *Chronicles of Alberich*
"Before the time of Antichrist the 'Tower of Babel' will be rebuilt, the 'Caspian Mountain' reopened, the River Ethan will flow again, and 'Mohammedanism' will die or be destroyed."

307. Johannes von Lilienthal
"At that time, the Church will suffer severe pressure, will practically lose all its wealth and will be severely oppressed by internal and external enemies ... "

308. St. Vincent Ferrer (d. 1418)
"Apostolic men will come, poor, simple, meek and humble, who are little in their own eyes, devoted to each other with a burning love, who only think of and have nothing on their lips but Jesus, i. e. Jesus Crucified, who do not bother about

140

the world, who forget themselves by uninterruptedly having in mind the honor of God and His Saints, who long for and expect death in order to possess the Highest Good . . . Then a happy time will arrive."

See also prophesy 111.

309. *Father Jerome Votin (d. 1420)*

"And after the end of five centuries (20th century) the servants of the altar will weep and suffer persecutions for the sake of justice. The shepherd (Pope) will be smitten and the fold scattered . . ." See also prophesy 112.

310. Prophesies 113b, 115, 116, 117, and 118 dating from this century may be read here.

311. Bernardine Von Busto (d. 1490)

a. "At the time when Antichrist is about twenty years old, most of the world will have lost the faith.

b. "Antichrist will be descended from the tribe of Dan. The people at that time will be very corrupt. He will preach to the people while flying through the air.

c. "Many fervent priests and religious in the wilderness and desert will be miraculously sustained by God. Some of them will travel about to encourage the Christians to remain firm in the faith till death.

d. "When a pious Christian is pleading to God for help before a crucifix in his room, Satan will disturb him in his prayers and confuse him. He will cause a voice to come from the crucifix saying: 'Why do you call on Me, as if I can help you? I am not God nor the Saviour of the world, but a sorceror, an instigator and deceiver of the people, for I was a false prophet and as a consequence I am damned to everlasting hell fire. Therefore, call on me no more, lest by calling on me you increase the pain that I must suffer in Hell. Through the power of Almighty God, whose gospel is now preached throughout the world, I am urged and compelled to tell you the truth and reveal to you that I am not the Son of God, but rather the greatest sorceror the world has ever had, and hence for all eternity I must suffer the severest pains without hope of redemption.' Also the pictures of the Mother of God at times will speak when someone will be praying before them: 'Cease your supplications. I am not the Mother of God. I have no power with God. I am only a miserable creature. You should take refuge with the true Mother of the Most High, whose teachings are being taught to you today.' It will be the same with the pictures of the Saints. That it is the devil who speaks from the crucifixes and pictures but few will perceive, on the contrary, many will run excitedly to the apostles of Antichrist, to accept the new religion. By order of those apostles they will trample on the crucifix and holy pictures and break them in pieces.

e. "When a mother has her infant in her arms or puts it in the cradle, in a clear and distinct voice it will begin to speak, acknowledging the diety of Antichrist and urging the mother to leave Christ and turn to Antichrist. The child will reproach the parents, that they, in spite of the many miracles of Antichrist, still persist in their wickedness and obstinacy. Oh how much anguish will those parents have to bear. Yet many Christians will remember that this was all foretold of Antichrist for centuries past, and perceive the fraud of Satan and refuse to be deceived. They will stand firm and enlighten the faint-hearted and console them."

(This may be intended to explain Scripture: 'Woe to them that are with child, and give suck in those days.' Mt. 24: 19)

312. St. Francis de Paul (d. 1507)

a. "A new Order will be founded, that of the Cruciferi, (cf. Pius XII) because its members will carry the cross on their banners. This Order will consist of three groups: the first group are the armed riders, the second group the priests, and the third group the nurses. The Crusaders will lead the Mohammedans, the teachers of heretical doctrines and bad Christians to Christ. (See also prophesy 114)

b. "Antichrist will restore the power of Islam (Mohammedanism) destroyed by the Great Monarch."

313. To this century belong several seers quoted before. See prophesies 121 (Catherine di Racconigi), 124 (Gameleo), 125 (Telesphorus).

314. Mother Shipton (d. 1551)

   a. "An ape shall appear in a leap year,
       That shall put all womankind in fear;
       And Adam's make shall be disputed;
       And Roman faith shall be uprooted.

       The fiery year as soon as o'er,
        Peace shall then be as before;
       Plenty everywhere be found,
       And men with swords shall plow the ground."

   b. A woman-child, an ape, a bear
       Hath topsy-turned all the sphere.
       Look where thou wilt, far and wide.
       Fire burns on every side.

       More I know but quake to tell,
       I know too much in knowing hell.
       From sixty till the Beast be dead,
       The heavens warm with fiery red.

       One hundred twenty to Amen
       One sixty six over one zero six to make an end,
       Six o'clock and six deal past
       The six days the Sabbath last

       This much time the Church hath got
       To bring them to their blessed lot

(One commentator thinks the figures given above are to be read $1666+106+120+66=1952$)

CHAPTER V

MODERN PROPHESY

315. Michael Nostradamus (d. 1566)

a. "He that the Principality shall keep by great cruelty; At last shall see a great army, by fire, blow most dangerously. The Purveyor shall put all in disorder, When Mars shall be in the sign of Aries, Joined with Saturn and Saturnith The Moon then shall be thy greatest misfortune, The sun being then in its exaltation.

b. "Because of the power of three realms the Holy See will be moved elsewhere. The blood of priests will flow in the streets and temples, as flows water after a furious rain. The Holy of Holies will be destroyed by Paganism and the Old and New Testament will be banished and burned.

c. "In a cycle of the lily (Bourbon) a great prince is born. He comes late (into the fray?), yet early (in age?) into his dominion. Saturn will be in Libra, its exaltation. (1951 is the next year for this occurence. This dates the zenith of his power).

d. "After the seat is held seventeen years (Pius XI, Feb. 1922 - Feb. 1939), five shall change in the same length of years. (That would be five popes between 1939 and 1956).

e. "When the two evil ones (Saturn and Mars) are conjoined in Scorpio, (this conjunction occurs in January 1954) the great personage (a king or pope) will die within his palace. There will be a scourge within the Church together with the newly-elected ruler in northern and lower Europe.

f. "Then the King of the North, hearing the complaint of the people from his chief state, will raise up a mighty army, and pass through the limits of his last progenitors and great-grandfathers, to him who will replace almost everything in its old condition. The great Vicar of the Cope shall be put back to his pristine state; but, desolated and abandoned by all, will return to the sanctuary destroyed by Paganism, when The Sacred Scriptures will be burnt. After that Antichrist will be the infernal prince. During this last epoch, all Christendom, as well as the infidel world, will be shaken during the space of twenty-five years, (World War

I and II) and the wars and battles will be most grievous, and the cities, castles, and other edifices will be destroyed with much effusion of blood, married women and widows violated, sucking children dashed and broken against the walls of towns; and so many evils will be committed by means of Satan, the infernal prince, that nearly all the world will become desolated. Before the events occur, however, strange birds (airplanes?) will cry in the air, 'to-day! to-day!' and after a time they will disappear. Shortly afterwards, there will be renewed another reign of Saturn, the age of gold. (Reign of Antichrist proper?) God the Creator shall say, hearing the affliction of His people, 'Satan shall be precipitated and bound in the bottomless abyss,' and then shall commence between God and men a universal peace. There he shall abide for the space of a thousand years, and after that he shall turn his greatest force against the power of the Church, and shall then be bound again.

g. "When the tomb of the Great Roman shall have been found, the day after shall be elected a Pontiff: hardly shall he be approved by the Cardinals when his blood shall be poisoned in the sacred chalice.

h. "At the foundation of the new party will be found the bones of the Great Roman, a fissure will reveal the marble of the sepulchre, ill covered, after an earthquake in April. When the source of the stream is traced a freshet will lay bare the marble and lead of the tomb, which will be that of the Great Roman (Peter?) whose motto was Deus in Me. (St. Peter's remains were found in 1949).

i. "By the appearance of a false holiness, the assembly shall be betrayed to the enemies. By reasons of quarrels and new schisms among the Cardinals when the Pope shall be elected, great amounts of false doctrine will be produced against him and Rome will be injured by the Mohammedans.

j. "Then shall begin the great empire of Antichrist who will come with a countless throng, so that the advent of the Holy Spirit, from the 48th parallel, will make a great change and chase away the abomination of Antichrist that made war on the sovereign Vicar of Christ (the Pope) and against his Church for a time and to the end of time. This

145

will be preceded by an eclipse of the Sun, of denser darkness than has ever been seen since the Creation and up to the passion and crucifixion of Jesus Christ, and from that time until the coming one. There will take place in the month of October a great translation made so that the earth will seem to lose the weight of its natural motion in an abyss of end-darkness. There will be premonitory signs in the spring, and there will be extreme changes, overthrows of kingdoms, and earthquakes."

316. Francisco Suarez (d. 1617)

"Suarez, (after St. Jerome, St. Ambrose, Sulpitius Severus, et al.) says that Antichrist shall be born of Jewish extraction, and will profess the Jewish religion; not through real devotion, but through hypocrisy, in order more easily to persuade the great majority of that mysterious race to receive him as their Messiah. He will have two important objects in doing this. In the first place, he will thus mimic Jesus Christ; in the second place, he will thus obtain the enthusiastic support and the wealth of the Jews, and through this material advantage be able to open the way to his ambition for high dignities and human power. The opinion of these Christian writers is derived from the following words of the New Testament. Our Divine Lord and Saviour said to the Jews: 'I am come in the name of my Father, and you receive me not. If another (Antichrist) shall come in his own name, you will receive him.' (St. John 5: 43) St. Paul also says: 'He whose coming is according to the working of Satan, in all power and signs and lying wonders, and in all seduction of iniquity to them that perish, because they receive not the love of truth (Jesus Christ) that they may be saved; therefore God (in punishment of it) will send them the operation of error (Antichrist), to believe a lie.' (Thess. 2: 9-10) Our Divine Lord and Saviour Jesus Christ was born from the Jewish race, and, preaching to them the truth, confirmed it with many incontestable miracles, yet they obstinately refused to believe in him or in his doctrines. Antichrist shall be born from the same people, who will allow themselves to be deceived by his satanic power, signs, and lying wonders, and will enthusiastically receive him as their long-expected Messiah. Thus we see how obstinacy in error leads men to greater crimes and to final reprobation. Because they receive not the love of truth, that they may be saved; therefore God sent them the operation of error to believe a lie."

317. The Sibylle, Queen Michaula of Saba (printed 1619)

"As Henoch and Elias will preach against the Antichrist and draw many away from him, he will, as soon as he perceives the damage, march towards Jerusalem in order to prove there that he be the true Messiah and God. He will kill both prophets in Jerusalem. Their bodies will remain lying in the streets unburied, but on the fourth day they will be resurrected by a voice from heaven, 'Henoch and Elias arise!' and ride to heaven in a cloud. Then the followers of Antichrist will regret having believed him and will repent their sins. Thereupon, Antichrist will make it known that after fifteen days he will also ascend into heaven, so that no one can doubt his divinity. On the appointed day he will majestically seat himself on a beautiful chair, on Mt. Olivet, in view of a large crowd, and before all the people will lift himself up towards heaven through the help of the devil. But, here at the command of God, the Archangel Michael will cast him down to earth by a stroke of lightning."

318. St. Robert Bellarmine (d. 1621)

"The executioners of Antichrist will work wonders while the Christians will be powerless in such matters."*

319. Cornelius a Lapide (d. 1637)

"He will cure the blind, dumb, deaf, lame, lepers, rheumatics and others, so that the world will be astounded, but he will not lay his hands on the sick until they have denied Christ. A great multitude of sick will flock to Antichrist and many will even make very long journeys to be cured by him."

---

*Note: According to St. Robert Bellarmine (Doctor of the Church), the return of Henoch and Elias before the last judgment is "most true," and adds that the opposite view is either heretical or approaching heresy. (Rom. Pont. 3:6; De Controv.).

320. Venerable Bartholomew Holzhauser (d. 1658)

d. "The triumph of the Church will only be short and merely last until he who is to come, shall come—the son of ruin and corruption, who will unleash Satan anew.

e. "And while I trembled exceedingly and was amazed, I saw how everything turned against God ... And I saw men and beasts being killed everywhere. A great wound was on earth and it was overflown with blood. The bloodhound will harass the Church, and the greatest distress and chaos will reign ...

f. "Antichrist will come as the Messiah from a land between two seas in the East.

g. "He will be born in the desert; his mother being a prostitute to the Jews and Hindus; he will be a lying and false prophet and will try to ride to heaven like Elias.

h. "He will begin work, in the East, as a soldier and preacher of religion when thirty years old.

i. "Antichrist and his army will conquer Rome, kill the Pope and take the throne.

j. "He will restore the Turkish regime destroyed by the Great Monarch. The Jews, knowing from the Bible that Jerusalem will be the seat of the Messiah, will come from everywhere, and accept Antichrist as the Messiah.

k. "He will be able to fly. His flight will take place from Mt. Calvary. He will tell the crowd he is going after Henoch and Elias (who had arisen from the dead) in order to kill them again.

l. "Antichrist will live fifty-five and one-half years, that is 666 months (his days are numbered).

m. See also prophesy 129.

321. Venerable Mary of Agreda (d. 1665)

a. "When the world will be drowned in terrible vices, Satan and all his devils will be let loose so that they may pave the way for the godless Antichrist to attain world dominion and final persecution.

b. "As mankind has lost its faith, the subjects of that time will be very much oppressed by their rulers and authorities. Then many people will come to the Antichrist, who will

148

pretend to be exceedingly kind and generous to all, and tell him their troubles. He will console the oppressed and promise them help. Finally the delegates of certain nations, the Jews, Turks and Tartars will beg him to personally free them from their unbearable yoke. He will now declare himself ready to fulfill their wishes, while at the same time he will arouse the neighboring nations to revolution. The Jews will finally bring him a costly crown and a kingly garment, as well as a scepter, and declare him as their freely elected king. The kings of the world, who will hear of this, will laugh at it and not pay any attention to this little horn. In the meantime he will build a powerful army and take up residence in Babylon, where a magnificent palace will be built for him. Many Jews will then stream to Babylon. Then the Antichrist will seek to enlarge his kingdom. He will, therefore, occupy with his troops various surrounding districts in Asia. Then, like a storm wind, he will appear in Egypt with his army and conquer this country, as well as Ethiopia. He will then endeavor to make himself loved by the subjugated nations by a friendly behavior, and by exacting a very small tribute from them. He will declare everywhere that he is destined to be the Saviour of all the oppressed. He will not in the least let it be known that he strives for a world kingdom. Thereupon he will march into the promised land and occupy Jerusalem. Now, at last the kings of the world will become frightened; they will recognize that they are dealing with the Antichrist, especially since the Jews of the whole world will make known the great talents and deeds of the Antichrist, so that his praise shall resound throughout the world. Then the kings will send armies to the Holy Land, but the Antichrist will slay them all."

c. (Taken from the "City of God" describing the Last Supper) . . . "Then also the angels of her guard, all the angels of heaven, and among them likewise the souls of Enoch and Elias, in their own name and in the name of the holy Patriarchs and Prophets of the old law, fell down in adoration of their Lord in the holy Sacrament."

. . . "The great high priest Christ raised up his own consecrated body and blood in order that all who were present at this first Mass might adore it in a special manner, as they also did. During this elevation his most pure Mother, Saint John, Enoch and Elias, were favored with an especial insight into the mystery of his presence in the sacred species."

. . . "The effects of holy Communion in the body of Christ were altogether miraculous and divine; for during a short space of time the gifts of glory flowed over in his body just as on mount Tabor, though the effects of this transfigura-tion were manifest only to his blessed Mother, and partly also to Saint John, Enoch, and Elias."

. . . "Then saint Peter, at the command of Christ the Lord, administered two of the particles of holy Communion to the two patriarchs, Enoch and Elias. This holy communion so rejoiced these two holy men, that they were encouraged anew in their hope of the beatific vision, which for them was to be deferred for so many ages, and they were strengthened to live on in this hope until the end of the world. Having given most fervent and humble thanks to the Almighty for this blessing, they were brought back to their abiding place by the hands of the holy angels. The Lord desired to work this miracle in order to pledge Himself to include the ancient natural and written laws in the benefits of the Incarnation, Redemption and general resurrection; since all these mys-teries were contained in the most holy Eucharist. By thus communicating Himself to the two holy men, Enoch and Elias, who were still in the motal flesh, these blessings were extended over the human race such as it existed under the natural and the written laws, while all the succeeding gen-erations were to be included in the new law of grace, the Apostles at the head. This was all well understood by Enoch and Elias, and, returning to the midst of their contempor-aries, they gave thanks to their and our Redeemer for this mysterious blessing."

d. See also prophesy 130.

322. Dionysius of Luxemberg (d. 1682)

a. "After the birth of Antichrist the people of the world will be very wicked and Godless. People of real virtue will be very scarce. Pastors in many places will neglect the service of God, and will live with women. Even the religious will crave for worldly things. The churches will be dreary and empty like deserted barns . . . at the time when Antichrist is about twenty years of age the whole world will be without faith, subjects will be oppressed by rulers and others in authority. In every period of tribulation God aids His Church, and He will do it in the time before the coming of Antichrist. From the midst of His Church He will raise up a Christian ruler who will perform most remarkable deeds. With divine assistance, this ruler will not only lead erring souls back to the true faith but also deal a heavy blow to the fces of the empire, the Turks, take away their empire and restore it to Christianity.

b. "The conception of Antichrist will be like Christ's except it will be by the devil* instead cf the Holy Ghost. He will have the devil's power like Christ had God's.

c. "Antichrist will present himself to the Jews as the Messiah. They will be his first followers. (2 Thess. 2: 9)

d. "Antichrist will have the powers of the devil from the beginning. He will be so evil it would seem his father was the devil. He will inherit his evil tendencies from his mother, who will also train him in evil.

e. "His wife will be a Jewess but he will have many women, especially the daughters of rulers. (Dan. 11: 27)

f. "Antichrist's life will be a mockery of Christ's. He will be a convincing speaker, have great knowledge, the gift of tongues (Apoc. 13: 5) and be a child wonder at six or seven.

g. "He will take the riches of the world to Jerusalem and appear to have power over natural laws.

h. "Antichrist will be an iconoclast (even against pagan images). Most of the world will adore him. He will teach that the Christian religion is false, change the ten commandments, confiscation of Christian property is legal, and that Saturday is to be observed instead of Sunday. All his wonders could not be written in a bock. They will be more wonderful than the Old and New Testaments. All with the mark of Antichrist will be possessed by the devil. There will be

---

* This is denied by St. Thomas and others.

151

persecution without rest for those who do not have the mark. He will read peoples' minds, raise the dead*, reward his followers and punish the rest."

i. "Elias will cause the rain, dew and snow to cease in those countries where the inhabitants oppose the two prophets and refuse to reject Antichrist. The first land to be so punished will be Palestine in order to win over the Jews.

"After Elias finds the 'Ark of the Covenant' of the Jews (hidden until the recall of the Jews to God), he and Henoch will place the Blessed Sacrament upon it. The Jews will then realize that Jesus Christ and not Antichrist is the true Messiah. They will desert Antichrist and make a pilgrimage to Mount Nebo (where the Ark is found) bewailing the hardheartedness of the ancestors. Thereafter they will accept the Christian faith."

j. "The Antichrist will kill Henoch and Elias and leave them unburied. These will, however, be resurrected after three and one-half days and ascend into heaven in a cloud in the presence of their enemy. This miraculous event will actually confuse Antichrist. In order that the nations will not abandon him, he will lift himself with great majesty into space on Mt. Olivet, with the purported intention to cast down the prophets who have ascended into heaven. But, in this moment Christ will strike him down. The earth will open and swallow him and his prophets alive. Then a large part of Jerusalem will fall into ruins from the earthquake."

k. "When Antichrist hears that the two prophets have miraculously ascended into heaven he will proclaim in Jerusalem that it was through witchcraft that they were able to ascend into heaven, but that he will follow and bring them back, to prove that, being God, their sorcery is subject to him. His ministers will assemble a vast crowd on Mt. Olivet, Antichrist will talk to the people and then, with the aid of Satan, he will ascend, like an Eagle, heavenwards."

323. Other prophesies from these years are numbers 131 (Rudolph Kekner), 136 (The Monk of Padua), 139 (Capuchin Friar).

---

* This is denied by St. Thomas and others.

324. Hermit of Nazara (18th Century)

"From day to day we may expect another universal chaos."

325. St. Louis de Montfort (d. 1716)

"The training and education of the great saints, who will appear towards the end of the world, is reserved for the Mother of God. These great saints will surpass in holiness the majority of the other saints like the cedar of Lebanon surpasses the lowly shrub. These great saints, full of grace and zeal, will be chosen in order to oppose the enemies of God who will appear everywhere. By their word and example these saints will bring the whole world to a true veneration of Mary. This will bring them many enemies, but also much blessing." See also prophesy 135.

326. Father Nectou, S. J. (d. 1772)

" 'The Venerable Abbe Nectou did not assign any precise time for all these events, (those given in prophesy 137) which he predicted to me,' says the Abbe Raux, his friend. 'He stated, however, that those persons who shall behold this last revolution will thank God for having preserved them to witness this glorious triumph of the Church.'

g. "Finally, the Venerable Nectou foretold, that when the above-mentioned events shall be near at hand, everything upon earth shall be so upset and confused, as if God had entirely withheld his providence from mankind, and that, during the worst crisis, the best that can be done would be to remain where God has placed us, and persevere in fervent prayer."

327. *Bernhardt Rembordt (d. 1783)*

a. "After a time of peace and prosperity, during the reign of the Great Monarch, the people will again become wicked. Then in punishment the precursor of Antichrist will come, and there will be more wars.

b. "They want to found a new kingdom of Christ, and all faith is to be banned and people do not care any more whether they go to church or not.

c. "They call themselves servants of God, but they are servants of the flesh.

153

d. "They take unto themselves one woman, then two, then three, and make a religion out of their sinfulness.

e. "For their belly is their God and the destruction of Christ their goal.

f. "With it the false prophets will fall. As such many will burn themselves with their wives and children. And four hundred of them will be strangled with intestines. And those that are left will be cast from a rock on the Rhine. That is the beginning of the blood-era. The Holy City of Cologne will then witness a frightful battle. Many strange people will be murdered here, and men and women will be fighting for their faith. And it will not be possible to avoid a horrible devastation of Cologne. And there one will wade in blood up to the ankle."

328. Jane Le Royer (d. 1798) Sister Mary of the Nativity

a. "Many precursors, false prophets, and members of infernal secret societies, worshippers of Satan, shall impugn the most sacred dogmas and doctrines of our holy religion, shall persecute the faithful, shall commit abominable actions; but the real and extreme abomination and desolation shall more fully be accomplished during the reign of Antichrist, which will last about three years and a half.

b. "Thereupon I saw a great power arising against the Church. It despoiled, plundered and laid waste to the vineyard of the Lord, made of it a foot-path for those passing over it, and derided it before the nations as an object of scorn and mockery. After desecrating the celibate and suppressing monasticism, this power boldly confiscated the properties of the Church and at the same time usurped the powers of the pope, whose person and laws they condemned.

c. "You will soon become aware of a great transformation. For the end has not as yet set in and they have not as yet reached the goal, as they suppose. To be sure, the dawn begins to break, but the age that follows will be stormy and full of suffering.

d. "Woe, woe, woe to the last century which is descending! What tribulations precede its commencements.

e. "Out of this mighty voice I recognized that these woeful tribulations will make their appearance in the age before the judgment. And as I pondered over and weighed, in God, the century, I saw, that which begins with 1800 will not yet be the last.

f. "I see that when the Second Coming of Christ approaches, a bad priest will do much harm to the Church.

g. "When the time of the reign of Antichrist is near, a false religion will appear which will be opposed to the unity of God and His Church. This will cause the greatest schism the world has ever known. The nearer the time of the end, the more the darkness of Satan will spread on Earth, the greater will be the number of the children of corruption, and the number of Just will correspondingly diminish.

h. "Antichrist will kill the Pope, probably by crucifixion. As a child of ten he will know more than anyone else in the world and when he is thirty he will begin his real work.

i. "The day of retribution will now (end of reign) begin, because, being full of the spirit of Lucifer, with the greatest presumption and self love he will consider himself God, and in his haughtiness he will endeavor, together with his followers, to solemnly arise to Heaven to the throne of God. The Almighty has already prepared St. Michael with power and justice and charged him to oppose Antichrist in the heavens. When the demon group with Antichrist in their midst arrives, St. Michael will descend from Heaven with great speed upon them, being filled with holy indignation. With his appearance great fear surges through the proud army. A terrible voice sounds forth from the mouth of St. Michael as the earth opens: 'Begone you cursed! Down into the deepest abyss of Hell!' A bolt of lightning from the cloud casts Antichrist and his cohorts into the fearful abyss of fire and flames with such force that the deepest foundations tremble and all Hell resounds. With the fall of Antichrist will come severe earthquakes, thick darkness will cover the Earth, the ground will open in thousands of places under the feet of the inhabitants and cities, towns, castles and an immense number of people will be swallowed up. One-half of that immense crowd on Mt. Olivet will be cast in the abyss with Antichrist. The ocean will move frightfully and waves arise heavenward overflowing the coast and inundate the earth. All these calamities are only to frighten the remaining into accepting the Grace and Mercy of God."

j. "Fifteen days after the ascension of Henoch and Elias into heaven, terrible catastrophes will come upon the earth: most severe earthquakes, tidal waves inundating much of the earth's surface, culminating in a thick darkness over the entire earth."

329. *Birch Tree Prophesy* (before 1800)

"There will come a time when the world is averse to God. Loyalty and faith rule no more. Then there will arise a general insurrection, so that the father will fight against the son and the son against the father. At this time attempts will be made to distort the dogmas of faith in Church and school. New books will be introduced. The Catholic Church will then be greatly oppressed and her enemies will cunningly strive to annihilate her altogether. But then it will not be long before a change takes place. A frightful war breaks out." See also prophesy 89.

330. Sister Marianne von Blois (d. 1804)

a. "Before the great combat the wicked shall be masters. They will perpetrate all the evils in their power, but not as much as they desire, because they shall not have the time. Good and faithful Catholics, less in number, shall be on the point of being annihilated, but a stroke from Heaven will save them. (Three days darkness?)

b. "O power of God! O power of God! All the wicked shall perish, and also many good men. O, how frightful shall these calamities be! The churches shall be closed, but only for the space of twenty-four hours. Religious women, being terrified, shall be on the point of abandoning the convent, but they shall remain. At this time such extraordinary events shall take place that the most incredulous will be forced to say, 'the finger of God is there.' O power of God! There shall be a terrible night, during which no one shall be able to sleep. These trials shall not last long, because no person could endure them. When all shall appear lost, all will be saved. It is then that dispatches shall arrive, announcing good news, when the Te Deum shall be sung, in a manner in which it has never been heard before. It is then that the

Prince shall reign, whom people will seek, that before did not esteem him. At that time the triumph of religion will be so great that no one has ever seen the equal. All injustices will be repaired, civil laws will be formed in harmony with the laws of God and of the Church. The instruction given to children will be most Christian; pious guilds for workmen shall be re-established; the triumph of the Church and of France shall be most glorious.

c. "One will have to pray much, because the wicked will try everything. Before the big battle they will be masters. They will do as much evil as they possibly can, however, not as much as they would want to do, because they will not have the time for it. A big battle will take place between the good and the wicked; it will be terrible. For nine hours continuously the thunder of canon will be heard. The less numerous good will be for a moment on the brink of being destroyed; but oh! the power of God! All the wicked will perish."

331. The Pinsk Prediction (1819)

"The Civilta Cattolica of Rome, 1864, related the follow-tested by a person worthy of confidence, that heard it from the Polish religious to whom the prophesy was made: 'In the year 1819, the Rev. Father Korzeniecki, a most zealous Dominican preacher, was most strictly forbidden by the Russian schismatical government to publish any writing, to preach, or even to hear confessions, under penalty of exile to Siberia. He was most afflicted in being thus deprived of

One evening, (1819) about nine o'clock, before going to rest, this holy religious opened the window of his cell in the monastery wherein he lived, and looking up towards heaven he made with great fervor the following prayer: 'O glorious martyr of Jesus Christ, Blessed Andrew Bobola! you who so many years since foretold the liberation and restoration of our Poland, you who see our masters determined to force her to become through schism an enemy of God, ah! do not allow such a scourge and humiliation to fall upon her. Obtain, holy martyr, from the omnipotence of God, that our common Catholic country may be delivered from her schismatic Protestant yoke.' Having after this prayer shut up the win-

dow and prepared to lay down on his humble bed, the holy
martyr appeared to him and said: 'Behold, I am the person
to whom you have addressed your prayer; open again the
same window and you will see . . .' The good religious, surprised and somewhat terrified, opened the window, when, to
his great amazement, the enclosed grounds and little garden
attached to the monastery had disappeared, but in their
stead he saw an immense plain. Then the blessed martyr,
resuming, said to him: 'You behold now the fields of Pinsk,
(northern Poland) where I had the glory of suffering martyrdom for the faith of Jesus Christ . . . Now, looking again
in the same direction, you will learn what you wish to know.'
The Rev. Father Korzeniecki once more turned his eyes towards the place indicated, and beheld that vast field covered
with Russian, Turkish, French, English, Austrian, and Prus-
sian armies, and others which he could not well discern, all
of them fighting in a most furious manner one against the
other.

Not being able to comprehend the meaning of this vision,
Saint Andrew explained it to him in the following words:
'When the war which you see shall end, then the kingdom
of Poland shall be established, and I shall be acknowledged
its principal patron. In token of the reality of this vision and
of the realization of this prophecy, behold my hand.' In saying this the blessed martyr places his hand flat upon the
little table in the cell, and disappeared. Amazed beyond expression, the pious religious was attempting to make some
short prayer in thanksgiving to God for the favor received,
and being entirely restored to his senses he looked immediately on the table and really beheld the impression of the
martyr's hand. With sentiments of lively devotion, he kissed it several times, after which he quietly retired to his needed rest. As soon as he awoke on the following morning, his
first impulse was to look again for the miraculous impression, which he found just the same as on the preceeding
evening, and this more than ever convinced him of the
reality of the vision of the previous night. Then, having
gathered in his room all the religious of the monastery, he
showed to them the miraculous sign of the hand, and re-

lated to them all that had happened to him the evening before."

332. Anna Catherine Emmerich (d. 1824)

a. "In the center of Hell I saw a dark and horrible looking abyss, and into this Lucifer was cast, after being first strongly secured with chains; thick clouds of sulphurous black smoke arose from its fearful depths, and enveloped his frightful form in the dismal folds, thus effectually concealing him from every beholder. God himself had decreed this: and I was likewise told, if I remember right, that he will be unchained for a time fifty or sixty years before the year of Christ 2000. The dates of many other events were pointed out to me which I do not now remember; but a certain number of demons are to be let loose much earlier than Lucifer, in order to tempt men, and to serve as instruments of the divine vengeance. I should think that some must be loosened even in the present day, and others will be set free in a short time.

b. "Antichrist will fight a successful battle at Mageddo in Palestine after which seven rulers, from fear will subject themselves to Antichrist and he will thereafter become lord of the world.

c. "I see new martyrs, not of the present time, but in the next century. I see them pursued. I see how here and there good and pious people and especially the religious orders, are tortured, imprisoned and murdered . . .

d. "I saw a picture of a dreadful battle. The entire field was covered with vapor. They shot everywhere out of thickets and the air, which were full of soldiers. The place was low-lying territory and in the distance were great cities. I saw St. Michael descending with a great multitude of angels and dispersing the combatants. That, however, will only happen when everything seems lost. There will be a leader who will invoke St. Michael and then victory will descend. The enemy were in the majority but the small loyal band overthrew whole lines. It was a frightful battle, and at last only a small band of good people were left and they became the victor.

159

e. "I wish the time were here when the Pope dressed in red will reign. I see the Apostles, not those of the past, but the apostles of the last times, and it seems to me, the Pope is among them.

f. "A pale faced man floated slowly over the earth and, loosening the cloths, which wrapped his sword, he threw them on sleeping cities, which were bound by them. This figure also dropped pestilence on Russia, Italy and Spain. A red noose lay around Berlin, and from there it came to Westphalia. Now the man's sword was naked, bands red as blood hung from its hilt and blood trickled from it on Westphalia.

g. "The Jews shall return to Palestine and become Christians towards the end of the world."

333. Elizabeth Canori-Mora (d. 1825)

"God will make use of the power of darkness in order to root out the followers of Sects and godless who want to shake and destroy the foundation of the Church . . . They will be punished by the cruelty of demons and die a tragic and barbarous death. Hereupon the grand triumph of the Catholic Church will follow and all stream into the fold of the Catholic Church, and recognize the Pope as the representative of God." See also prophesy 150.

334. To this period belong prophesies 152 (Belez), 153 (Wittman), 154 (Bufals), 158 (Lataste), 161 (Clausi), 168 c. d, (Porzat), 162 (Mayence), 164 (Steiner).

335. Blessed Anna Maria Taigi (d. 1837)

a. "God will decree two afflictions. One will originate on earth, namely; wars, revolutions and other evils. The other judgment comes from the air.

b. "A very thick darkness shall envelop the earth during three days. This awful darkness shall be impregnated with such pestilential vapors, and filled with such frightful apparitions, that they will cause, in a more special manner, the death of the hypocritical or avowed enemies of the Holy Church.

c. "On this terrible occasion so many of these wicked men, enemies of his Church and of their God, shall be killed by this divine scourge, that their corpses round Rome will be as numerous as the fish which a (then) recent innundation of Tiber had carried into the city. All the enemies of the Church, secret as well as known, will perish over the whole earth during that universal darkness, with the exception of some few, whom God will soon after convert. The air shall be infested by demons, who will appear under all sorts of hideous forms.

d. "During this darkness artificial light will be impossible. Only blessed candles can be lighted and will afford illumination. He who out of curiosity opens his window to look out or leaves his house will fall dead on the spot. During these three days the people should remain in their homes, pray the Rosary and beg God for mercy.

e. "A heavenly apparition shall come to reassure the faithful. St. Peter and St. Paul will appear on the clouds, and all men shall see them; and, in a supernatural manner, faith shall return to their hearts. Innumerable conversions of heretics shall cause universal edification.

f. "One day, Anna Maria, while shedding a torrent of tears, prayed and offered her actions and sufferings for the conversion cf sinners, for the destruction of sin, and that God might be known and loved by all men. Then God manifested to her the horrible sins of persons of every condition, and how grievously he was offended. At this sight the servant of God experienced a profound sorrow, and sighing, she exclaimed: 'Dearly beloved! what is the remedy for this disaster?' Jesus Christ answered: 'My child, the Church, my spouse, my Father, and myself shall remedy everything. For after a punishment . . . those who shall survive shall have to conduct themselves well.' At this point she saw innumerable conversions of heretics, who will return to the bosom of the Church; she saw, also, the edifying conduct of their lives, as well as that of all other Catholics.

g. "During several successive days, Anna Maria beheld a most excessive darkness spreading itself over the whole world. She likewise saw falling ruins of walls, accompanied by much dust, as if a great edifice had tumbled down. This scourge was shown to her on divers occasions. This may indicate the ruins caused by frightful earthquakes, or the destruction effected by the wicked Communists. We presume, and assume as pretty certain, that this darkness will be sensible, similar to that of Egypt, mentioned in Exodus, tenth chapter, and that it shall continue during three days.

h. "Religious shall be persecuted, priests shall be massacred, the churches shall be closed, but only for a short time; the Holy Father shall be obliged to abandon Rome.

i. "Our Lord said to her: 'First five big trees must be cut down in order that the triumph of the Church may come. These five trees are five great heresies.' Then the Servant of God said: 'Two hundred years are hardly sufficient that all of this may happen.' And Our Lord replied: 'It won't take as long as you think!'

j. "First, several EARTHLY scourges will come. They are going to be dreadful, but they will be mitigated and shortened by the prayers and penances of many holy souls. There will be great wars in which millions of people will perish through iron. But, after these earthly scourges will come the HEAVENLY one, which will be directed solely against the impenitent. This scourge will be far more frightful and terrible; it will be mitigated by nothing, but it will take place and act in its full rigor. However, in what this heavenly scourge will consist, God did not reveal to anyone, not even His most intimate friends."

336. Franciscan Friar of Mt. Sinai (d. 1840)

a. "A terrible war will break out throughout Europe; they will tear each other to pieces and blood will flow in streams.

b. "Spain and Portugal both have to efface a debt of blood, partly because of the inhumaness with which they conquered America, murdering so many thousands in a cruel manner, all because of vain gold, and partly because they captured so many innocent people in Africa, all images of God, and sold them into slavery like cattle. The potentates of these two thrones will be murdered. Then both countries will unite and establish a common Republic. All inhabitants will return to peace and order; but their foreign possessions will sever themselves from these two countries. The Catholic religion will again bloom as originally.

c. "France will be involved in a foreign war. As soon as this is over, however, the people will revolt and murder the President, whereupon a terrible blood bath will ensue. More than half of the city of Paris will be turned into ashes.

d. "England, this country of merchants which supports all injustices for the sake of gain, will become the scene of the greatest cruelties. Ireland and Scotland will invade England and destroy it. The royal family will be driven out and half of the population murdered. Poverty will come and all colonies will sever themselves from England.

e. "Italy, Italy, thou beautiful country! I cry over thee! A part of your prosperous cities will be destroyed; here so many Germans find their grave.

f. "Blessed years will then again make their appearance, and the year 1957 will heal all wounds. Blessed are they who live to see this year."

337. La Salette Prophecy (1846)

a. "There will be a kind of false peace before the advent of Antichrist. Man's only thought will be upon diversions and amusements. The wicked will indulge in all sorts of sin, but the children of the Holy Church, the children of the faith, My sincere followers, will wax strong in the love of God and in the virtues that are dear to me. Happy the humble souls that are guided by the Holy Ghost. I will fight with them until they shall have reached the completion of age.

b. "Italy will be severely punished for her efforts to shake off the yoke of the Most High Lord. She will become the play-ball of war. On every side blood will flow. The temples will either be closed or desecrated. Priests and members of religious orders will be put to flight. They will be beaten to death and otherwise die cruel deaths.

c. "The Vicar of my Son will be compelled to suffer much because for a time the Church will be delivered to great persecutions. That will be the hour of darkness, and the Church will experience a frightful crisis. The powerful officials of the State and the Church will be suppressed and done away with, and all law and order as well as justice which exist. Then will be murder, hate, envy and deceit, with no love or regard for one's country or family.

d. "The priests, ministers of my Son, through their bad lives, through their irreverences, and their impiety, whilst celebrating the holy mysteries, through their love of money, love of honors, and pleasure, yes, priests cry for vengeance, and vengeance is suspended over their heads. Woe to the priests, and to persons consecrated to God! who through their infidelity and their bad lives crucify again my Son. The sins of persons consecrated to God, cry to heaven, and call for vengeance, and behold vengeance is at their doors. For no person is any more to implore the mercy and pardon of God in behalf of the people; there are no more generous souls, no more any person worthy of offering the Immaculate Victim to the Eternal Father in behalf of the world. God is going to punish in a manner without example. Woe to the inhabitants of the earth! God is going to exhaust his wrath, and nobody shall be able to evade so many combined evils. At the first stroke of his fulminating sword the mountains and the whole nature shall shake with terror, because the disorders and crimes of men pierce the very vaults of the heavens. The earth shall be stricken with every kind of plagues. (Besides the pestilence and famine, which shall be general.) There shall be wars until the last war, which shall be waged by the ten kings of Antichrist. All these kings shall have a common design, and they only shall govern the world. Priests and religious shall be hunted; they shall be butchered in a cruel manner. Many shall abondon the faith, and great shall be the number of priests and religious who shall separate themselves from the true religion; among these there will be found likewise several bishops. Let the Pope be upon his guard against miracle-workers, for the time is arrived when the most astounding prodigies will take place on the earth and in the air.

e. "Lucifer, with a very great number of demons, will be unchained from hell. By degrees they shall abolish the faith, even among persons consecrated to God. They shall blind them in such a manner that, without very special graces, these persons shall imbibe the spirit of those wicked angels. Many religious houses will entirely lose the faith, and shall be the cause of the loss of many persons. In the monasteries, the Flowers of the Church, will mould and rot. The superiors of religious communities should be alert regarding the ones they take into the community, for the devil will use all malice, to bring persons into the orders who are addicted to sin.

f. "Bad books will abound upon the earth; and the spirit of darkness shall spread over the earth a universal relaxation about everything relating to the service of God. Satan shall have very great power over nature (God's punishment for the crimes of men); temples will be erected for the worship of these demons. Some persons shall be transported from one place to another by these wicked spirits, even some priests, because these will not be animated by the holy spirit of the gospel, which is a spirit of humility, charity, and zeal for the glory of God.

g. "Some will make the dead rise* and appear as holy persons. The souls of the damned shall also be summoned, and shall appear as united to their bodies. (Such persons, resurrected through the agency of demons, shall assume the figure of holy persons, who are known to have been upon earth, in order more easily to deceive them. These self-styled resuscitated persons shall be nothing but demons under their forms. In this way they shall preach a Gospel contrary to that of Jesus Christ, denying the existence of heaven.)

h. "In every place there shall be seen extraordinary prodigies, because the true faith has been extinguished, and a pale light shines in the world.

i. "My Son's Vicar shall have much to suffer, because for a time the Church shall be exposed to very great persecutions. This shall be the time of darkness. The Church shall have to pass through an awful crisis. France, Italy, Spain,

---

*This is denied by St. Thomas and others. In the Catholic Encyclopedia article on "La Salette", it states the the original message (1851) and that given the public years later (1879) were probably not identical. The later version is thought to have been influenced by apocalytic literature.

and England shall have civil war. Blood shall flow through the streets. French shall fight French. Italians against Italians. After this there will be a frightful general war. For a time God shall not remember France, nor Italy, (for two years or for one?) because the gospel of Jesus Christ is no more understood. The Holy Father will suffer much. I will be with him to the end to receive his sacrifice. The wicked shall many times attempt his life.

Nature demands vengeance against men, and she trembles with fright in expectation of what will befall the earth sullied with crimes. Tremble, O earth! And tremble you also who make profession of serving Jesus Christ, but inwardly worship yourselves, because God has delivered you to his enemies, because corruption is in holy places.

j. "The abomination shall be seen in holy places, in convents, and then the demon shall make himself as the king of hearts. It will be about that time that Antichrist shall be born from . . . At his birth he shall vomit blasphemies. He shall have teeth; in a word, he shall be like an incarnate demon; he shall utter frightful screams; he shall work prodigies; and he shall feed on impure things. He shall have brothers, who, though not incarnate demons like him, shall nevertheless be children of iniquity. At the age of twelve years they shall have become remarkable for valiant victories, which they shall achieve; very soon each of them will be at the head of armies. Paris shall be burned, and Marseilles shall be submerged; many great cities shall be shattered and swallowed up by earthquakes. The populace will believe that everything is lost, will see nothing but murder, and will hear only the clang of arms and sacrilegious blasphemies.

k. "I address a pressing appeal to the earth. I call upon the true disciples of the living God, who reigns in the heavens; I call upon the true imitators of Christ made man, the only true Saviour of mankind; I call upon my children, those who are truly devoted to me, those who have offered themselves to me that I may lead them to my Son, those whom I carry as it were in my arms, those who have been animated by my spirit. Finally, I call on the apostles of

166

these last days, these faithful disciples of Jesus Christ, who have lived despising the world and themselves, in poverty and humility, in contempt and in silence, in prayer and mortification, in chastity and union with God, in suffering and unknown to the world. It is time for them to come out and enlighten the world. Go ye forth and manifest yourselves as my darling children; I am with you and within you, so that your faith may be the light which illumines you in these unhappy days, and that your zeal may make you hankering for the glory and honor of the Most High. Fight, ye children of light; combat, ye small band that can see, for this is the time of times, the end of ends.

1. "The seasons of the year will change, the earth will produce only bad fruits, the stars will depart from their regular course, the moon will give only a weak, reddish light. Water and fire in the interior of the earth will rage violently and cause terrible earthquakes, whereby mountains and cities will sink into the depths. Earthquakes will also devour whole countries. Together with the Antichrist the demons will work great false miracles on earth and in the air. Voices will be heard in the air. Then men will desert religion and become worse and worse. Men will let themselves be deceived because they refused to adore the real Christ Who lives bodily amongst them. Woe to the inhabitants of the earth! Bloody wars, famines, pestilence and contagious diseases will develop. Terrible rain and hail will come with animals falling from the heavens, thunder and lightning burning down entire cities. The whole universe will be gripped by fear. Finally the sun will be darkened and faith alone will give light.

m. "A certain precursor of Antichrist, together with his followers from many nations, will fight the real Christ, the only Saviour of the world. He will endeavor to eliminate the adoration of God in order to be considered as God himself. Much blood will flow. Then the earth will be visited by all kinds of blows, from constant wars until the last war which finally will be made by the ten kings of the Antichrist.

n. "During the time of the arrival of Antichrist, the

gospel will be preached everywhere, and all peoples and nations will then recognize the Truth.

o. "Rome will lose the faith and become the seat of Antichrist. Yet the Heathen Rome will disappear. See, here is the Beast with its subjects that claims to be the Saviour of the world. Proudly it rises in the air to go straight to Heaven, but it will be strangled by the breath of the Archangel Michael and cast down. And the earth, which for the past three days was in continuous convulsions, opens her fiery jaws and swallows him with all his cohorts forever into its hellish abyss. Eventually will water and fire cleanse the earth and the works of human pride will be destroyed and all will be renewed. Then will all serve God and glorify Him.

p. "The just will have much to suffer; their prayers, works of penance and tears will ascend to heaven. All of God's people will cry for forgiveness and grace and beg my help and intercession. Then Jesus Christ will command His angels, by a special act of His Justice and Mercy, to deliver all His enemies to death. Then suddenly all persecutors of the Church of Jesus Christ and all evil doers will perish, and rest and peace between God and man will appear. Jesus Christ will be served, adored and glorified. Love of neighbor will begin to flourish all over. The new kings will be on the right hand of the Church which will grow strong, and which will be humble, pious, poor, zealous and followers of the virtues. All over, the Gospel will now be preached, people will make great progress in faith; there will be unity amongst the laborers of Jesus Christ, and people will live in the fear of God.

q. "What I shall tell you now will not always remain a secret. You are allowed to publish it after the year 1858.

r. "Behold the reign of the ten kings! Woe to the inhabitants of the earth; there shall be sanguinary wars, and famine, and plagues, and contagious maladies; there shall be showers of a frightful hail of animals; thunder shall shake entire cities; earthquakes which shall swallow up some countries; voices shall be heard in the air; men (in despair) shall knock their heads against the walls; they shall call on death; and death shall be their torment; blood shall flow from every side. Who shall be able to overcome (all these evils)? Fire shall rain from heaven, and shall destroy three cities. The whole world shall be struck with terror, and many will allow themselves to be seduced, because they have not believed the true Christ living among them. The sun becomes dark. Faith only shall survive. So the time! the abyss opens. Behold the king of the kings of darkness! Behold the beast with his subjects!...

s. **Words of Melanie:** "The great chastisement will come, because men will not be converted; yet it is only their conversion that can hinder these scourges. God will begin to strike men by inflicting lighter punishments in order to open their eyes; then he will stop, or may repeat his former warnings to give place for repentance. But sinners will not avail themselves of these opportunities; he will, in consequence, send more severe castigations, anxious to move sinners to penance, but all in vain. Finally, the obduracy of sinners shall draw upon their heads the greatest and most terrible calamities.

t. **Extract from a letter written by Melanie:** "We are all guilty! Penance is not done, and sin increases daily. Those who should come forward to do good are retained by fear. Evil is great. A moderate punishment serves only to irritate the spirits, because they view all things with human eyes. God could work a miracle to convert and change the aspect of the earth without chastisement. God will work a miracle; it will be a stroke of his mercy; but after the wicked shall have inebriated themselves with blood, the scourge shall arrive.

u. "What countries shall be preserved from such calamities? Where shall we go for refuge? I, in my turn, shall ask, What is the country that observes the commandments of God? What country is not influenced by human fear where the interest of the Church and the glory of God are at stake? (Ah, indeed! what country, what nation upon earth?) In behalf of my Superior and myself, I have often asked myself where could we go for refuge, had we the means for the journey and for our subsistence, on condition that no person were to know it? But I renounce these useless thoughts. We are very guilty! In consequence of this, it is necessary that a very great and terrible scourge should come to revive our faith, and to restore to us our very reason, which we have almost entirely lost. Wicked men are devoured by a thirst for exercising their cruelty; but when they shall have reached the uttermost point of their barbarity, God himself shall extend his hand to stop them, and very soon after, a complete change shall be effected in all surviving persons. Then they will sing the Te Deum Laudamus with the most lively gratitude and love. The Virgin Mary, our Mother, shall be our liberatrix. Peace shall reign, and the charity of Jesus Christ shall unite all hearts ... Let us pray; let us pray. God does not wish to chastise us severly. He speaks to us in so many, so many ways to make us return to him. How long shall we remain stubborn? Let us pray, let us pray; let us never cease praying and doing penance. Let us pray for our Holy Father the Pope, the only light for the faithful in these times of darkness. O yes, let us by all means pray much. Let us pray to the good, sweet, merciful Virgin Mary; for we stand in great need of her powerful hands over our heads."

v. **Secret of Maximin Giraud:** "Afterwards this peace shall be disturbed by the monster (Antichrist?).

w. "The monster shall arrive (be born?) at the end of this nineteenth century, or at latest, at the commencement of the twentieth.

x. "In this time the Antichrist will be born of a nun of Hebraic descent, a false virgin, who will have intercourse with the ancient serpent, with the master of impurity and putrefaction. His father will be a bishop. He will perform false miracles and subsist only on vitiating faith. He will have brethren, who will be children of evil but not incarnate devils like himself. Soon they will be at the head of armies, supported by the legions of hell.

y. "Up, ye children of light, and fight! For behold, the age of ages, the end, the extremity is at hand! The Church passes into darkness. The world will be in a state of consternation, perplexity and confusion."

z. **On Henoch and Elias.** "They will suddenly appear on

earth full of the spirit of God, when the Church becomes darkened and the world in terrible agony. They will convert those of good will and comfort the oppressed Christians. With the help of the Holy Ghost they will have great success against the heresies of Antichrist. But in the end they will be delivered unto death."

338. Sister Rose Colomba Asdenti of Taggia (d. 1847)

"A great enemy of the Church, a precursor of Antichrist, will take the title of Saviour. Heretics will join this precursor of Antichrist and persecute the true Church of Christ. Their cunning will be great, so great in fact that they will be able to draw many righteous men to their side. The Bishops in general will remain faithful, but all will, on account of their courage and faithfulness to the Church, suffer much, yet many Protestants will console the children of God by their conversion to the Catholic Church. Immediately preceding Antichrist there will be starvation and earthquakes."

See also prophesy 15 g.

339. John Baptist Stickelmeyer (1848)

"The Shepherd foretold the coming of the Reds, in which he foresaw the Berlin-Moscow pact and the partition of Poland. He then warned that it would be time to take to the woods, for the time of Universal Killing would be at hand. He warns the people not to leave the woods, for the Universal Killing will be followed by the Universal Dying caused by starvation and pestilence. Following these times, people may leave the woods in safety, for the Great White King will come and once more there will be peace."

340. Sister Bertina Bouquillion (d. 1850)

a. "I have seen the holy patriarch Henoch, one of the two just men who shall have to fight against Antichrist, and sustain the faithful during their severe trials at the end of the world. He was dressed like a missionary, ready, as it were, to start for his great approaching difficult mission; the end of the world."

b. "The coming of Antichrist will be unobserved by most people."

c. "The end of time is nearing and Antichrist will not

171

delay in coming. However, neither we nor those sisters who come after us will see him, but those who come after them will fall under his reign. At the time of his coming nothing will change in this house. All will be in its usual order. The religious exercises, the work, the occupations in the wards — all will be done in the customary manner, when suddenly all the sisters will be aware that Antichrist is master of the world. The beginning of the End will not come in the nineteenth century but certainly in the twentieth century."

341. John O'Connell (1858)

"Lest the deceptions, snares and danger of Antichrist should fall upon the Irish; He promised to send a deluge over Ireland, Seven years previous to the burning of the spheres."

342. St. John Mary Vianney (d. 1859)

"A time will come when people will believe that the end is near. It will be a sign of the last Judgment. Paris and two or three other cities will experience a transformation. Paris will be demolished but not altogether. However, one will behold still more frightful things to come. There is, nevertheless, a limit beyond which the demolition will not progress." See also prophesy 163.

343. Palma Maria Addolorata Matarelli (d. 1863)

a. "The massacre of priests, as also of some dignitaries of the Church.

b. "A short but furious war, during which the enemies of religion and of mankind shall be universally destroyed.

c. "Rome shall have to endure severe trials from the malice of wicked men. But at the critical moment, when the rebellious Republicans shall attempt to take possession of the Holy City, they shall be suddenly arrested at the gates and forced to fly away in terror, crushed under the deadly blows of the exterminating angel.

d.' "The destruction of Paris. The civil war, which will, in consequence, break out in these countries, accompanied by other dreadful punishments, as pestilence and famine.

e. "Supernatural prodigies which shall appear in the heavens. There shall be three days' darkness. Not one demon shall be left in hell. They shall all come out, either to excite the wicked murderers, or to dishearten the just and shall cause the death of large multitudes of incredulous and wicked men. For this awful occasion, which, sooner or later, will certainly arrive, Palma Maria recommends the use of blessed candles, which alone shall be able to give light and preserve the faithful Catholics from this impending dreadful scourge. This shall be frightful! frightful!! but a grand cross shall appear, and the triumphs of the Church will make people quickly forget all evils."

344. Rev. Frederick William Faber (d. 1863)

a. "From the first, all the troubles of the Church were regarded as types of Antichrist, as Christ had His types; so we naturally conclude with this. It is not an idle speculation; Scripture puts it before us.

b. The person of Antichrist.

1. A single person. 'The man of sin, the son of perdition, that wicked one.' (2 Thess. 2: 3) 'This is Antichrist, who denieth the Father and the Son.' (1 John 2:22)
2. Many believed in a demoniacal incarnation — this will not be so — but he will be a man utterly possessed. (Card. Berulle.)
3. Not come yet — Mahomet was not he — the signs are not fulfilled.
4. He is to be a king — his kingdom in visible antagonism to the kingdom of Christ — so all civil oppositions have been precursors of Antichrist.
5. Certainly a Jew — uncertain if of tribe of Dan — origin probably obscure.
6. With zeal for the temple, gives himself out as the Messias.
7. With immense talents, awfully assisted by the devil — immense wealth, Dan. xi — immoral, Dan vii.; and xi. unparalleled in deceit — deceiving even the elect.
8. His doctrine an apparent contradiction of no religion, yet a new religion. Comparison with French Revolution. (1) He denies the divinity of Christ. (2) Asserts that he is the Messias. (3) Worship of devils. (4) He is an atheist, (5) but begins by affecting respect for the

law of Moses. (6) Lying miracles, false resurrection, mock ascension. (7) He has an attendant pontiff so separating regal and prophetic office.

c. His kingdom.
1. Not hereditary — got by degrees, by fraud, talent, and iniquitous diplomacy.
2. It will begin at Babylon. (Zach. v. 11.)
3. It will extend in influence over the whole civilized world.
4. Jerusalem will be the metropolis.
5. When his empire is at its full, it will last only three years and a half.

d. His persecution.
1. Unparalleled horror of it. (Apoc. xx.)
2. In spiritual things—(1) there will be hardly any mass, (2) but the worship of his image and the wearing of his mark; (3) Majority of Christians will apostatize, (4) but the Church will not be destroyed.
3. Saints will be greater than ever — martyrs greater, as the first fought against men, the latter will fight against devils, our Lady's Saints, vide Grignon de Montfort.
4. Enoch and Elias, now confirmed in grace, and waiting — they will preach in sackcloth — for as long a time as Christ, i.e. three years and a half less nineteen days — their martyrdom — they will lie unburied.
5. Jesus kills him, and comes to the doom forty-five days after; some say that St. Michael will kill him on Mount Olivet.

c. Protestantism an anticipation of Antichrist.
(1) Its attitude towards the Blessed Virgin Mary, (2) the Mass, (3) sign of the cross. (4) All its sects unite against the Church. (5) Its carelessness about Baptism; sixth angel drying up Euphrates. (6) It blasphemes Saints.

f. The Five-and-Forty Days.
(1) Space for repentance. (2) Full of signs. (3) The Lord comes and the weary world is judged and burnt.

g. Lessons.

1. The reign of Antichrist is to be the last temporal reign: so the Church's last enemy is to be a kingdom, the consummation of the wickedness of all kingdoms; how significant!

2. What part should we take in this persecution? Let us measure it by the boldness of our profession now — by our strictness with ourselves — by our self-denial in charity for others — by our perseverance in the practices of penance — by the fervor and the frequency of our prayers — by the rigorousness of the examinations of our conscience. It is always to each of us the five-and-forty days; Chirst will come — He will not tarry — let us have our loins girded and our lamps burning, that when the midnight cry is raised, and the Bridegroom cometh, we may go forward with holy awe to meet our Saviour and our Judge."

345. Mother Alphonse Eppinger (1867)

a. "In the impending revolutionary chaos eminent religious will be assassinated by dignitaries. Rome will see blood of priests flowing. Convents will be sacked. Churches laid waste. Laws will be enacted against religion and the worship of God. Through the stroke of the scourge the Lord wishes to re-awaken the right spirit among those in holy and sacred positions. Secretly conducted agitations, revolts, insurrections, slaughter and the creation of a state of alarm and anxiety within the ranks of general society will be characteristic signs of the times when the evil ones shall have established themselves in power. God wishes to administer punishment for allowing faith to wane and for the sins that engulf the world, and therefore permits the raging passions of man to have free reign until they reach a point where they will subside of themselves . . .

b. "A great persecution of priests will break out, but it will not be so severe in Alsace and, therefore, many foreign priests will fly thither . . . For many clergymen are no longer zealous for the glory of God and the salvation of souls. Their hearts are set on the specious goods of this life. Through chastisement they must be torn away from these things in order to bring about a change in their point of view . . .

    c. For the rest see prophesy 166.

346. Maria von Merl (d. 1868)

"The fourth successor of Pope Pius IX will live to see the great revolution within the Church."

347. Anonymous Prophecy Found in the Public Library of Piacenza (before 1873)

"Bella, fames, pestis, fraudes Saturnia regna
    Sternet, et veteres pellentur ubique tyranni.
Pastor erit claves, non regna gubernans.
    Monstra loquor! Tum cum pariet bos rubeus hydram,
Nec Deus extinguet flammas, nec deseret jram,
    Nisi prius Ausoniae feriant mala singula gentes.
Tempus erit prope lustrum. Mox aliger ingens
    Surget ut e somno, rostro metuendus et ungue.
Colla bovis caedet, sitibundus iniqui draconis
    Viscera depascet. Gallorum trina colorum
Sternet humi; statuet in propria reges.
    Galatia genitus terra Vir justus et aequus
Pastor erit: toto surget Concordia Mundo.
    Una fides, unus regnabit in omnia Princeps."

Translation: "Famine, pestilence, war, and frauds shall prostrate the Italian kingdoms, and the ancient kings shall everywhere be expelled. The Supreme Pastor will hold the keys of Heaven, but shall be deprived of earthly kingdoms.

"Horrible spectacle! When the red ox (Communism) shall give birth to the hydra (Anarchy) God will not extinguish the flames nor calm his anger until all these calamities shall have stricken the people of Ausonia (Italy). This state of affairs shall last about five years.

"Then an enormous bird (Great Monarch) shall awake, as from a sleep, and with its terrible bill and claws shall sever the ox's neck, and shall eagerly devour the intestines of the wicked dragon. He shall drag to the mud the tricolor flag of the French and restore to their dominions the legitimate kings. A just and pious man born in Gallicia shall be the Supreme Pontiff; then the whole world shall be united and

176

prosperous. One faith only and one emperor shall reign over the whole earth."

348. The Pious Dupont of Tours (d. 1876)
"Satan will become so violent because he feels that he will be beaten."

349. Bishop of Mainz (d. 1877)
"There will come no peace but rather more wars amongst all nations of the earth; bloodier and more terrible than that which we now (1870) have before our eyes."

350. Other late 19th and early 20th century prophesies are numbers 169b (Pius IX), 170 (Baourdi), 171 (Pie), 173 (Bosco), 176 (Tilly), 178a (Chambau), 177 (Christine).

351. Marie Deluil Martiny (d. 1884)
a. "I shall perform miracles. Neither the efforts of Satan nor the unworthiness cf men will prevent me. Before time expires I desire to be compensated for everything which has been inflicted upon me. I want to pour out all graces which have been rejected. I am like a swollen stream which nothing can stop from overflowing its banks.

b. "Let us hasten the triumph of Christ over hell and the hostile powers through prayer and sacrifice."

351. Marie Julie Jahenny of La Faudais (d. 1891)
"During the time of the approach of the punishments announced at La Salette, an unlimited amount of false revelations will arise from hell like a swarm of flies; a last attempt of Satan to choke and destroy the belief in the true revelations by false ones." See also prophesy 174.

352. Paul de Moll (d. 1896)
"France will be cleansed through great punishments."

353. L'Abbe Joseph Maitre *Prophecy of the Popes*, (Imprimatur 1898)
a. "Let us re-read the grave warnings which St. Paul sent to the Thessalonians on the subject of the Man of Sin: 2 Thess. 2: 1-16 'But there is one entreaty we would make of you, brethren, as you look forward to the time when our Lord Jesus Christ will come, and gather us in to himself. Do

not be terrified out of your senses all at once, and thrown into confusion, by any spiritual utterance, any message or letter purporting to come from us, which suggests that the day of the Lord is close at hand. Do not let anyone find the means of leading you astray. The apostasy must come first; the champion of wickedness must appear first, destined to inherit perdition. This is the rebel who is to lift up his head above every divine name, above all that men hold in reverence, till at last he enthrones himself in God's temple, and proclaims himself as God. Do not you remember my telling you of this, before I left your company? At present there is a power (you know what I mean) which holds him in check, so that he may not shew himself before the time appointed to him; meanwhile, the conspiracy of revolt is already at work; only, he who checks it now will be able to check it, until he is removed from the enemy's path. Then it is that the rebel will shew himself; and the Lord Jesus will destroy him with the breath of his mouth, overwhelming him with the brightness of his presence. He will come, when he comes, with all Satan's influence to aid him; there will be no lack of power of counterfeit signs and wonders; and his wickedness will deceive the souls that are doomed, to punish them for refusing that fellowship in the truth which would have saved them. That is why God is letting loose among them a deceiving influence, so that they give credit to falsehood; he will single out for judgment all those who refused credence to the truth, and took their pleasure in wrong-doing.

b. "'We must always give thanks in your name, brethren whom the Lord has so favoured. God has picked you out as the first-fruits in the harvest of salvation, by sanctifying your spirits and convincing you of his truth; he has called you, through our preaching, to attain the glory of our Lord Jesus Christ. Stand firm, then, brethren, and hold by the traditions you have learned, in word or in writing, from us. So may our Lord Jesus Christ himself, so may God our Father, who has shewn such love to us, giving us unfailing comfort and welcome hope through his grace, encourage your hearts, and confirm you in every right habit of action and speech.'

THE INTERPRETATION

"In this obscure passage many points remain mysterious. Is it not the case with all prophecies till they are fulfilled? We can however extract more than one precious truth.

c. TRADITIONAL TEACHING — "At the epoch of St. Paul the time for the second coming of Our Lord had not arrived. Instead of proving it, as our modern theologians try to do by more or less human reasons, St. Paul tells the faithful of Thessalonica, to judge everything by the light of Faith and to guard the holy traditions.

"What do these traditions teach us? They teach says the Apostle that Evil is to first triumph by a general apostacy: A man will appear who will stand up definitely against God and His Christ: he will be the right arm of Satan and he will seduce by false miracles those who will have abandoned the Faith. A terrible chastisement for impiety and unbelief!

"This sign has not appeared yet in its proper and absolute sense. The sacred text appears to give to the Man of Sin such particular marks, a power of seduction so terrible, that we cannot recognize him in the history of the past, nor in contemporary happenings.

d. THE MYSTERY OF INIQUITY — ITS ACTION THROUGHOUT THE AGES — "But this great apostacy is not to come without preparation. Already in the Apostolic times St. Paul tells us, the mystery of iniquity was doing its work. What was the hidden force which the Apostle wished to make known by those words? It was without doubt heresy, which even in the time of the Apostles had its chiefs and its adepts.

"'Already the "Simonians" and the "Gnostics" had separated from Jesus Christ.' (L'Abbe Drach)

"However we must see in this work of Evil more than just isolated revolts. It is a hidden force which without ceasing opposes the Church. It betrays itself in the course of time by the successive defections of the heresiarchs and

179

by the incessant attacks of which Christianity is the object; especially it has taken root in the impious and brutal sect which since the seventh century, opposes to the Cross, the symbolical cresent, as a perpetual menace.

"This mystery of iniquity which acts in the dark is the reign of Satan, which only waits for the permission of God to manifest itself.

e. THE ACTION OF EVIL IN MODERN SOCIETY — "Studying this question from this point of view we can find that Evil has made great headway especially since the coming of Protestantism.

"In the 18th century, Naturalism and Rationalism had been directly opposed to the reign of Jesus Christ in the world; the Secret Societies were directing the struggle.

"In the 19th century, the fruit of that detestable work of destruction was gathered. More and more, modern society turns away from Jesus Christ and His religion. Protestantism in our day is no more than a form of Rationalism.

"Can we not recognize in this spirit, alas! too general a terrible symptom if we refer to it the words of St. Paul.

THE FINAL APOSTACY—ANTICHRIST

f. JESUS, MASTER OF THE WORLD, STILL PREVENTS THE MANIFESTATION OF THE GREATEST EVIL — "The words which follow this warning are very obscure: He who checks it now will be able to check it, until he is removed from the enemy's path.

"A great number of interpretations are given about these words. Many refer them to the Roman Empire which exercised its power in the world at the time of St. Paul.

g. SOCIETY WILL DENY JESUS AGAIN — "But Monsignor L'Abbe Drach, whom we follow here, thinks that this interpretation is contrary to the text as well as to history. He brings together the words (who checks) with those (which holds him in check). He who checks is he who prevents the mystery of evil from developing, it is at the same time He who takes possession of the world, Jesus Christ Himself.

"Now Jesus who has transformed the world by His teachings and the action of His grace, will be again one day repudiated, denied by those to whom He brought hope and salvation. It is thus that the end of (v.7) the object of the remark (until he is removed from the enemy's path) brings together the idea put in relief by the Apostle.

"When the social reign of Jesus will have come to an end, when ungrateful humanity will have abandoned its God, then, the impious man, the man of sin, the Antichrist will come. By his seductions and his cursed charms he will make for himself adepts, and the **first chastisement of unbelief,** in the divine teachings **will be its opposite,** an unbelievable BELIEF in the superstition, and in the religion of Satan.

"From this point of view, we can recognize many characteristic traits in our epoch.

"One wishes, it is true, to speak of God, of religion. But religion for many is nothing more than a vague Deism which makes of the SUPREME BEING a sort of abstraction, afar off, indifferent to human affairs and the things of humanity.

"One speaks of love of men, of civism and of patriotism. But under these grand words the most odious egotism lies hidden. A vain philanthropy has replaced Christian Charity, the cult of reason and of matter has taken the place of the adoration of Christ and of respect for His Church, the source of true Charity.

"And however the strong spirits, the independents allow themselves to be enchained by tyrannical bands, and abdicate their liberty for the benefit of those cursed societies which lead the modern world, Free masonry, secret societies of every kind. These men who mock at the SUPERNATURAL, have an excessive faith when things relating to occult sciences or black magic are in question.

"Alas! the relations of the demon with humanity are only too real and we should take care to beware of laughing at the strange manifestations which are produced by magnetism or Spiritism: We should also beware of trying to find out explanations either natural or scientific of these phenomena.

"We believe then, we also, in the reality of very many happenings which seem to betray the intervention from the world of Spirits. But is it not strange to see men, who pretend to be independents and under the pretext of freedom of reason, shake off the yoke of all positive religion whilst they give themselves up blindly to practices which are made up by the intervention of hidden forces frightening in their effects as well as suspect in their nature.

"All these signs correspond from afar with those described by St. Paul as the time when the mystery of iniquity will be unveiled."

CHAPTER VI

TWENTIETH CENTURY PROPHETS

354. Sister Gertrude Marie of Angers (1907)

"I saw the triumph of the Church in the near future. How magnificent it will be! It will be the kingdom of the Sacred Heart. How many saints there will be! However, before that there will be many victims. Heresy will be destroyed; its plans will be destroyed, its efforts rendered fruitless, and just at the hour when it was believed to have accomplished everything."

355. Pius X (d. 1914)

"I see Russians in Genoa." See also prophesy 179.

356. *Sacred Heart Picture—Mirebeau, France*

a. (1914) " . . . The war will be so long and destructive that one has to look back very far to find its equal. But, the time after the war will be more terrible than the war itself.

b. (1917) "I shall conquer all nations, but I shall destroy the tool of which I made use.

c. (1917) "Plundering and death shall make their entrance there. (Vatican) The grave of my apostle shall be desecrated . . . They will all be dispersed.

d. (1919) "Two thrones are shaking, the throne of England and the throne of Spain. England is in danger; she is like a volcano. She will suffer the chastisement of her apostasy. The mighty will be robbed of their power. The prayer and penance of the saints of England ascend to Me in powerful supplication. May she return to Me; I would know how to protect her."

357. *Mrs. Marie Mesmin*

a. (1902) "Poor children! If you knew what will happen to you, you would be afraid and fearful. A war is coming the like of which has never before been experienced. It will be terrible. Up to the age of fifty years all men will have to go to war. I see, how big birds drop fire on the cities. Besides war, also pestilence and other entirely unknown diseases will come about which the physicians know nothing. Big earthquakes will come and mountains will move. Famine and revolution will come; one will be forced to hide . . . The day is coming when there will be no more food to eat. The rich will suffer just as much as the poor. Money will have no value.

b. "We stand on the eve of judgment. We have departed from the good Lord in order to serve the evil one. He will now serve us in his fashion. It is not God who wants to visit us . . . The moment has come when the evil one wishes to satisfy his passions, and since he likes only blood and crime, oh how many tears and sufferings, what horrible things will come! Finally the nations will tear each other to pieces: English against English, Italian against Italian, Spaniard against Spaniard, French against French. It will be terrible. Catastrophe will follow catastrophe!

c. (Nov. 7, 1918) "Do not believe, my children, that now all is ended in this apparent calm. Where are the converted people? Did the world return to God? . . . If the people would do penance one could say: soon will come the liberation, the renovation and a new prosperity in everything. But that is not the case, and dreadful evils await us . . .

d. "As revealed by the Mother of God: 'By my tears (in LaSalette and Bordeaux) I wanted to make you understand that prayer and penance can keep away the punishments . . . If one would pray nothing would happen. God is powerful enough to govern mankind; all would be renewed in peace without the terrible punishments which will exterminate three-fourths of mankind. God does not lack the means whereby to let those disappear who act against His law. If you could obtain a mitigation of the punishment, you would already have attained much'."

358. *Apparition of Our Lady at Fatima (1917)*

a. **Preparation by the Angel:** "Fear not, I am the Angel of Peace. Pray with me. 'My God, I believe, I adore, I hope, I love you! I ask pardon for those who do not believe, nor adore, nor hope, nor love you.'

"Offer continually to the Lord prayers and sacrifices in reparation for the numerous sins which offend Him, and in supplication for the conversion of sinners. Try then to bring

184

peace to your country. I am its Guardian Angel. Above all accept and bear with submission the sufferings which it will please the Lord to send you.

"The Angel appeared holding a Chalice in his hand surmounted by a Host, from which drops of Blood flowed into the Chalice. Leaving the Chalice and Host suspended in mid-air, the Angel knelt beside the children and made them recite three times the following prayer: 'Most Holy Trinity, Father, Son and Holy Ghost, I adore You profoundly! I offer You the most Precious Body and Blood, Soul and Divinity of Our Lord Jesus Christ, present in all the tabernacles of the world, in reparation for all the outrages committed against It; and, by the infinite merits of His Sacred Heart, through the intercession of the Immaculate Heart of Mary, I pray for the conversion of poor sinners.'

"Then rising, he took the Host which he gave to Lucy, and the Chalice which he divided between Jacinta and Francis, saying: 'Receive the Body and Blood of Jesus Christ horribly outraged by ungrateful men. Make reparation for their sins and console your God'."

b. **Words of Our Lady:** "You must recite the Rosary every day in honour of the Blessed Virgin, to obtain the end of the war through Her intercession, for only She can help you.'

"'Sacrifice yourselves for sinners, and say often, especially when you make sacrifices: Oh Jesus, it is for love of You, for the conversion of sinners, and in reparation for the offences committed against the Immaculate Heart of Mary.'

"'When reciting the Rosary, say after each decade: Oh my Jesus, forgive us our sins, save us from the fire of hell, and lead all souls to heaven, especially those who have most need of Thy mercy.'

"'Pray, pray very much, make sacrifices for sinners. Remember that many souls are lost because there is nobody to pray and to make sacrifices for them.'

"'Men must amend their lives, and ask pardon for their sins.'

"'Men must no longer offend Our Divine Lord, Who is already offended too much.'

"'I promise to help at the hour of death with the graces needed for their salvation, whoever on the first Saturday of five consecutive months, shall confess and receive Holy Communion, recite five decades of the Rosary, and keep me company for fifteen minutes while meditating on the fifteen mysteries of the Rosary with the intention of making reparation to me'."

c. **The Secret of Fatima:** "The children were shown a vision of hell, in all its horror, after which the Blessed Virgin said to them: 'You have just seen hell where the souls of poor sinners go. To save them the Lord wishes to establish in the world the devotion to My Immaculate Heart. If people do what I shall tell you, many souls will be saved and there will be Peace.

The war [World War I—1914-1918] will soon end. But if men do not stop offending the Lord it will not be long before another and worse one begins; that will be in the Pontificate of Pius XI.

When you see the night illuminated by an unknown light, know that it is the great sign which God is giving you, indicating that the world, on account of its innumerable crimes, will soon be punished by war, famine, and persecutions against the Church and the Holy Father.

In order to prevent it I shall come to ask for the consecration of Russia to my Immaculate Heart, as well as Communions of Reparation on the First Saturdays of the month.

If my requests are granted Russia will be converted and there will be peace. Otherwise Russia will spread her errors through the world fomenting wars and persecutions against the Church. Many will be martyred, the Holy Father will have much to suffer; several nations will be destroyed.

In the end my Immaculate Heart will triumph. The Holy Father will consecrate Russia to me, Russia will be converted, and there will be a certain period of peace'."

d. **Words of Jacinta:** "'The sins that lead most souls to hell are sins of the flesh! . . .

"'Certain fashions will be introduced which will offend Our Divine Lord very much. Those who serve God ought not to follow these fashions . . .

"'The sins of the world are too great! The Blessed Virgin

186

has said that there will be many wars and disturbances in the world: wars are only punishments for the sins of the world.'

"'The Blessed Virgin can no longer restrain the arm of Her Divine Son, which will strike the world . . .

"Men must do penance . . . If they amend their lives, Our Lord will still forgive them; but if they do not reform, the punishment will surely come.

"'. . . So many lives will be lost, and almost all will go to hell. So many houses will be destroyed, and so many priests will be killed.

"'Have you seen the Holy Father? . . . I do not know how it happened, but I saw him in a very large house, kneeling before a little table, weeping, with his head between his hands. Outside there was a crowd . . . Poor Holy Father!'"

e. "The children never failed to add three Hail Marys to their rosary for the Holy Father.

"The salvation of the world depends on the fulfillment of the three requests of the Blessed Virgin at Fatima: (1) Sacrifice — fulfillment of daily duty — make sacrifices necessary to avoid sin (2) Daily recitation of the Rosary and devotion to the Five Saturdays (3) Consecration to the Immaculate Heart of Mary."

359. Berry (published 1920) — *Interpretation of the Apocalypse*

a. "When applied to the last days of the world these verses bear a more literal interpretation.* Then shall 'the sun be darkened and the moon shall not give her light, and the stars shall fall from heaven, and the powers of heaven shall be moved.' The sun will probably be obscured by volcanic ashes sent up from many places as the result of terrible earthquakes and eruptions of volcanoes. The veiled light of the moon will appear red as blood. Myriads of meteors resembling stars will fall to earth, kindling the whole world into flames. The heavens shall be rolled up as the scroll of a book. In other words, the atmosphere will be so obscured that the sun and moon will become invisible as at

---

* See Apocalypse quoted above in No. 231.

187

the beginning of creation. The mountains and continents shall be overturned and the whole world shall return to chaos.

"Comparing this description with the first chapter of Genesis we find the confusion of elements occuring in inverse order to that of their unfolding at creation. The faithful who witness these terrible convulsions of nature will prepare for the judgment of God. They shall be more terrified at the anger of God and of His Christ than by the upheaval of the material world.

"'Then shall men wither away from fear and expectation of what shall come upon the whole world.' They will cry out in their terror: 'O ye mountains, fall upon us! Ye hills, cover us!' for 'who shall be able to withstand the wrath of God?' This thought is beautifully expressed in the sequence of Massess for the dead: 'Day of wrath, O day of mourning, Lo, the world in ashes burning. Seer and Sybil gave the warning. What Shall I, frail man be pleading? Who for me be interceding When the just are mercy needing?'"

b. "The prophecies of this chapter have been fulfilled many times in the past. No doubt they will often be verified in the future. It should be noted, however, that a progressive accumulation of evils is predicted. At first it affects individuals only. (v.7) Then a nation or an entire church is involved, (v.8) and a number of great heretics fall away from the Faith. (v.10) Finally the whole Church suffers from a weakening of Faith and discipline. (v.12) This gradual progression of evil, 'this mystery of iniquity' which was working even in the days of St. Paul, will finally usher in the Antichrist.

"An eagle appears in mid-heaven proclaiming three great woes to follow the sounding of the remaining trumpets. Two interpretations are permissable. The first recognizes in the eagle a powerful nation which shall be an instrument of God's judgments upon the world. The other interpretation sees in the eagle a symbol of new preachers of the Gospel. God raises up new saints or religious orders to arouse the faithful to renewed faith and zeal in his service. Neverthe-

188

less, three great evils shall afflict the Church before her final victory over the world and the devil.

"Whatever interpretation be adopted, there can be no doubt that this verse heralds the beginning of a new and important epoch in the history of the Church."

c. "The invasion of the locusts is the first woe predicted by the eagle. The two yet to come will fill up the 'mystery of iniquity' with the appearance of Antichrist and his prophet.

"God sends a sixth angel to instruct and guide the Church. This mission will still further reveal the thoughts of many hearts. The wicked continue to be separated from the just.

"A voice from the golden altar commands the captive angels of the Euphrates to be released. As noted above, the altar is Christ who makes trials and tribulations a means of sanctification for souls and an increase of fervor and holiness in the Church. They also serve to spread the blessings of the Gospel for as Tertullian says: 'The blood of martyrs is the seed of Christians.'

"Christ Himself gives command to release the captive angels thus showing that the enemies of the Church have no power against her unless God permits. The Church can say to her enemies as Christ said to Pilate: 'Thou shouldst not have any power against me, unless it were given thee from above.'

"The captive angels are demons who will arouse new enmities against the Church. In a figurative sense they represent the new enemies thus aroused against the Church, whether they be nations, individuals, or secret societies hostile to her. Four, the number of universality, indicates how widespread will be their influence.

"With the prophets of old the region of the Euphrates was ever the country whence came the enemies of God's people. Its mention here indicates that these new enemies will arise among nations already hostile to the Church. In a secondary sense the term may be taken literally to represent peoples from that region who are hostile to the Church.

"The four angels of the Euphrates, now ordered to be released, may be the same as those whom Christ forbade to injure the earth until the Church could be firmly established after the persecutions.

"Even the time for the manifestations of these evil spirits and their minions has been accurately fixed in the designs of Providence. The very day and hour has been determined.

"Great numbers will be done to death in the religious wars and revolutions stirred up by these angels from the Euphrates. The prophecy may also mean that large numbers will be led into new errors and schisms. Both interpretations are fully justified by the history of the pretended Reformation and the wars that followed it.

"These scourges shall be more terrible than any yet predicted. The first plagues were brought to earth by four horsemen. Then we saw four charioteers, the four winds, ready to scourge mankind. Here we find a vast array of cavalry. The chastisements sent upon the world increase with the growth of iniquity and the approach of Antichrist.

"The description of horses and riders in this vision gives some idea of their boldness, strength, and cunning ferocity. They inflict upon men the plagues of fire, smoke and sulphur. The fire is persecution and war. Smoke symbolizes the obscuring of doctrine and the weakening of faith; sulphur, the moral depravity which follows.

"The fire, smoke and sulphur issue from the mouth of the horses. From the mouth should proceed words of wisdom; instead there come forth heresies, and incitements to revolt and revolution. It should be noted that Luther openly preached revolt and revolutions to the peasants of Germany, but when they put his words into practice, he turned to the princes and urged them to stamp out the revolt with fire and sword.

"The horses of this vision inflict injuries with their tails which resemble serpents. Amongst all peoples the serpent is a symbol of lying and hypocrisy. These vices have ever characterized the enemies of the Church.

"There is no question here of real artillery as some have imagined. St. John is giving only the broad outlines of the Church's history. He is not concerned with the material means employed by men to wage war against her.

"The vision of locusts and the vision of cavalry horses are not two representations of one and the same event. They foreshadow two distinct events that follow one another in the order of time. The one is the great revolt against the Church brought about by the fallen star. The other consists of wars and disturbances which follow in the wake of that revolt.

"After these plagues have passed there still remain many who worship idols, and many guilty of robbery, murder and immorality. This is verified today. Although nineteen hundred years have elapsed since the first preaching of the Gospel, whole nations are still steeped in idolatry, and Christendom seems hopelessly divided by heresy and schism."

d. "An Angel coming in clouds of grace and glory brings to St. John a book of further prophecies. The rainbow about his head symbolizes mercy, while the brightness of his countenance expresses the power of his teachings to enlighten souls. The feet as of fire indicate that he shall lead the Church in the ways of truth and justice as the pillar of fire guided the Israelites in the wilderness.

"The book is open to signify that the prophecies therein revealed to St. John are intelligible and shall be understood in due time according to the needs of the Church. The angel places one foot upon the sea, the other upon the land to express God's supreme dominion over all things.

"The voice like the roar of a lion is the voice of the Gospel which shall penetrate to the very ends of the earth teaching divine truth, condemning error, and threatening persecutors with the vengeance of God. Here, as elsewhere, the thunders may symbolize the anathemas of the Church against all wickedness and error; but it would be useless to comment on their exact meaning since St. John was commanded to seal up the words of his prophecies until the time appointed by God for their publication. The words of the seven thunders may also have been such as St. Paul heard — 'secret words which it is not granted to man to utter.'

"Lifting his hand to heaven the angel calls upon the

191

God of all creation to witness the truth of his words that time shall be no more. This does not mean that the end of the world is at hand, but that the time for judgment against obstinate sinners and persecutors has arrived.

"This judgment shall be the great persecution of Antichrist and its attendant evils. Then shall be accomplished the 'mystery of God' which has been announced (evangelized) by the prophets of old. To evangelize is to announce good tidings, hence this 'mystery of God' is probably the plentitude of the Redemption applied to all nations of earth. After the destruction of Antichrist and his kingdom all peoples shall accept the Gospels and the Church of Christ shall reign peacefully over all nations.

"Eating the book symbolizes an intimate union with the Holy Ghost by which the mind of the Apostle is illuminated with the spirit of prophecy. St. John finds the book sweet to the taste because it announces mercy to the elect and the final triumph of the Church. It is bitter in so far as it predicts dire persecutions for the Church and terrible punishments for the wicked."

e. "As the two prophets are taken up to heaven, Jerusalem is shaken with a mighty earthquake in which seven thousand people perish and a tenth part of the city is destroyed. At the sight of these prodigies all who survive are converted and begin to praise and glorify God. Here is seen the great Mercy of God who punishes not to destroy but to convert and save."

f. 'In the foregoing chapters St. John outlines the history of the Church from the coming of Antichrist until the end of the world in order to give a connected account of the two prophets Henoch and Elias, (or Moses) and the result of their labors. In this chapter he shows us the true nature of that conflict. It shall be war unto death between the Church and the powers of darkness in a final effort of Satan to destroy the Church and thus prevent the universal reign of Christ on earth.

"Satan will first attempt to destroy the power of the Papacy and bring about the downfall of the Church through heresies, schisms and persecutions that must surely follow.

Failing in this he will then attack the Church from without. For this purpose he will raise up Antichrist and his prophet to lead the faithful into error and destroy those who remain steadfast.

"The Church, the faithful spouse of Jesus Christ, is represented as a woman clothed in the glory of divine grace. In the Canticle of Canticles the Church is likewise described as 'she that cometh forth as the morning rising, fair as the moon, bright as the sun.' The brightness of the sun is a fitting symbol for the enlightening power of the Church's teachings.

"The moon was beneath her feet. St. Gregory the Great and St. Augustine see in this dominion of the Church over the whole world, and her contempt for the perishable goods of this life. The moon with its ever changing phases is a figure of the transitory things of earth.

"The crown of twelve stars represents the twelve Apostles and through them the whole ministry of the Church. It may also denote the assembly of faithful nations symbolized by the mystic number twelve.

"The Church is ever in labor to bring forth children to eternal life. In the sad days here predicted the sorrows and pains of delivery shall be increased many fold. In this passage there is an evident allusion to some particular son of the Church whose power and influence shall be such that Satan will seek his destruction at any cost. This person can be none other than the **Pope to be elected in those days.** The Papacy will be attacked by all the powers of hell. In consequence the Church will suffer great trials and afflictions in securing a successor upon the throne of Peter.

"The words of St. Paul to the Thessalonians may be a reference to the Papacy as the obstacle to the coming of Antichrist: 'You know what withholdeth, that he may be revealed in his time. For the mystery of iniquity already worketh; only that he who now holdeth, do hold, until he be taken out of the way. And then that wicked one shall be revealed.'

"St. John now sees in heaven a red dragon with seven heads and ten horns; each head bearing a diadem. (Communism?) The dragon is Satan red with the blood of martyrs which he will cause to flow. The meaning of the seven heads and ten horns must be sought in the description of the beast that represents Antichrist where they symbolize kings or worldly powers. Those of the dragon must have a similar meaning, and indicate that Satan's attacks against the Church will be organized and carried out by the governments and ruling powers of those days.

"With the beast of Antichrist only the horns have diadems as symbols of royalty or governing power. The heads are branded with names of blasphemy. Hence they symbolize the sins and errors that will afflict the Church. Seven, the number of universality, indicates that in this final struggle to prevent the universal reign of Christ all forms of sin and error will be marshalled against the Church. A prelude to this may be seen in the errors of Modernism which has been rightly designated 'a synthesis of all heresies.' The number seven is also appropriate since all sins are included in the seven capital sins. In like manner all errors that have afflicted the Church may be summed up in these seven: Judaism, paganism, Arianism, Mohammedism, Protestantism, rationalism, and atheism.

"The dragon is seen in heaven which is here a symbol of the Church, the kingdom of heaven on earth. This indicates that the first troubles of those days will be inaugurated within the Church by apostate bishops, priests, and peoples — the stars dragged down by the tail of the dragon.

"The tail of the dragon represents the cunning hypocrisy with which he succeeds in deceiving a large number of people and pastors — a third part of the stars. Arianism led away many bishops, priests, and peoples. The pretended Reformation of the sixteenth century claimed still larger numbers but these cannot be compared to the numbers seduced by Satan in the days of Antichrist.

"The dragon stands before the woman ready to devour the child that is brought forth. In other words, the powers of hell seek by all means to destroy the Pope elected in those days.

"The woman brings forth a son to rule the nations with

a rod of iron. These are the identical words of prophecy uttered by the Psalmist concerning our Saviour Jesus Christ. They confirm our application of this vision to the Pope, the vicar of Christ on earth to rule the nations in His stead and by His power.

"It is now the hour for the powers of darkness. The new born Son of the Church is taken 'to God and to his throne.' Scarcely has the newly elected Pope been enthroned when he is snatched away my martyrdom. The 'mystery of iniquity' gradually developing through the centuries, cannot be fully consummated while the power of the Papacy endures, but now he that 'withholdeth is taken out of the way.' During the interegnum 'that wicked one shall be revealed' in his fury against the Church.

"It is a matter of history that the most disastrous periods for the Church were times when the Papal throne was vacant, or when anti-popes contended with the legitimate head of the Church. Thus also shall it be in those evil days to come.

"The Church deprived of her chief pastor must seek sanctuary in solitude there to be guided by God himself during those trying days. This place of refuge prepared for the Church is probably some nation, or nations, that remain faithful to her. In those days the Church shall also find refuge and consolation in faithful souls, especially in the seclusion of the religious life.

"St. Michael, the guardian angel of the Church, shall come with his hosts to defend her against the onslaughts of Satan and his minions. The followers of St. Michael are the angelic hosts of heaven and all faithful bishops and priests of the Church. The minions of Satan are the fallen angels with the leaders of heresy, schism, and persecution.

"The battle is waged in the Church, the kingdom of heaven, from which the dragon and his angels are cast out and hurled down to earth. The earth symbolizes the nations hostile to the Church — the world over which Satan rules. By the aid of St. Michael the Church shall purge herself of all heretics, schismatics and apostates. A similar work was accomplished by the Council of Trent in the sixteenth century."

g. "The Church is called upon to rejoice over the defeat of the dragon and the glorious martyrdom of her children; but woe to the earth and the sea — all mankind. Realizing that the time of his power is short, Satan will now loose upon earth all his rage and fury in a last effort against the Church. His attempt to destroy her from within having failed, he will now seek to crush her by hatred and persecution from without.

"In this new danger the Church shall receive the wings of an eagle to defend her and carry her to the place of refuge which God has prepared. The wings are probably two armies sent in defense of the Church by some nation that remains faithful. This interpretation seems justified by verse 16.

"In a spiritual sense the two wings are faith and prayer. In the faith and prayer of her children, and especially in the contemplative life of religious orders the Church shall find a refuge of consolation which Satan cannot violate. The desolation of those three and one-half years may be compared to that of the three days following our Lord's death on the cross. The faith and prayers of Mary, of the holy women, and of the Apostles afforded the only consolation in those days of anguish.

"This chapter indicates that the Church shall find refuge for three and one-half years on two different occasions; the one during the internal warfare against the Church and the other after the dragon has been cast out. It is possible that the two-fold attack against the Church will be carried on simultaneously, making the refuge mentioned in verse 6 coincide with the one mentioned here. However, the whole context seems to be against such an interpretation.

"The dragon now seeks to overwhelm the Church with a veritable flood of tribulations, but some faithful nation, or nations, (the earth) comes to her rescue. This verse proves that the great revolt of nations mentioned by St. Paul will not be universal. God will preserve at least one nation to defend the Church in that hour when, humanly speaking, everything seems hopeless.

"Satan now realizes that victory will be difficult. His first attempt failed miserably. In this second conflict new tactics must be employed. He will now seek to lead the faithful astray by a false Messias whom he will raise up in the person of Antichrist. This new adversary is to spring from the sea — the nations already hostile to the Church — hence Satan takes his stand by the shore to call forth the man of sin, the son of perdition.

"It is a solemn moment of 'fear and expectation of what shall come upon the whole world.'"

h. "The beast from the sea is Antichrist who was foretold by Daniel, the prophet, in a vision quite similar to this of St. John. Our study of the Apocalypse thus far makes it certain that a beast cannot be identified with the Roman Empire as many interpreters have done. Others, following the opinion of St. Augustine, take the beast as a symbol of all the wicked and unfaithful. This interpretation is true in a measure since Antichrist could not accomplish his nefarious work without disciples and followers. Hence the beast may be taken by extension to represent the whole empire of Antichrist. Nevertheless it is certain, in fact Suarez holds it as an article of faith, that Antichrist is a definite individual. The words of St. Paul to the Thessalonians leave no room for doubt in this matter.

"It is a very general opinion that Antichrist will set himself up as the Messias. This opinion seems to be supported by the words of our Saviour: 'I am come in the name of my Father, and you receive me not: if another shall come in his own name, him you will receive.' This pretension to Messiasship will make it necessary that he spring from the Jewish race.

"The coming of Antichrist opens the decisive conflict between the Church and the powers of hell. It shall be the complete realization of the prophecy of Genesis: 'I will put enmities between thee and the woman and thy seed and her seed.' The seed of the serpent is Antichrist and his followers; the seed of Mary, the woman, is Jesus Christ and his faithful disciples.

"The beast has seven heads and ten horns like those of the dragon. As the representative of Satan, Antichrist will be aided and abetted by the same kings and rulers symbolized in both instances by the horns and diadems. Antichrist will follow in the footsteps of his master by employing every form of sin and error to seduce the faithful. Hence each head is branded with a name descriptive of the sin or error it represents. All heresies blaspheme by denying some dogma of Faith; thus, for example, atheism denies the existence of God; Arianism rejects the divinity of Christ; Mohammedanism denies both the divinity of Christ and the Trinity of God, while Judaism refuses to recognize our Lord as Messias.

"The beast resembles a leopard in cruelty. The feet of a bear are symbols of stealth, while the mouth of a lion is an emblem of that strength and power which Satan confers upon his representative. Through the power of Satan, Antichrist will perform great wonders to deceive the people and lead them to accept him as the true Messias. St. Paul says that the coming of Antichrist will be 'according to the working of Satan, in all power, and signs, and lying wonders.' Our Lord also warns the faithful of false miracles in those days: 'For there shall rise false Christs, and false prophets, and shall show signs and wonders insomuch as to deceive (if possible) even the elect. Behold I have told it to you beforehand.'

"The head wounded unto death but healed in a marvelous manner signifies that one of the powers supporting the cause of Antichrist shall be overcome by the sword in its conflict with the Church. But to the surprise of all, this power will quickly rally its forces and thereby lead many to believe in Antichrist. As noted above, the heads represent spiritual rather than temporal powers. Since the heads of the dragon wear the diadem of royalty they may symbolize powers that combine both the spiritual and the temporal.

"Those who adore Antichrist on account of his 'lying wonders' thereby adore Satan who gives the power to perform them. Power and material prosperity are the rewards for those who serve him as the devil signified to Christ on the mountain: 'All these (kingdoms) will I give to thee, if falling down thou wilt adore me.' Antichrist accepts this infamous bargain and receives the empire of the world — 'Who shall be able to fight against him?'

"The power of Antichrist will be of short duration (three and one-half years), but during this time he will pour out blasphemies against God and against the Blessed Sacrament of the altar (the tabernacle of God.) He will also malign and vilify those who remain faithful to God and to His Church. He will be given power to wage war against the Church and to overcome it for a time. He shall rule over many nations and many peoples will adore him; his kingdom shall have the semblance of catholicity or universality. This is the great revolt of the nations foretold by St. Paul, but it shall not be truly universal; one nation at least, shall remain faithful to the Church in those days, and the elect whose names are written in the book of life will not adore Antichrist.

"These two verses contain consoling promises to the faithful, but dire warnings for the wicked; hence, the solemn admonition: 'If any one have an ear, let him hear.' Antichrist and his followers, at first victorious, shall soon be overcome and destroyed. As they have meted out to others, it shall be measured unto them. They who have led the faithful into captivity and put them to death, shall themselves be made captives and put to the sword. Hence the faithful must suffer in patience with full confidence of victory."

i. "The beast arising from the earth is the false prophet — the prophet of Antichrist (Lucifer). Our divine Saviour has a representative on earth in the person of the Pope upon whom He has conferred full powers to teach and govern. Likewise Antichrist will have his representative in the false prophet who will be endowed with the plentitude of satanic powers to deceive the nations.

"If Antichrist be of Jewish extraction, as he probably will, the sea from which he arises signifies Judaism. Then the earth whence comes the second beast is a symbol of the

Gentile nations in revolt against the Church. The two horns denote a twofold authority — spiritual and temporal. As indicated by the resemblance to a lamb, the prophet will probably set himself up in Rome as a sort of anti-pope during the vacancy of the papal throne mentioned above. But the elect will not allow themselves to be deceived; they will recall the words of our Lord: 'Then if any man shall say to you: Lo here is Christ, or there, do not believe him.'

"Antichrist will establish himself in Jerusalem where a great number of Jews will have gathered through some such movement as Zionism. The vast majority of Jews have ever clung to the belief that God will one day restore the kingdom of Israel through a Messias — an 'Anointed one' — of the house of David. When Antichrist manifests himself to those in Jerusalem with his 'lying wonders' they will immediately proclaim him their king and Messias. Then through the power of false miracles the prophet will soon lead the Gentile nations to adore him as the true Messias promised of old by the prophets. St. Paul clearly states that Antichrist will give himself out as God: 'He opposeth, and is lifted up above all that is called God, or that is worshipped, so that he sitteth in the temple of God, shewing himself as if he were God.

"Many theologians believe that Antichrist will rebuild the temple of Jerusalem in which he will establish his throne and be worshipped as God. The words of St. Paul, cited above, certainly seem to favor this belief, and there can be no doubt that such an achievement would secure immediate recognition for Antichrist and his projects. On the other hand the prophecy of Daniel seems to preclude such a possibility: 'And there shall be in the temple the abomination of desolation: and the desolation shall continue even to the consummation, and to the end.' It matters not how scholars interpret this abomination, the words of Christ clearly prove that it was to lead directly to the destruction of the temple by the Roman army in 70 A.D. The destruction then wrought shall be final — it shall 'continue even to the consummation, and to the end.'

"Julian the Apostate attempted to rebuild the temple in

the fourth century but the undertaking was frustrated in a miraculous manner. 'The place was made inaccessible by fearful balls of fire that broke out near the foundations and so scorched and burned the workmen that they were forced to retire. The frequent attacks finally caused the work to be abandoned.'

"The 'temple of God' in the above passage from St. Paul probably means all places of Catholic worship in general, and in particular the churches of Rome and Jerusalem. The 'abomination of desolation' has been wrought in many Catholic churches by heretics and apostates who have broken altars, scattered the relics of martyrs and desecrated the Blessed Sacrament. At the time of the French Revolution a lewd woman was seated upon the altar of the cathedral in Paris and worshipped as the goddess of reason. Such things but faintly foreshadow the abominations that will desecrate churches in these sorrowful days when Antichrist will seat himself at the altar to be adored as God.

"The prophet, of course, shall have power to perform the wonderful works of his master. Among other prodigies he will bring down fire from heaven, probably to offset the preaching and miracles of Elias, and thus seduce great numbers. He will also have statues of Antichrist erected to be adored by those whom he has seduced. These statues will give out oracles as did those of ancient paganism. In fact the reign of Antichrist and his prophet will be a veritable renewal of paganism throughout the world.

"The followers of Antichrist will be marked with a character in imitation of the sign that St. John saw upon the foreheads of the servants of God. This indicates that Antichrist and his prophet will introduce ceremonies to imitate the Sacraments of the Church. In fact there will be a complete organization — a church of Satan set up in opposition to the Church of Christ. Satan will assume the part of God the Father; Antichrist will be honored as Savior, and his prophet will usurp the role of Pope. Their ceremonies will counterfeit the Sacraments and their works of magic be heralded as miracles. A similar project was attempted in the fourth century when Julian the Apostate counterfeited Catholic

201

worship with pagan ceremonies in honor of Mithras and Cybele. He established a priesthood and instituted ceremonies in imitation of Baptism and Confirmation.

"During the persecution under Diocletian statues of the gods were set up in stores and market places where customers were obliged to honor them and offer incense. None could buy or sell without the contamination of pagan worship. In the days of Antichrist the false prophet will adopt similar tactics to accomplish the downfall of the faithful. No one will be able to buy or sell the necessities of life without implicating himself in the worship of Antichrist.

"For the name of Antichrist, St. John gives a cryptogram that will enable the faithful to recognize him as soon as he makes his appearance in the world. This cryptogram consists of the numerical value of the letters in his name. St. John says that it is the number of a man. This may mean that the name is that of a definite individual, thus showing that Antichrist is not to be identified with the Roman Empire nor with the wicked generally as some maintain.

"In computing the number of Antichrist authors are divided in their opinions as to whether the Latin, Greek or Hebrew letters should be used. The prevailing opinion today regards the use of Hebrew as the most probable. In the new Jewish kingdom of Jerusalem the use of Hebrew will certainly be encouraged if not made obligatory. Even today Hebrew is one of the recognized languages of Palestine, and is widely used by the Jews living there.

"At present, the majority of scholars, both Catholic and Protestant, interpret the number 666 as a cryptogram for Nero Caesar as written in Hebrew characters. But according to our interpretation this is an impossible solution because the days of Antichrist are still in the future. Furthermore, the career of Nero does not correspond to that of Antichrist except in so far as he persecuted the Church. His coming was not 'in all power, and signs and lying wonders' as St. Paul predicts concerning Antichrist.

"Father Sloet of Holland proposed a solution based upon the title of Antichrist as king of Israel. The Jews have ever looked forward to the Messias as a great leader to restore the kingdom of Israel. They rejected our Lord because He did not fulfill this expectation. We may be sure that the pretensions of Antichrist will not be wanting in this regard. He will be king of a restored Israel — not only king, but the king par excellence. In Hebrew this idea could be expressed by the words 'hammelek l'Yisrael,' which have the requisite numerical value of **666**; but in order to obtain this number kaph medial must be used in melek (king) instead of kaph final. Since he will be a king under false pretenses, this interpretation could readily be accepted."

j. "A third angel threatens all followers of Antichrist with eternal damnation. They shall be punished with all the rigors of God's infinite justice untempered by mercy. The wine of wrath shall be poured into the cup unmixed with the water of mercy. This is a reference to the ancient custom of mixing water with wine for drinking.

"These verses clearly prove that the pains of hell are eternal, and without respite. 'The smoke of their torments shall ascend up forever and ever: neither have they rest day nor night.'"

k. "The followers of Antichrist have been warned of defeat and eternal punishment; the faithful have been encouraged by promise of victory here and eternal happiness hereafter. The time of judgment is at hand; the final conflict now begins. The separation of the good from the bad will be still further accomplished. As on the last day, Christ sends forth His angels to gather the wheat into the barns while the cockle is being bound into bundles for the fire. The gathering in of the good through martyrdom is represented as a harvest. The destruction of the wicked is depicted as the vintage of God's wrath. The realization of this judgment will be found in the complete destruction of the kingdom of Antichrist in subsequent chapters.

"The reaper sitting upon a bright cloud, is an angel who comes in the name of Christ to execute His orders. Hence he bears the resemblance of Christ and is surrounded by a cloud of glory. He also wears a crown of gold, the emblem of royalty, because as representative of Christ he exercises dominion over all peoples.

"The cloud of glory and the crown of royalty might lead one to accept the reaper as Christ Himself. Yet the context makes it plain that the reaper cannot be identified with Christ since he is commanded by an angel to thrust in his sickle. Furthermore, Christ has told us in the Gospel that angels shall be commissioned to separate the wheat from the cockle.

"The voice from beneath the altar, commanding the vintage to be gathered is the voice of a martyr whose blood cries to heaven for vengeance. This martyr who has 'power over fire' is probably Elias who will destroy Antichrist by sending down fire from heaven. The prophet Joel also describes the judgments of God against unholy nations as a vintage and a treading of the wine-press.

"The wine-press of divine wrath shall be trodden outside the city of Jerusalem. Final victory over Antichrist will be won through great slaughter and bloodshed in a battle near the Holy City, perhaps in the Valley of Josaphat. The prophecy of Joel may refer to this event instead of the last judgment; 'Let the nations come up into the Valley of Josaphat: for there I will sit to judge all nations round about . . . in the valley of destruction; for the day of the Lord is near.'"

m. "The first vial is poured out upon earth to inflict malignant sores upon those who follow Antichrist. This resembles the sixth plague sent upon Egypt in which 'there came boils with swelling blains in men and beasts.' God also threatened the unfaithful Jews in the wilderness with like punishment: 'May the Lord strike thee with a very sore ulcer in the knees and in the legs, and be thou incurable from the sole of the foot to the top of the head.' Herod Arippa was similarly stricken when he allowed himself to be hailed as God.

"In a moral sense this plague refers to the shame and confusion of those who harden their hearts and close their ears to the voice of the Church. In this sense it refers especially to the Jews who rejected the true Messias and become leaders against His Church in the days of Antichrist.

"The second plague changes the waters of the sea into

blood and destroys all living things therein. This may be taken literally as in the first Egyptian plague when Moses turned the water of all Egypt into blood. In a figurative sense the sea represents the nations in revolt against the Church. They shall be chastised by war and revolution almost to extermination. But if the destruction of 'every living soul' be taken literally the sea must refer to particular nations or peoples.

"The streams and their sources shall likewise be changed into blood. In a symbolic meaning this signifies that the teachers of error and blasphemy shall be slain.

"The Church teaches that nations as well as individuals have angels to guide and protect them. The Bible speaks of the guardian angels of the Persians and Macedonians. The angel of the waters mentioned here must be the guardian of those nations hostile to the Church. He is forced to acknowledge the justice of God's judgment against them. It is just retribution for the blood of martyrs which they have shed. What they meted out to others is now measured unto themselves."

n. "The fourth vial is emptied on the sun which thereupon sends forth its scorching rays to torture the wicked; but Pharao-like instead of being converted they harden their hearts and blaspheme God.

"In a figurative sense the burning rays of the sun are the rigors of God's justice. Christ, the sun of justice, is a guiding light to the faithful, but a consuming fire to the wicked.

"The fifth plague is directed against Jerusalem, the residence of Antichrist and the capital of his kingdom. This kingdom of darkness shall be made still darker by the confusion and ruin. The enemies of the Church shall bite their tongues in anger and despair, yet they will not repent of their sins.

"As in 9:14, the Euphrates symbolizes nations in revolt against the Church. Here they are the Gentile nations subject to Antichrist. The vision probably means that these nations shall be so reduced in strength by the sixth plague that kings from the East will not hesitate to march against them. These eastern kings probably represent nations that remain faithful to the Church and now come to her defense.

"Antichrist and his prophets prepare to resist this attack by sending out messengers with the power of false miracles. By means of these prodigies kings and people are rallied to the cause of Antichrist and march to his defense against the invading armies.

"This verse is a warning to the faithful to be prepared for the great conflict. They must guard well their garments of good works lest they be found without God's grace in that evil day. Our Lord gave a similar warning when He foretold the destruction of Jerusalem: 'Watch ye therefore, because you know not what hour your Lord will come.'

"The armies from the East will meet the forces of Antichrist near Jerusalem. The scene of carnage that follows makes the field of battle another Mageddo, where the invading armies are completely victorious. A further description of the battle is found in Ch. 19. It seems that it will occur after the fall of Rome.

"Armagedon is the Greek for Har-Mageddo (Mount Mageddo), a place often drenched with Israel's blood. The defeat of Antichrist may be accomplished on this very battle ground."

o. "As the seventh angel pours out his vial upon the air, a great voice from the temple cries out 'It is done.' This voice, mentioned in v. 1, now proclaims the defeat of Antichrist and the destruction of his empire. The lightnings flashing and the thunders rolling in heaven are symbols of divine judgments. The great earthquake is the social upheaval following the fall of Antichrist.

"Perhaps the thunder and lightning, and the hail mentioned below should be taken literally like the disturbance of the elements described in Exodus: 'The Lord sent thundei and hail, and lightning running along the ground: and the Lord rained hail upon the land of Egypt. And the hail and fire mixed drove cn together: and it was of so great bigness, as never before was seen in the whole land of Egypt.'

"The great city (Jerusalem) is divided into three sections by yawning chasms caused by the earthquake. A simi-

206

lar punishment befell Jerusalem after the death of the two witnesses when one-tenth of the city was destroyed and seven thousand persons perished. The rending of the rocks by an earthquake at the time of our Lord's death upon the cross warrants the belief that these later disturbances will be actual upheavals of the earth.

"In a figurative sense the division of the city may refer to rival factions warring amongst themselves. During the siege of Jerusalem by the Roman army in 70 A. D. the greatest sufferings were caused by warring factions within the walls of the city.

"Rome, the great Babylon, is also destroyed and the cities of the Gentiles are laid waste. These cities are probably the capitals of those nations that submit to the domination of the neo-pagan empire of Rome and thus become parts of the empire of Antichrist."

p. "The fall and devastation of Rome* were mentioned in the preceding chapter, but its importance as the seat of the false prophet and the capital of a world-wide empire under Antichrist demands a more detailed account. Hence St. John now describes at length the new pagan empire of Rome (Ch. 17) and foretells its complete and final destruction (Ch. 18).

"The great harlot sitting by many waters is Rome holding sway over many nations that share in her corruption and infidelity to God. Ancient Tyre and Ninive were likewise designated as harlots by the prophets Isaias and Nahum. St. John simply follows out the symbolism in which infidelity to God is called fornication and adultery.

---

* This author's conviction that Rome, Italy is to become again the capital of a pagan empire and be utterly destroyed is by no means a necessary conclusion. Just as Rome is said to be Babylon yet is not, so the false prophet's capital is said to be Rome but need not be. Pagan Rome inherited Babylon's ignominy and the false prophet's capital shall inherit that of both Babylon and pagan Rome and shall· suffer as did Babylon and as Rome would have suffered had she not been converted by becoming Christian. Where the Antichrist will establish the seat of his religion we do not know. We do not say that it will not be at Rome but only that it need not be as far as this text is concerned.

"St. John is led into a desert which foreshadows the great devastation and desolation that shall be wrought upon the unfaithful city. There he beholds a harlot seated upon a scarlet beast having seven heads and ten horns and covered over with names of blasphemy. This is evidently the beast from the sea — a symbol of Antichrist. Hence the vision indicates that the new pagan empire of Rome holds sway over the nations through the power and influence of Antichrist.

"Scarlet is the emblem of imperial power — a power exercised over the nations by Antichrist through his prophet in Rome. Scarlet is also the color of blood and forebodes terrible persecutions in which the blood of martyrs will flow in copious streams. The significance of the heads and horns and the names of blasphemy has been explained in connection with the beast from the sea. A further development is found in verses 9, 17.

"The harlot wears a mantle of purple and gold, an emblem of the imperial power possessed by Rome as capital of a vast empire. The gems and gold cup imply riches and material prosperity, but the cup is filled with every iniquity and immorality. Riches and luxury have ever been the great demoralizers of nations as well as of individuals.

"Through her power and riches Rome leads other nations to worship Antichrist and imitate her own immoralities. Hence the harlot bears upon her forehead the mystic title: 'Babylon the Great, Mother of the Fornications and the Abominations of the Earth.' It seems that Roman harlots often wore upon their foreheads a label whereon their names were conspicuously displayed. Here the name is a mystery showing that Babylon is used figuratively for Rome as in the Epistle of St. Peter and other early literature.

"The woman glutted with the blood of martyrs is a warning to the faithful of great persecutions at Rome and throughout the empire during the reign of Antichrist and his prophet.

"The angel's interpretation bristles with difficulties. He says the beast was, and is not, but shall come forth from the abyss only to perish again after a short time. In verse 2 the beast is identified with one of the heads which shall be is the eighth although it is one of the seven, and shall quickly go into destruction. Further on (v. 16), it is said that the ten horns of the beast (in Greek, 'the ten horns and the beast') will fight against the harlot and destroy her by fire.

"Those who take Nero to be the Antichrist find an explanation for these mysteries, which at first sight, seems quite plausible. They have recourse to a popular legend that Nero, after attempting suicide, fled to the East and would soon reappear with the Parthian armies to conquer Rome and regain his throne. The writing of the Apocalypse is assigned to the reign of Vespasian who thus becomes the sixth head — the one who 'now is,' — Titus is the seventh who is yet to come. His short reign fulfills the prediction: 'He must remain a short time.' Then Nero, one of the five who have fallen, returns with the kings of Parthia (the ten horns) to regain his throne and establish himself as the eighth although he is one of the seven.

"This interpretation is ingenious but impossible, as already noted, Nero cannot be identified with Antichrist. But the insuperable difficulty lies in the fact that it destroys inspiration. The use of a legend in an inspired work might be admitted, incongruous though it seems, but a prophecy without fulfillment cannot be inspired. Yet according to the above widely received interpretation the prophecy remains unfulfilled except in so far as Domitian was known as a second Nero on account of his cruelty. If the ten horns be interpreted as the Parthian kings, or astraps, there is no ground in history for representing Domitian or any other Emperor, as their leader. Neither was Rome ever destroyed by a Parthian invasion.

"The settled conviction of many scholars that Nero was Antichrist makes it necessary to refer this whole prophecy to the time of St. John and interpret the seven heads as Roman Emperors. But the context shows that the prophecy concerns events that are still in the future, and most probably the seven kings will not be emperors of Rome. The 'one who now is' refers not to the time of St. John, but to the time when the prophecy shall be fulfilled.

"St. John says there will be many Antichrists; in fact there were many even in his day: 'Even now there are become many Antichrists; whereby we know that it is the last hour.' Again he writes: 'And every spirit that dissolveth Jesus is not of God: and this is Antichrist of whom you have heard that he cometh and he is now already in the world.' According to these words of St. John every teacher of error and every adversary of the Church is an Antichrist.

"Nero has ever been considered one of the principal Antichrists. Sts. Peter and Paul were the two witnesses raised up against him. Arius, leader of the first great heresy may well be called an Antichrist with St. Athanasius and St. Hilary as the witnesses opposed to him. Mohammed, Luther, and Voltaire are often enumerated as Antichrists and many others could be added to the list.

"These few examples are sufficient to show that Antichrist will be like the true Messias in having forerunners who typify him in various ways; and since they are types of Antichrist it is not surprising that the prophecies concerning him can often be applied to them also in one or more particulars. But in Antichrist alone will they be realized in every particular. Hence the faithful will recognize him and avoid his snares, but the rest of mankind will be deceived by his 'lying wonders.'

"The angel tells St. John that the seven heads are seven mountains and seven kings. The seven mountains upon which the harlot sits are quite generally interpreted as the seven hills of Rome. The only apparent reason for mentioning the seven hills would be to show that the name Babylon is used figuratively for Rome, but the usage seems to have been well known to the early Christians. The connection of kings and mountains under one symbol suggests the imagery of the ancient prophecies where mountains so often figure as symbols of kingdoms and empires. Hence the seven heads, which are seven mountains, may be seven principal nations subject to Rome in the days of Antichrist.

"One of the seven kings devotes himself and his kingdom

so completely to the cause of Antichrist that he can rightly be identified with the beast as is done in Verse 11. This is the head which St. John saw in a former vision where it was wounded unto death but revived and healed in a mysterious manner to the astonishment of all.

"Five are fallen, one is, and the other is not yet come,' and the 'beast which was, and is not; the same also is the eighth, and is of the seven, and goeth into destruction.' Any attempt to explain this mysterious prophecy before its accomplishment can be nothing more than speculation. Nevertheless we may find a solution that has some degree of probability.

"Verse 10 may mean that five nations supporting the cause of Antichrist are overcome, one still maintains the conflict, and a seventh has not yet submitted to the domination of Rome. but will soon do so only to be defeated after a short time. Through the infleunce of Antichrist and his lying wonders, the nations most devoted to his cause will rally from defeat and be organized anew as the eighth kingdom although it is really one of the seven. It shall soon go down to destruction in the final defeat of Antichrist and the destruction of his empire.

"Again the prophecy may be interpreted of the rulers instead of their kingdoms. In this sense 'five are fallen,' etc., would probably mean that the rulers of five nations have fallen from power, presumably by violent means, but the sixth still holds his throne. In the seventh kingdom a ruler is yet to come who will use his power in support of Antichrist.

"One of the five kings, identified with the beast on account of his great devotion to the cause of Antichrist, has received a sword wound unto death but is quickly healed and reorganizes his kingdom, or obtains power over another nation. Thus he becomes the eighth, yet in reality he is one of the seven. The sword wound unto death may be understood literally thus making this extraordinary recovery one of the 'lying wonders' of Antichrist, or his prophet, to deceive the nations.

"The ten horns are ten kings or princes who shall come to the assistance of Antichrist for a short time. They will place all their power and resources at his command to accomplish the one object in view — the destruction of the Church. Despite their efforts they shall be overcome by the faithful of Christ who is Lord of lords and King of kings.

"As in other visions the waters, or the sea, symbolizes human society. Here they represent in particular the peoples and nations subject to Rome and with her in revolt against the Church. The seven principal ones were symbolized above by seven mountains.

"After a time the beast and his allied kings (the ten horns) will make war upon Rome and lay it waste with fire and sword. The barbarian invasions of Rome in the fourth and fifth centuries give some idea of the manner in which Rome shall become the prey of a 'scourge of God' in punishment for revolt against the Church and for its worship of Antichrist. St. John gives no reason why Antichrist and his allies turn against Rome except that God put it into their hearts to accomplish His purposes.

"According to the vulgate, only the ten kings will make war upon Rome: 'The ten horns which thou sawest in the beast: these shall hate the harlot,' etc. The Greek text reads: 'The ten horns which thou sawest and the beast: these shall hate,' etc. This is evidently the better reading, as it fits into the context, God put it into the hearts of the ten kings to give their power to the beast to do His words. The 'words of God' can be nothing else than the destruction of Rome."

q. "The mighty angel is probably a great saint or prophet raised up to enlighten the Church by his teaching and to foretell the destruction of Rome as Jonas foretold the fall of Ninive, and Daniel that of ancient Babylon. But if 'angel' be taken literally it is probably St. Michael, the guardian of the Church or St. Gabriel, the mighty one of God.

"The angel speaks of the fall of Rome as something already accomplished to show that it must surely come to pass. It shall be left so desolate that wild beasts will find it a fitting abode and unclean birds will hover about its ruins. Thus also did Isaias prophecy concerning ancient Babylon: 'Wild beasts shall rest there and their houses shall be filled with serpents . . . and owls shall answer one another there, in the house thereof, and sirens in the temples of pleasure.'

"Some interpreters take the words of the angel to mean that the ruins of Rome shall become the lurking place of evil spirits according to the words of Christ: 'When an unclean spirit is gone out of a man he walketh through dry places seeking rest.'

"The terrible destruction and desolation of Rome is a punishment for her many sins and for the sins into which she has led other nations. The kings and merchants of the earth have been led into the sins and vices of Rome, and with her they have upheld Antichrist in his efforts against the Church.

"Another voice from heaven — a voice of mercy — warns the faithful of the impending ruin and exhorts them to seek safety in flight. In like manner did our Lord warn His disciples to flee from Jerusalem upon the approach of the Roman army. Heeding these words of warning the faithful fled to Pella in Peraea and thus escaped the terrible sufferings of the siege.

"These verses are an apostrophe to the ministers of God's judgments, apparently the ten kings of the preceding chapter. They are to punish the wicked and unfaithful city for all the evils she has heaped upon them, presumably the evils resulting from apostacy and adherence to Antichrist. They shall punish her also for her own apostacy and worship of Antichrist: 'Double unto her double according to her works: in the cup wherein she hath mingled mingle ye double unto her.'

"The ruin and desolation of Rome shall be commensurate with her former glory, riches and power. The proud city that 'sits a queen' with neither fear nor anxiety, shall be humbled in the dust.

"The kings of earth who have shared her guilt shall lament the fate of the city, but they stand afar off fearing to come to her assistance. Such is usually the friendship between nations!"

r. "In response to the summons given above, (18:20), St. John hears the voices of praise from great multitudes.

They are the martyrs in heaven and the faithful on earth singing the praises of God for the manifestation of His justice in the fall of Rome. The ruins of the city shall remain as a lasting memorial of God's judgments upon unfaithful nations and peoples: 'Her smoke ascendeth for ever and ever'."

s. "Antichrist and his allied kings now make a last effort against the forces of Christ and His Church. 'I saw the beast and the kings of the earth and their armies gathered together to make war with him that sat upon the horse.' This seems to be a reference to the battle at Armagedon mentioned above (16:16). Three false prophets were sent as messengers of Antichrist to gather the kings of earth to battle but Antichrist and his forces are overcome and a voice from the temple cries out 'It is done.' Antichrist and his prophet are cast into hell, and their allies put to the sword. It is the last battle in the great conflict between the Church and the powers of darkness."

360. Sebastian Michaeliz (before 1922)
"Beelzebub shall accompany Antichrist in the form of a bird with four feet and a bull's head. He is the son of Beelzebub. He will torture Christians like demons are tortured. He will be able to fly, speak all languages, and will have various names."

361. *Apparitions of the Blessed Virgin at Beauraing* (1932-1933)
"I am the Mother of God and the Queen of Heaven. Pray a great deal. Pray always. I shall convert sinners."

362. *Apparitions of the Blessed Virgin at Banneux* (1933)
"I am the Blessed Virgin of the Poor. I have come to relieve suffering. Believe in me, I will believe in you. Pray a great deal!"

363. Sister Faustina (d. 1938)
"About the year 1931 Our Lord demanded of Sister Faustina the painting of a picture and indicated to her what it should be like. Unable to paint the picture herself, she was given permission by the Superiors to instruct an artist in

the painting of the picture of the "Mercy of God." Following are the promises of Our Lord made to Sister Faustina:

"I promise that the soul which shall venerate this picture will not perish. I further promise that soul victory over its enemies already here on earth and especially in the hour of death. I myself shall defend that soul as my own glory ... I am giving to people a vessel, with which they should come to fetch graces from the font of Mercy. That vessel is this picture with the subscription: 'Jesus, I trust in Thee.' I desire that the first Sunday after Easter be celebrated as the Feast of Mercy ... Anyone who approaches on this day the source of Life, will obtain complete remission of punishment and sin. Mankind will not find peace, unless it turns with confidence to My Mercy. Before I come as a just judge I will reveal myself as the King of Mercy so that no one will be able to excuse himself on the Day of Judgment, which is slowly approaching."

364. *Apparitions of the Blessed Virgin at Heede* (1937-1940)

"The Blessed Virgin ordered prayer, MUCH PRAYER especially for the conversion of sinners."

During Lent, 1946 Our Lord appeared saying: "Men did not listen to my Most Holy Mother at Fatima when She appeared to them and admonished them to do penance. Now, I myself am coming at the last hour to warn and admonish mankind. The times are very serious! Men should finally do penance, turn away from their sins and pray, pray much in order that the wrath of God may be mitigated; particularly the holy rosary should be prayed very often! The rosary is very powerful with God! Worldly pleasures and amusements should be restricted."

When a dance was planned and assigned for October 2, 1945, our Saviour said to Gretchen Gansforth, the privileged one: "Tell the pastor — I command that this dancing party may not take place. He must announce it publicly in church. Woe to those parents who nevertheless allow their daughters to go there. They shall at once have a very severe account to render!"

"I want Heede to become a model parish. All abuses should

b₂ redressed and the inhabitants should give a good example to the pilgrims."

365. *Apparitions of the Blessed Virgin at Bonate* (1944)

The Blessed Virgin appeared to Adelaide Roncalli and instructed her "To tell bad mothers to stop committing ugly sins, to pray and do penance, and then, after a little time, the Madonna will bring to an end the troubles that are afflicting us now."

"Everybody — the just and sinners — must pray, pray without tiring for the world in its suffering!"

366. *Apparitions of the Blessed Virgin at Pfaffenhofen* (1940-1946)

a. **April 25, 1946** The "beautiful lady" urged the girls to trust her, saying "Wherever it is being taught that I am all-powerful, I will spread peace, for peace will be where all men have faith in my power.

"I am the Sign of the Living God and my children will carry the imprint on their brows, and while the Star will persecute the imprint, my imprint will conquer the Star." (The word **Star** appears to stand for Lucifer, as would be concluded from later messages.)

b. **May 25, 1946** "I am the great Mediatrix of Grace. Just as the world cannot gain the Father's mercy except by the sacrifice of the Son, so you, too, cannot be heard by my Son except through my intercession. Christ is so little known because I am not known. The Father cast His wrath over the nations of the earth because they cast out His Son. The world was consecrated to my Immaculate Heart, but this consecration has become a terrible responsibility for many. I demand that the world live that consecration! Have absolute faith in my Immaculate Heart. Have faith that mine is all power with the Son. Replace your sinful hearts by my immaculate one, then I will be the one who attracts the power of God, and the love of the Father anew will bring Christ to perfection within you. Do fulfill my prayer so that Christ may rule soon as King of Peace. The world must empty the chalice of divine wrath to its depth because of the countless sins which offend my heart.

The Star of the Abyss (Lucifer?) will roar more violently than ever and cause terrible destruction because it knows that its time is short and because it sees already many have gathered about my Sign. He has no power over it even though it will kill the bodies of many. But from this sacrifice accomplished for me my power will grow to lead those who remain to the victory for Christ. Some have received my imprint, and there will be many more. In the bloodiest of days I will warn you, my children, not to forget that this very cross is a grace. Thank the Father for this grace time and again. Pray and sacrifice for sinners. Sacrifice yourselves and all your works through the Father! Surrender yourselves to me entirely! Pray the rosary! Do not pray so much for material goods! There is more at stake today. And do not expect signs and miracles! I want to accomplish things in hiding, as the great Mediatrix of Grace. I want to convey to you peace of heart, if you accept my demands. Only on such a peace can the peace of nations be established. Then Christ will rule as the King of Peace, over all peoples.

"See to it that my wishes are conveyed to the world. I will give you the necessary strength to do it."

c. **June 25, 1946** "I am the great Mediatrix of Grace. The Father wants the world to recognize His handmaid. Men must believe that I am the eternal bride of the Holy Ghost, the faithful Mediatrix of all graces. My sign is about to appear. Thus God wills it. Only my children recognize it because it manifests itself in hiding, and therefore they honor the Eternal One. I cannot reveal my power to the world as yet. I must go into retirement with my children. In hiding I will perform miracles in the souls until the (ordained?) number of victims is complete. It is up to you to shorten the days of darkness. Your prayers and sacrifices will destroy the image of the Beast. Then I will be able to reveal myself, in honor of the Almighty. Choose a sign for yourself in order that the Trinity may soon be adored and honored by all! Pray and sacrifice through me! Pray always! Pray the rosary! Pray to the Father for everything through My Immaculate Heart! If it is for His honor He will give it

217

to you. Pray the Immaculate Rosary as I have shown it to you. Do not pray it for material rewards, but pray for graces in favor of individual souls, for your communities, for the peoples of the earth, in order that all may love and honor the Divine Heart. Observe the Holy Saturday devoted to me the way I have suggested it. The apostles and priests ought to devote themselves to me especially in order that the great sacrifices which the Inscrutable One demands from them very particularly may grow in holiness and worthiness when they are laid into my hands. Make many sacrifices for me and make your prayer a sacrifice. Be selfless.

"The only thing that matters today is that the Eternal One be honored and that atonement be made to Him. If you devote yourselves to this completely, I will take care of everything else. I will impose crosses upon my children that will be as heavy and deep as the sea because I love them in my sacrificed Son. I pray, be prepared to bear the cross in order that soon the Trinity may be honored. I demand that men soon fulfill my wishes because it is the will of the Father and because it is necessary for His greater honor and glory today and forever. A frightful woe the Father holds in store for those who will not submit to my will.

d. Answering the request that "the woman" give some outward sign, this reply was given: "I have provided so many signs already and spoken so often, but men have not understood. Upon the manifestation of outward signs great masses of people always came who were not concerned with the things that are essential. Were I to give outward signs many people would carry a heavy responsibilty because they would not accept my will.

"This revelation is to go to everybody, but the rank and file will not take it seriously. This will lead to a condition in any case where these revelations will be reserved to a small group. In this small group I will perform signs and miracles which the world does not see. Only those will see them who see what is hidden. Where a small group begins to do my will I shall perform miracles in the souls such as never before, but only my children will see these miracles. I am pleased that first in your country a small group was found which recognizes my position and has formed their lives accordingly and fulfilled my wishes. I am pleased that this small flock conveys the Father's thoughts to the world. Not only I myself want to intercede with the Father. Many must intercede with the Father. That is why I need many to make reparation. I need many children who are prepared to help.

"Already a small group has made many sacrifices for me on this spot. I was pleased by them and have accepted them. A sanctuary should be built here such as this group plans it. I want my message to be conveyed to everybody textually. Then there will be a division of minds. When my message is spread, details and subordinate aspects of it should not be emphasized, but my will should be made manifest as the will of the Father. A small flock will understand the message rightly and absorb it. The great mass of people will reject it and not take it seriously and even take offense at it. However, you must not be afraid, for I am always with you. A small flock of those who understand my thoughts already is at hand, represented in all countries. They will receive my message and spread it and take it seriously. They have properly understood my position as wonderful Mother and Mediatrix of Graces. I am pleased by that and I will show them hidden mysteries."

e. The "Immaculate Rosary" requested by "the woman" provided for inserting the following mysteries between the individual decades: "By Thy Immaculate Conception — Save our Country! — Protect our country! — Sanctify our country! — Rule our country!" However, "country" could be substituted for by some other intention.

f. **Prayer of the Angels, who surrounded "the woman,"** — "Hail, Eternal Lord, Living God who always was a terrible, rightful Judge, merciful Father always benign! Thine now and always be adoration, praise and honor and glory through Thy sun-clad daughter, our wonderful Mother!

"Hail, sacrificed God-Man, bleeding Lamb, King of Peace, Tree of Life, our Head, gate to the Father's heart, eternally born of Life, eternally united with the One that Is, Ruler! Thine be now and always glory and greatness and adoration, atonement and praise through Thy Immaculate Mother and our wonderful Mother!

"Hail, Spirit of the Eternal God, always holy, God manifesting and effecting Itself since all eternity! Burning fire from the Father to the Son, thunderous storm who conveyeth power and light and fervor to the members of the eternal Body, eternally burning Love, God-Spirit forming all the living, red stream of fire in the eternally Loving One toward the mortals. To Him be always anew and in all eternity power and glory and splendor through Thy Bride crowned with the stars, our Mother.

"You, great Mediatrix of Grace! Pray for us."

367. *The Apparition of Tre Fontane* (1947)

"I am she who is in the Divine Trinity; I am the Virgin of the Revelation. You persecute me. Now, it is enough. Enter the holy fold, the heavenly court on earth. The nine Fridays of the Sacred Heart have saved you. You must be like the flowers which Isola (his daughter) has picked; no lamentation is made, they are silent and do not rebel . . . The prayers' out of the mouth of him who prays with faith, are like golden arrows which reach into the Heart of Jesus . . . With this dirt of sin I shall perform powerful miracles for the conversion of unbelievers."

"Love one another. Let us love one another always for the good of the whole world.".

Long and lovingly she spoke to him, the merciful Mother to the prodigal son. She showed him all that God, in His Revelation, had taught us of her graces and her privileges from the beginning of her existence until "my Son and the angels came to take me at the moment of my passing." She spoke eloquently of prayer "a golden arrow going out from the mouth of the Christian and piercing the Heart of God." She urged him to avoid the sins of the flesh which so greatly disgust and offend God, infinite purity, and her, Virgin without stain. She assured him that by means of the dust, of the earth, of this cave, where so many sins had been committed ("sinful soil") she would obtain marvels of conversion and of healing. She urged him to pray much and to obtain prayers, especially for three ends: the conversion of sinners, the enlightenment of unbelievers, the return of all Christians to the unity of the faith. And the prayer she urged him to say is the prayer she had so earnestly recommended at Lourdes, at Fatima, and on so many other occasions: the rosary."

368. Lipa (1948)

Manila.—The "finger of God" had no part in the alleged rain of rose petals and the apparitions of the Blessed Virgin reported to have taken place at Lipa in late 1948. This is the decision of a special commission of Philippine Bishops, who studied the case under the direction of Archbishop Gabriel M. Reyes, the highest-ranking member of the Islands' Hierarchy.

"We, the undersigned Archbishop and Bishops," the commission's statement declared, "constituting for the purpose a special commission, having attentively examined and reviewed the evidence and testimonies collected in the course of repeated, long, and careful investigations, have reached the unanimous conclusion and hereby officially declare that the above-mentioned evidence and testimonies exclude any supernatural intervention in the reported extraordinary happenings—including the shower of petals—at the Carmel of Lipa."

In addition to Archbishop Reyes, the statement was signed by Bishops Cesar Guerrero of San Fernando, Mariano Madriaga of Lingayan, Rufino Santos, Apostolic Administrator of Lipa; Juan Sison, Auxiliary of Nueva Segovia; and Vicente Reyes, Auxiliary of Manila.

The central figure in the rose petal mystery at Lipa was reported at the time of its alleged occurrence as Teresita Castillo, then a 21-year-old Carmelite postulant. According to her testimony at the time, she was walking in the convent garden on the afternoon of September 12, 1948, when her attention was attracted by a vine swaying though there was no breeze.

She said she saw no one but heard a voice urging her to come to the spot for 15 consecutive days. The next day she allegedly saw a lady in white. The following days she was reportedly accompanied by other nuns, who were said to

221

see mysterious rose petals scattered over the ground. The postulant alone saw the vision of a lady, it was reported.

Later a shower of the mysterious rose petals allegedly fell in the convent cells and on the staircase, and were also said to have been seen by people outside the cloister.

When the alleged phenomenon attracted wide attention both in the Philippines and other parts of the world, an official ecclesiastical investigation was launched, first by the Lipa diocesan authorities and then by members of the Philippine Hierarchy. (NCWC Radio and Wire, April 2, 1951).

369. Rev. Theophilus Reisinger, O.M. Cap. (d. 1941)

Letter written by Father Reisinger to the author, April 18, 1940, for publication:

"About Antichrist: In my exorcisms the evil spirits, and among them Lucifer, had made it known that Antichrist is already born. But be sure Rev. Father, I wanted the truth from the mouth of the infallible truth, from Christ Himself. Many things Christ had revealed already but only during the Mass, therefore I told my 'Mystic': Ask Christ whether Antichrist is already born. Christ appeared to the Mystic during the Mass at the Consecration, lifted up on the Cross, bleeding from all the wounds. After the Consecration He approached her and remained until the Agnus Dei and gave the following answer: 'Yes, Antichrist is already born, but he is yet too small and too young, wherefore, he cannot appear yet publicly. At the age of 33 years, he will begin his persecution against the Church and this will fall into the year 1952 and his end will come in the year 1955.'

"After some years, I had Christ asked something about Antichrist, but He answered: 'These questions cannot be answered, tell your Confessor: He knows that Antichrist is already born; he knows where he lives; he knows when he will begin his persecution, when his end shall come; he knows his name 666 and this should suffice him.'

"I had to perform another Exorcism and one of the evil spirits spoke out of the body, very loud: 'Ha! in the year 1952, Antichrist will begin his persecution.'

"Antichrist will have his 20th birthday this year. Judas

222

Iscariot possesses the man, who will appear as Antichrist. Antichrist should have been here already according to St. Francis de Paul and Bartholomew Holzhouser, and Franz Ferdinand cf Austria was appointed as the Great Monarch. But there were many souls of Atonement and the coming of Antichrist was postponed and the appointment for the Great Monarch went over to Otto of Hapsburg. Christ says: He will accomplish great things in the time of Antichrist and the 2nd Verse of Apoc. Chapter VI means Otto. The time for Antichrist can no more be postponed because he is already born. Now dear Father, whatever I have written down here are the words of Christ. That Antichrist should begin in 1965 is not quoted right. Many priests and people believe that the destruction of Antichrist is the end of the world. This is only the first act of the General Judgment. After this follows the time 'One flock and One Shepherd.' And then the final end." Editor's note: Despite the assurance given here this is still one man's opinion.

370. *Apparition of Our Lady at Gimigliano, Italy* (April-May 1948)

Our Lady appeared to 12 year old Anita Frederici on 25 different occasions frcm April 18th to May 23rd. On five previous occasions, from April 3rd, an angel appeared to the child. Nine secrets were entrusted to Anita by Our Lady: three are to be revealed on Easter Sunday, 1953; and six on the feast of Our Lady of Sorrows, 1963.

The principal message of Our Lady was this:

1. Pray for priests;
2. Pray for sinners;
3. Say the Rosary;
4. Pray for the conversion of Russia; (particularly emphasized)
5. Pray for the Holy Father.

Similar to the great miracle at Fatima, phenomena of the sun were noted not only at Gimigliano, but at places as far distant as thirty miles, by thousands of people.

371. Other modern seers and commentators will be found quoted in prophesies 181 (Benedict XV), 183 (Lamy), 184 (de Billiante), 187 (Neumann), 188 (Pius XI), 189 and

Appendix I (Pius XII), also 185, 186, 190, 191, 195, 197, 198, and 199 (all anonymous).

The long prophesy attributed to Father Pio is omitted because it is repudiated by Father Pio and his superiors. Likewise we omit reference to several other interesting phenomena either because the material does not relate to the subject of the book or because we have not been able to get reliable information on the events.

372. In closing this book we feel that it is wise to point out again the very great danger of being deceived by phenomena which seem to be beyond nature. In this connection we quote a warning which appeared in the press of the world under the date line Vatican City, February 3, 1951—"Catholics were warned today against false assertions of the supernatural whose widespread prevalence threatens to "discredit the true miracle."

"The warning was given in a front page article in the Vatican's L'Osservatore Romano by Monsignor Alfred Ottaviani, assessor of the Supreme Holy Office—one of 11 congregations which govern Roman Catholic Church affairs.

"'Pretexts and uncontrolled assertions of supernatural manifestations,' he wrote, 'are these days springing forth a little bit everywhere.

"'This has progressed to the point where there has occurred deplorable disobedience of ecclestical authority that had intervened to apply needed curbs.'

"Msgr. Ottaviani said: 'We are witnessing for years an increase of popular passion for the marvelous, even in religion, throngs of faithful go to scenes of presumed visions and prodigious pretexts, deserting, instead, the church, the sacraments and sermons.'

"This, the monsignor said, occurred in Italy, following assertions of visions in Voltago, in Belgium at Hamsur-Sambre, in Germany at Heroldsbach and in the United States in Necedah. Msgr. Ottaviani said he could list other examples in other countries, both near and far. He added:

"The Church certainly does not want to put in shadow that which God does that is prodigious, but wishes only to hold the faithful alert on that which comes from God and that which does not come from God. She (the Church) is the enemy of false miracles." (No. 372 is added by the editor)

BIBLIOGRAPHY

The bibliography prepared for this work by Father Culleton cannot be found. What follows is a list of books and manuscripts on prophecy and allied subjects by Catholics found in his library or mentioned in his notes. A few non-Catholic books and one or other work published since 1949 are added. A star indicates that the book is still in print, (NC) that the author seems to be a non-Catholic.

*American Eccl. Review, Jan. 1951 "The Jewish Road to Rome"

*Ancient Christian Writers edited by Quasten and Plumpe

Anti-Nicene Fathers edited by Roberts and Donaldson (NC)

Apocrypha, *Apocryphal New Testament edited by James (NC), *Apocrypha . . . of the Old Testament edited by Charles (NC)

*Barthas and Fonseca: Our Lady of Light (Fatima)

Bell: Peasant Life in Old German Epics (NC)

*Benson: Lord of the World

Berry: Apocalypse of St. John

*Bible, The Old Testament, Douay Version; The New Testament, Confraternity Version

Billuart: Theologia Juxta Mentem D. Thomae

Boost: Die Geschichte und die Propheten . . .

Brooks: The Jews in the Light of Prophecy (NC)

*Catholic Biblical Quarterly, Vol. XIII, No. 1.

Cheyne and Black: Encyclopaedia Biblica (NC)

Clericus: Das Buch der Wahr- und Weissagungen

*D'Ales: Dictionaire Apologetique de la Foi Catholique

Eichinger: Die Ehrwurdige . . . Elizabeth Canori-Mora

*Fathers of the Church edited by Schopp, Deferrari, et al.

Fonseca: Nossa Senhora de Fatima

Forbes: A Little Sister of the Sacred Heart (Lateau)

*Furfey: The Mystery of Iniquity

Galua: Futura Grandeza de Espana . . .

Hastings: Dictionary of the Bible (NC)

Izard: Louise Lateau

(Kapsner): Begone Satan; Mary Crushes the Serpent

Konzinator: La Salette und die Nachste Zukunft

Krogh-Tonning: Die Hl. Brigitta von Schweden

*Lucken: Antichrist and the Prophets . . . in the Chester Cycle

*Luddy: Life of St. Malachy

Luetzenburg: Vita Antichristi

Mackenzie: The Popes of St. Malachy's Prophecy (NC)

Maitre: La Prophetie des Papes; Les Papes et La Papaute . . .

Manning: The Four Great Evils of the Day

*Marchi: The Crusade of Fatima

Martindale: Antichrist

*McGlynn: Vision of Fatima

*McGrath: Fatima or World Suicide

Neuman, Therese. Works on this mystic are numerous, e.g. De Houre, Messmer, Schimberg, Theodorowicz, Thomas, Waitz, Witt. *Von Lama has several works.

*Newman: Essays Critical and Historical

*Norton: Visitations of Our Lady

Nostradamus. This author has numerous translators and commentators, e.g., *Allen, Lamont, *McCann, Roberts, Ward (all NC except Allen)

*Oca: More about Fatima

*Oesterreicher: Seeds of Hope (on the Mystery of Israel)

Parent: Le Secret Complet de La Salette

Patrologiae . . . Cursus Completus edited by Migne. See index P.L. Vol. 220, Coll. 266-308

Pelligrino: The Christian Trumpet . . .

*Prat: Theology of St. Paul (vol. 1)

Ratton: Antichrist, An Historical Review

*Ryan: Our Lady of Fatima

Sardi: Leben des . . . Kaspar del Bufalo

*Schneweis: Angels and Demons according to Lactantius

Spirago: Genaues uber den Antichrist; Die Malachias—Weissagung . . .; Der Weltuntergang; Die Zukumft Deutschlands . . .

*Thomas Aquinas: In Omnes S. Pauli Ap. Epistolas Commentaria; Summa Theologica . . . Translated . . . First American Edition.

Ullathorne: The Holy Mountain of La Salette

*Vacant et al.: Dictionaire de Theologie Catholique

*Vigouroux-Pirot: Dictionaire de la Bible

Wetzel: Die Falschen Propheten . . .

Other works are listed in The Prophets and Our Times

MANUSCRIPTS

INDEX
to Prophecies and Commentators

/